GERALD du MAURIER
the last actor-manager

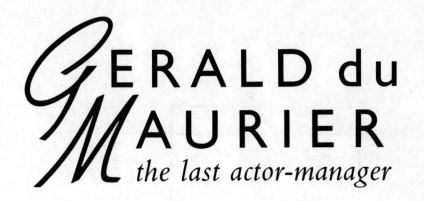

GERALD du MAURIER
the last actor-manager

JAMES HARDING

Hodder & Stoughton
LONDON SYDNEY AUCKLAND TORONTO

British Library Cataloguing in Publication Data
Harding, James, *1929–*
    Gerald du Maurier : the last actor-manager.
    1. Great Britain. Theatre. Acting.
    Du Maurier, Sir Gerald 1873–1934
    I. Title
    792'.028'0924

ISBN 0-340-42382-X

Published by Hodder & Stoughton,
a division of Hodder & Stoughton Ltd,
Mill Road, Dunton Green, Sevenoaks, Kent TN13 2YA.
Editorial Office: 47 Bedford Square, London WC1B 3DP.

Typeset by Hewer Text Composition Services, Edinburgh.
Printed in Great Britain by St Edmundsbury Press, Bury St Edmunds, Suffolk

This biography of a decidedly
Anglo-Saxon personality is
dedicated to
ZAID NOH
and his family.

Hutang emas boleh dibayar,
hutang budi dibawa mati.

Irving was always Irving, with this
important proviso; that there were
at least twenty Irvings, and all of
them different . . . 'Leave Irving
out of it,' you say impatiently.
'What about Gerald du Maurier?
Was he not always himself?'
Yes. But himself in a way that
what he put on the stage was an urgent,
heightened, *theatrical* presentation
of Geraldism . . .

JAMES AGATE

He was such a great actor . . .

JOHN GIELGUD

. . . brilliant actor that he was . . .
he was a genius of a technician . . .

LAURENCE OLIVIER

Contents

ACKNOWLEDGMENTS

While Dame Daphne du Maurier approved in principle of the suggestion for a book about her father, she felt that she had said all she had to say on the subject in her own published writings. This biography therefore has no family sanction, and the opinions expressed in it are entirely the author's own.

The paths of the biographer often cross and interweave. Mrs Mary Butterfield, whose uncle was James Agate's friend Leo Pavia and whose mother was one of Mr Cochran's Young Ladies, thus has links with two of my recent biographies and kindly provided me with clues to be followed up for this one. I am also grateful to Mrs Maureen Baker-Munton for her interest. Mr Charles Duff gave me valuable information about Audrey Carten and had many stimulating observations to make on the actor's craft.

I must also record my gratitude for documentation and/or memories to Mr Andrew Birkin; Mr Jimmy Edmundson; Miss Elaine R. Garwood; Mr Michael Kingsley; Mr M. J. Mathews; Mr James McConnel; Mr and Mrs Jake Taylor who worked with Gracie Fields; Mr Christopher Wade, Curator of the Hampstead Museum; and Mr Ken Woodward.

As always, my special thanks go to Mrs Lynda Saunders and Mrs Pauline Skinner for their patient and adroit interpretation of the hieroglyphics which comprised the original manuscript.

J.H.

ILLUSTRATIONS

The photograph of Gerald du Maurier (front cover) by Howard Coster and the watercolour of George du Maurier by Leslie Ward are reproduced by kind permission of the National Portrait Gallery, London.

The author has kindly allowed the editor to select pictures for this book from his own albums. It has not always been possible to trace copyright. The publishers apologise for any inadvertent infringement and will be happy to include an acknowledgment in any future edition.

FOREWORD

'The moment at which I speak,' said Pascal, 'is already far away from me.' Once an actor has delivered his speech and made his exit the illusion he created has vanished. It may, or may not, flicker on, growing dimmer with time, in the minds of his audience. No film or tape will ever recapture the performance which for a moment held the imagination of those who saw and heard him.

Evanescent, elusive, the actor's creation dies with him. Gerald du Maurier knew this. It coloured the melancholy which beset him at the end of his days and gave him a feeling of bitter impotence. His father's example made him all the more aware of his dissatisfaction. George du Maurier was, like his son, popular and famous, but he left behind him a permanent reminder of his achievement. Despite being blind in one eye he produced drawings which are a valuable social record of his time, and at least one classic joke ('the curate's egg') which has become a part of English idiom. He also wrote novels that can still be read with pleasure, including the enormously successful *Trilby*. Besides contributing a new word to the language it introduced a character, Svengali, who takes his place in literature alongside Sherlock Holmes and Mr Pickwick, to be quoted even by those who do not know the novel. Gerald could show nothing like this.

Success came easily, too easily. Few English actors can have been so naturally gifted as he was. He never saw the inside of a drama school and never took lessons in any branch of the dramatic art. Everything he did was achieved through an inborn talent nurtured by intuition and observation. He liked to pretend that he only went on the stage because he would have been bored by the routine of a nine-to-five office job. The impression of nonchalance, of lazy grace, was, however, the result of long rehearsal and painstaking sessions in front of a mirror. Even his famous 'throwaway' technique was limited to appearance only, for he could place a line and point it as clearly and audibly as any of his flamboyant predecessors. This is something which his younger imitators overlooked, and for years inaudibility was mistaken for naturalness. As a director, too, or producer as it was called then, he was accomplished.

He lacked the dazzling good looks of a Henry Ainley or an Owen Nares. This he made up for with a charm and a magnetism which enslaved those around him. When as a young man he joined Mrs Patrick Campbell's company, she thought, and said in her typically out-spoken way, that he was ugly. If the daunting Mrs Pat had a love scene with him, she would mutter: 'Good God! To have to play a scene like this with a face like that!' Yet even she, although she taught him much about the stage and about life, could not help falling in love with him, as did many other much less talented and strong-minded women.

Gerald never had to struggle. After a few agreeable years under the benevolent eye of John Hare, Squire Bancroft, Tree and Forbes-Robertson, he emerged as a fully fledged leading man. Not for him were the ardours of Crewe Junction on a wet Sunday morning and the low life of theatrical digs. Apart from a few youthful excursions into the provinces, when hard beds and lumpy soup were regarded as a bit of a lark, he glittered fixedly as an ornament of the West End. Henry Irving, by contrast, served an exhausting apprenticeship in the provinces. During his two and a half years in Edinburgh repertory he played four hundred and twenty-eight different rôles. He was hampered, in addition, by a speech impediment resulting from a childhood stammer and by an awkward, ungainly walk. In the battle to overcome these obstacles he made himself an inimitable actor and the greatest of his day.

Gerald was faced with no such disadvantages to conquer. He soon found an admiring audience who delighted in his understated manner. They did not want him in Shakespeare or Chekhov. They wanted him as Raffles the Old Harrovian crook, as Arsène Lupin the gentleman burglar, as Bull-Dog Drummond. So he gave them what they asked for. As an actor-manager upon whom many employees depended for a livelihood he used his brilliant stagecraft to transform sub-quality material and to fill his beloved Wyndham's Theatre. Since, except for a few minor appearances when young, he never played Shakespeare or any of the big classic rôles, he has not received the credit he deserves. His true genius only came out intermittently, in isolated scenes from minor plays and in Barrie. Setting aside his Captain Hook, a bravura tour de force, he portrayed a memorably Scottish anti-hero in *What Every Woman Knows* and a moving failed artist in *Dear Brutus*. To these may be added the grandfather in *Pantaloon* and the silent butler in *Shall We Join The Ladies?*, where, denied the help of words, he conveyed every emotion by face and manner alone.

His real contribution to the theatre was a novel style of acting which crystallised the reaction against the school of Irving and Tree. Where they had been expansive and grandiloquent, he was intimate and playful. Where they stood full face to the audience and met them head-on, Gerald treated spectators with a careless look and an amiable glint in the eye. They spoke in rolling periods and paraded with a conquering air. He conversed in staccato accents and loped around the furniture with a quick stride. As John Gielgud has remarked, he swept away a lot of fustian. It would have been impossible, anyway, said Gerald, to play modern drama in the style they had evolved for the theatre of their time. A new voice was needed, a new approach, and he supplied these in his own unique fashion. Beneath his deceptively casual appearance he contrived to suggest hidden reserves of power. His detractors and his less able followers did not understand that you cannot imply restraint if there is nothing to restrain.

He died an unhappy and disappointed man. Despite the honour and acclaim which made him the head of his profession, despite a happy family and a wife who unselfishly devoted her existence to his greater comfort and ease, he remained unsatisfied. The money problems which darkened his last years and obliged him to make paltry films were not the main cause of his frustration. The trouble went deeper than that. A parallel with his father again suggests itself. George du Maurier had wanted to be a great artist. Instead, denied the use of his left eye, he was condemned to earn his living as cartoonist, illustrator and novelist. The feeling of regret endured until his death. When Gerald died a few weeks after his sixty-first birthday he felt he had squandered his gifts. Success made him take the easy option and he sensed that he had not displayed the full measure of his ability. He left everything too late. Moreover, the thought of growing old filled him with horrified despair. He wanted to stay eternally young. He was no Captain Hook. He was, really, Peter Pan.

J.H.

GERALD du MAURIER

the last actor-manager

CHAPTER I

THE FRENCH CONNECTION

[i]

Slut in a Frying Pan

In 1922 His Majesty King George V went to the theatre sixteen times, which was probably more often than most of his subjects. Yet the theatre bored him and he only attended out of duty or if his Queen, who rather enjoyed the footlights, nagged him into going. That year, at the direction of those fellows in government who decide such things, he conferred a knighthood on Mr Gerald du Maurier, the famous actor-manager whom he had often seen at the charity matinées and gala performances he was condemned to grace with his unwilling presence. The knighthood officially confirmed Sir Gerald as the brightest star of his profession and, like Irving in his time, the public embodiment of theatre. Sir Gerald, Old Harrovian, member of exclusive clubs, jealous upholder of the theatre's respectability, would not, we may be sure, have discussed with his monarch the only thing he had in common with him. This mutual bond was Sir Gerald's great-grandmother, Mary Anne Clarke, an avaricious whore who, a hundred years or so before, had been the blackmailing mistress of King George's ancestor, the then Duke of York.

Satirists in the 1800s enjoyed a riotous liberty of speech that their modern descendants would envy. No libel law cabined their picturesque venom and no thought of good taste affected their malice. In 1810 they found a very promising target for their barbs. Hawkers roamed the streets of London selling lampoons which included such verses as:

And when I strove to chaunt my Mrs Clarke
With rhyme, confused, I knew not which was which,
But, as I went on fumbling in the dark,
I set down bitch for Clarke and Clarke for bitch.

I

On Guy Fawkes night a troop of ragamuffins burnt the effigy of a woman as they carolled discordantly:

> Mary Anne, Mary Anne,
> Cook the slut in a frying pan.

A doll with a lacy nightcap on its turnip head twisted, broke up and shrivelled among roaring flames.

Mrs Mary Anne Clarke was a prostitute from the slums who had known the inside of Newgate Gaol. At the age of sixteen she married a person from the mercantile class and almost immediately deserted him for gentlemen of fashion better able to accommodate her expensive tastes. Swiftly she worked her way through the minor ranks of the aristocracy via knights, baronets and viscounts whom she entranced with her sparkling good humour and seductiveness. She had a particular fondness for military men whose lack of intelligence was compensated for by their dashing uniforms and manly physique. Eventually she won the greatest prize of all and became mistress to the Duke of York, brother of King George III.

For some time her soft curly hair and white shoulders fascinated His Royal Highness. He, bloated, pot-bellied, bulging-eyed, showered upon her gorgeous presents which included a mansion in Gloucester Place. The season was spent at modish watering-places and in London town houses. Party succeeded party, rout followed on rout while Mrs Clarke shrewdly amassed jewellery and possessions, for she knew that such bounty could not last. In 1809 the idyll ended when it was discovered that she had also taken bribes from officers keen on promotion and anxious to profit by her influence with the Duke of York who was then Commander-in-Chief of the army. An official enquiry was held at the House of Commons and Mrs Clarke gave evidence. The Duke was obliged to resign and Mrs Clarke performed at the enquiry with an impudent wit that silenced her inquisitors.

Within a short space of time, however, the Duke regained his former position and Mrs Clarke was out of favour. She no longer enjoyed a ducal allowance and creditors were beginning to press. Infamy now covered her name, boys chanted rude couplets outside her window and the gazettes printed scathing verse about her. Although she was forced to sell off many of her belongings she still owned something of great value: the Duke of York's love letters to her. When she threatened to publish her memoirs she was offered a settlement of ten thousand pounds, an annuity of four hundred pounds and another of two hundred apiece for each of her daughters. At various points in her tempestuous career she had given birth to five children. History knows of only two, her youngest daughter Ellen and a son called George who was destined for an army career probably arranged by the Duke of York. Mrs Clarke took the money, settled her debts and prepared for exile in Paris with Ellen. She was a prudent woman and took with her across the Channel a dozen or so royal love letters which she had thoughtfully preserved from destruction. They would, she reckoned, be a useful insurance against the future.

In Paris Mary Anne set up a comfortable residence. She sent the twelve-year-old Ellen to school in the rue Neuve-St-Etienne, a building once the house of noble families who had left and never come back. There Ellen befriended her teacher, Mademoiselle Louise Busson du Maurier. Louise and her family were émigrés who fled their native country at the Revolution and had but lately returned from London in more settled times. She spoke vaguely of a grandfather who once owned a glass factory and of a château in Sarthe which no longer existed. Her brother Robert stayed in London. Another worked in Hamburg. The other four members of the family, including Louise and her brother Louis-Mathurin, lived in the home of their widowed mother. They, too, had the benefit of a royal annuity in the shape of a civil pension granted by King Louis XVIII as a reward for what was termed loyalty to the crown. In fact, their emigration to England in 1789 was inspired by the business failure of Louise's deceased parent, a happy-go-lucky speculator who had already been imprisoned on charges of fraud. In London he was to undergo another gaol sentence. Eventually he deserted his family and ended his days in Tours as a schoolmaster though still cherishing delusions of grandeur without the means to sustain them.

Louise introduced Ellen to her best friend, Mademoiselle Eugénie St Just, who was a boarder at the school. The three of them soon were intimate, and their relationship, forged in childhood, was to endure all their lives. Louise was a gentle creature, deeply pious, Eugénie was sensitive and romantic. Ellen, whom life with her outrageous mother had early turned into a realist, brought a sharp practical sense to the trio. All three were convinced royalists, Ellen perhaps the most firmly. Often when she looked at a mirror she fancied she could detect a likeness to a certain royal personage. The notion was one that her descendants from time to time nourished. Unfortunately the dates do not agree, for the Duke of York only met

Mrs Clarke several years after the birth of Ellen and of her brother. No one but Mrs Clarke would have been able to say who the girl's father was, and even she, given her eventful private life, could not be entirely certain.

Eugénie was the first of them to fall in love and marry. Her bridegroom was the Duc de Palmella, scion of a rich Portuguese family. Louise, now more than ever religious, burned candles and prayed for their future happiness. At the wedding, a grand and pompous affair, she met Mr Geoffrey Wallace, a secretary in the English legation, handsome, Scottish, well-born, it seemed. As soon as the Duc de Palmella and his Duchess had whisked away on their honeymoon Mr Wallace pressed his suit with Louise. He was charmed by her sweet character, the story of her life and the royalist devotion which had been recognised with a pension from King Louis XVIII. Soon afterwards they, too, were married, despite Mrs Clarke's urgent but unheeded advice about the need for a proper financial settlement. On their wedding night Mr Wallace appeared somewhat disturbed. Perhaps a headache or the excitement of the occasion had upset him? He confessed that he was penniless. His father some time ago had disinherited him. He did not even have enough to pay for their hotel accommodation. However, he was sure that Louise would be able to help, especially with her allowance from the King. She disillusioned him. It was only two hundred francs a year, she told him, and she was not an heiress. He turned pale and vanished. She never saw him again.

Mademoiselle Louise Busson du Maurier, now Madame Wallace, accepted an invitation from her old friend Eugénie to leave France and settle with the Palmella family where she could live as companion and governess to Eugénie's children. She was now thirty-five and persuaded by her unhappy romance that her purpose in life was to serve others. From Portugal she wrote to her brother, Louis-Mathurin, asking him to thank the good-hearted Mrs Clarke who had, through her solicitor, tried to discover the whereabouts of her ignoble husband. Louis-Mathurin conveyed her message to the Clarke household and, to his surprise, what he envisaged as a chore became an agreeable social occasion. He enjoyed meeting Mrs Clarke who, though raddled and given to hiccups which, she explained, like the Beatrice Lillie of a later age, were caused by wind round the heart, possessed a salty humour and took a roguish delight in the company of young men. Ellen he found, if not beautiful, then attractive in an austere kind of way. They had both spent their childhood in England, and, they learned in conversation, even come to France on the same date and in the same boat. What a delightful coincidence!

His visits to the Clarkes in their Auteuil apartment multiplied. To Ellen's accompaniment on the harp he sang, rather beautifully, songs by Schubert, melodies from Provence and English ballads which he and Ellen knew from their childhood. Having given up his early ambition to appear in opera he had become a scientist, and he spoke to them eloquently of the brilliant inventions he could make if only people with money had the daring and the imagination to support him. His blue eyes flashed and his curly hair drooped most becomingly. Mrs Clarke and her daughter thought him a highly engaging young man. For all her cynicism, for all her sophisticated knowledge of the world, Mrs Clarke adored him. Alas, he had no money. On the other hand, Ellen was over thirty and not exactly beautiful. Yet if they married and set up on their own she, Mary Anne, would be lonely with her soldier son abroad. Ellen, for her part, was fascinated by the blend of sadness and gaiety that tinged his moods. He awoke an odd sort of maternal feeling in her. An understanding arose between her and Louis-Mathurin. Mrs Clarke spoke to him about practicalities. She would make Ellen an allowance and, of course, at her death the money would pass to her daughter. Louis-Mathurin, who had not known of this, heard her attentively. He was a man of science, an intellectual, a dreamer for whom money and the sordid realities of life did not exist. Everyone knew that. He acted fast. Within a week he proposed to Ellen.

Miss Ellen Jocelyn Cécile Clarke was translated into Madame Louis-Mathurin Busson du Maurier at the British Embassy. Her mother returned to England while the couple honeymooned in Brittany where they strolled on the rocks, listened to the song of the waves and read Chateaubriand aloud to each other. They took an apartment at No. 80 in the Champs-Elysées and lived on the allowance Mrs Clarke gave Ellen together with occasional, very occasional, earnings by Louis-Mathurin. As he often told his wife, but for the Revolution he would have been a grand seigneur with his own château and rolling acres tilled by deferent peasants bowing low as he passed by in his golden carriage. He was not born to work and slave. A Gallic combination of Harold Skimpole and Mr Micawber, Louis-Mathurin regarded money as a wretched subject no true gentleman ever bothered his head about. Something would always turn up. Meanwhile he spent much time in cafés discussing what he described to Ellen as 'business' and pottering in his 'laboratory'.

A son was born to them in 1834. They called him George after his maternal uncle, Louis after his father and Palmella after Ellen's great friend Eugénie. For a time the family stayed in England with Mrs Clarke and Uncle George from whom Louis-Mathurin borrowed money which Ellen had to repay out of her exiguous allowance. There followed three years in Brussels where the Duc de Palmella had just been made Portuguese Ambassador. He created some sort of position in his retinue for Louis-Mathurin who was able to live very comfortably without, for once, borrowing. Ellen, too, enjoyed herself because she renewed acquaintance with her dear friends Louise and Eugénie. The Flemish nurse who looked after George du Maurier called him 'manneken', a term which his childish tongue converted into 'Kicky'. When a second son was born, to be named Eugène, George christened him 'Gyggy'. Isabella, the third and last child, came into the world three years later. By that time the Duc de Palmella was long since recalled to Lisbon and Louis-Mathurin, his occupation gone, had come back with his family to Paris and dreams of finding the philosopher's stone.

He remembered his brother Robert who stayed behind in London to follow a career for himself. The du Mauriers accordingly descended upon him for a sojourn abruptly cut short when Louis-Mathurin, with his usual nonchalance, offended him by a tactless remark that he was going off his head. Since Robert was subject to bouts of melancholia and dreaded insanity, the observation killed the brotherly feeling he had up to then displayed and the family returned once more to France. The strain of supporting her careless husband and the constant, excruciating shortage of money tormented Ellen's nerves. She lost her temper easily and snapped at people. Mrs Clarke deplored the situation and had an idea. Those letters from the Duke of York, yellowed now and fraying, were still in her possession. The Duke had recently passed away. Why not publish and be damned? Her departed lover's brother was very much alive and, if discreetly sounded out, might well be ready to talk money. The response to her approach was uncompromising: if she published anything her annuity would be cancelled immediately. She burst into a foul-mouthed passion which only subsided when Ellen, just as angry but for different reasons, pointed out that should she persist with her mad project the whole family would be doomed and have no money whatsoever. Some years later, undaunted, Mrs Clarke had her memoirs put into French and published them in Paris in the decent obscurity of a foreign tongue. The annuity was safe.

The boys, too, were causing Ellen trouble. Neither of them

did well at school and their reports continually bore the dismal comments, *médiocre, peu attentif, très léger.* They larked about in class, learned nothing and George, in particular, disgraced himself by covering the pages of his exercise book with naughty little caricatures of the headmaster. Louis-Mathurin intended him to be a 'scientist' like himself, although the boy was more interested in poetry, especially the scandalous works of Byron. At the age of seventeen George sat his baccalauréat exam and failed. Ellen fulminated. He must give up his silly sketching and concentrate on his education. She would send him to London where his father was at the moment – Louis-Mathurin had discovered a new and absorbing pursuit, that of financial speculation which, more instantly rewarding than chemistry, took him on extensive tours between the stock exchanges of Europe – and George would have to tell him the bad news in person. Reluctantly he left behind him the familiar sights of Paris and endured a Channel crossing black with fear about what his angry father would say. At London Bridge Louis-Mathurin awaited him amid drizzle and seething mist. A glance at his son's miserable expression told him immediately the purpose of the visit. He laughed exuberantly and, waggling his scarlet umbrella, invited him to forget his sorrows in a joyous dinner *tête-à-tête.* There were times, it must be conceded, when Louis-Mathurin's heedless *je m'en foutisme* came as a relief.

Louis-Mathurin had rented a house in Pentonville at 44, Wharton Street. The rest of the family came over with their five cats from France and joined him there while George was sent to study chemistry at University College. Although he enjoyed dabbling in substances with mysterious names and pouring strange mixtures out of test tubes, he soon was bored and nostalgic for Paris. The lugubrious air of Pentonville depressed him, the family home and its perpetual arguments over money saddened him, and he felt unutterably lonely. Only in music did he find consolation, and, like his father at an early age, he thought of becoming an opera singer. Here was a further irritation for his long-suffering mother. 'He has no initiative, no energy,' Ellen wrote. 'He sits about and dreams. Always a pencil in his hand – and I think of the money wasted on his education.' One morning in 1852 a letter arrived for her. It brought news of her mother's death. She did not find it easy to repress the feeling of thankfulness that arose within her. Now, at last, the Duke of York's annuity would pass entirely into her hands and money would no longer be a problem. Or would it? Louis-Mathurin beamed at her and started laying plans for more ambitious schemes.

Four hundred pounds a year! George's university fees were paid in a lump sum instead of by monthly instalments, and having completed his last term he emerged as a diffident but hopeful analytical chemist. A company which reckoned to have found gold deposits in Devon employed him on consultancy work. No ore was ever dug up but George was delighted by a pastoral interlude of 'golden peace and plenty' among the friendly Devonians. Few other people seemed anxious to use his services and Louis-Mathurin toyed with the idea of sending him to Paris where he could learn a new technique of instantaneous photography. The project was foiled when George went down with measles. His brother Eugène was, however, making rather more progress in his chosen career of the army. He had just been promoted to *brigadier*, a step which appears gratifying until you remember that the term is merely a *faux-ami* meaning 'corporal'.*

A short while afterwards, Louis-Mathurin found himself enmeshed in the toils of a long and complex action about one of his inventions, something to do with a method of fertilising the soil or extracting moonbeams from cucumbers. He jaunted off to France, borrowed money for his expenses from sister Louise and even, through her good graces, from the Duc de Palmella. It was not enough. Lawyers came and went, new and better particulars were demanded, rebuttal was met with surrebuttal. Louis-Mathurin began to flag. He no longer smiled, no longer chattered gaily of the wonderful future to come, and for days sat mute and solitary. The case was lost and he took to his bed. An unusually cold winter played up his asthma. *'Je suis si fatigué . . .'* he would murmur, his blank eyes staring at the ceiling. George sat beside him and read aloud, tried to cheer him up with jokes and showed him his latest caricatures in the attempt to shake him out of his depression. He did not react. *'Je suis si fatigué . . .'* he repeated. Winter passed into spring and still he sank. In the summer of 1856 he died at the age of fifty-nine and confirmed the tradition that no male du Maurier ever reached old age.

Ellen mourned him sincerely. Her experience of life had made her hard and formidable. While Louis-Mathurin floated serenely along on a cloud she was the one who had kept her feet on the ground, held the family together and dealt with practical things. His feckless ways maddened her, his foolish optimism grated on her, yet, womanlike, she loved him with all his faults. He was buried in Stoke Newington

* Just as de Gaulle was never a 'General' in the English sense but only a *général de brigade*, or 'Brigadier'.

and, such was the family's haste to regain Paris, the grave was left unmarked.

For George his father's death was a release and meant that he could no longer be forced into some uncongenial profession. He looked forward to studying in the Parisian atelier of the well-known artist Charles Gleyre and to revisiting the scenes of his childhood. Years later, in his novel *Peter Ibbetson*, he wrote nostalgically of:

Dark, narrow, silent, deserted streets that would turn up afterward in many a nightmare – with the gutter in the middle and towerlets and stone posts all along the sides; and high fantastic walls (where it was *défendu d'afficher*), with bits of old battlements at the top, and overhanging boughs of sycamore and lime, and behind them grey old gardens that dated from the days of Louis le Hutin and beyond! And suggestive names printed in old rusty iron letters at the street corners – 'Rue Videgousset', 'Rue Coupe-Gorge', 'Rue de la Vieille Truanderie', 'Impasse de la Tour de Nesle', etc, that appealed to the imagination like a chapter from Hugo or Dumas. And the way to these was by long, tortuous, busy thoroughfares, most irregularly flagged, and all alive with strange, delightful people in blue blouses, brown woollen tricots, wooden shoes, red and white cotton nightcaps, rags and patches; most graceful girls, with pretty, self-respecting feet, and flashing eyes, and no head-dress but their own hair . . .

But the Paris of Hugo's romances had been transformed by the pitiless incursions of Louis-Napoléon's architect Haussmann. Wide boulevards slashed their way through the city, and the jumble of medieval alleyways and turreted buildings of George's childhood had vanished. The Bois de Boulogne, which he knew as an enchanting place of overgrown thickets and ferneries, was now disciplined with an artificial lake and a rockery daunting in its symmetrical neatness. The return to Paris was the first big disillusionment of his life.

Still, the year he spent in Gleyre's studio was a happy one. His was not the impoverished existence described in Henri Murger's romantic novel *Scènes de la vie de Bohème*, later musicked by Puccini as *La Bohème*, but a comfortable routine divided between lodging with his mother and days spent in the cheerful company of fellow students, many of them, curiously enough, English rather than French. The most dazzling of his young friends was the American James Whistler who dominated the group with his startling avant-garde theories and, even then, outrageous wit. In *Trilby* du Maurier was later to describe him as

. . . the idle apprentice, the king of Bohemia, *le roi des truands*, to whom everything was forgiven, as to François Villon, 'à cause de ses gentillesses . . .' Always in debt, like Svengali; like Svengali, vain, witty, and a most exquisite and original artist; and also eccentric in his attire (though clean), so that people would stare at him as he walked along – which he adored! But (unlike Svengali) he was genial, caressing, sympathetic, charming; the most irresistible friend in the world as long as his friendship lasted – but that was not for ever!

Inevitably, when this description appeared in 1894, the prickly Whistler, whom age had not mellowed, was to erupt in a flurry of invective and litigation.

After a year of what he called 'my happy student life' in Paris George continued his studies at the Antwerp Academy of Fine Arts. Here, one morning, while drawing from a model, it seemed that the girl's head shrank to the size of a walnut. When he put his hand over his left eye he could see as well as ever. When he did the same with his right he knew what had happened: the sight of his left eye had gone. The retina had become detached and a haemorrhage spread over the back of the eye. The treatment of the day had no effect. Among the specialists he consulted was a Belgian who, in return for a large fee, blandly assured him that his right eye was failing as well.

A musician who becomes deaf can still, more or less, continue with his profession. An artist who goes blind cannot. George knew now that he must give up his ambition to be a great painter and that, at best, he must be content with illustrating books. Advice from a German doctor assured him that, with care, his right eye would last out, and he set about reconciling himself to the new and bitter reality that had soured his life. In time he regained his exuberant spirits, his gaiety that made him the best of companions, but an underlying melancholy, a melancholy that was never far from the surface in all the du Mauriers, henceforward tainted his attitude. The lost happiness of childhood for which he continually yearned seemed further away than ever.

Once the early shock of his semi-blindness was over he began to revise his ideas about a possible career. His Anglo-French upbringing had given him affinities with both countries. Yet on balance, perhaps, his sympathy lay more with England now. The France of his childhood had evaporated and was only a cherished memory locked in his heart. Most of his artist friends were English. Why should he not chance his luck as an illustrator in London, where magazines like *Punch* and the *Illustrated London News* depended heavily on a constant flow of black and white pictures for their contents? Illustration had become a recognised career. And there was, too, a pretty girl called Emma Wightwick who lived in London, a tall, wide-eyed, graceful creature, dark-haired and characterful, whom he had already met and been attracted to while she holidayed with her family abroad.

In London he first shared a studio with his friend Whistler at 70, Newman Street off the Tottenham Court Road. Here came other rising talents, young artists who, like Whistler, had begun to make their names and aspired to the Royal Academy, goal of all right-thinking painters at the time. George gained many friends among them. They thought him a good fellow, bright, amusing, a welcome guest at any party where his lively talk and the songs he sang enchanted those who heard him. He was already contributing to magazines, some of them quite famous like the *Cornhill*, and occasionally even *Punch* accepted his work. An added spur to success was Miss Wightwick. At the end of a day's hard work it was pleasant to visit the family home and, while Mr and Mrs Wightwick dozed in their chairs, to hear Emma read aloud or to talk with her at ease. Even pleasanter, he thought, would be a place of his own with Emma as his wife to support and comfort him.

Gradually he tired of Whistler, his sharp tongue, his boisterousness, his urge to dominate the company. After a year or so he moved to his own quarters in Berners Street nearby. Many false starts had convinced him that he should establish himself with one of the leading magazines and avoid the host of minor ones that paid neither well nor regularly. He laid siege to *Punch*, contributing at first ornamental initial letters and taking seriously the well-meant criticisms of its editor Mark Lemon. After a theatre matinée he proposed to Emma and she placidly accepted him. As an afterthought she enquired whether he was sure he would not change his mind?

Certainly he was, he answered, and he gave himself a target of a thousand pounds to be earned so that they could set themselves up in marriage. Since his drawings were not selling very well he wrote a short story and placed it with *Once A Week*. Encouraged, he drafted a tale about his student days in the Latin Quarter which prefigured *Trilby*. No editor would take it and he fell back on illustrating again. Money remained very short, his eye troubled him, and he went through all the symptoms of a nervous breakdown. By 1863, two years after his proposal to Emma, he had still not earned the promised thousand pounds. There was, however, a possibility of Mark Lemon taking him on as a regular member of the *Punch* staff. Grudgingly the Wightwick parents gave their consent, and in January, at Marylebone Parish Church, Emma married her George. They honeymooned in Boulogne.

'Once married I am safe,' George remarked to a friend. He had found, at last, the domestic routine which assured him the peace, the comfort, the regularity he so ardently craved.

The married couple took a damp little house in Bloomsbury at Great Russell Street. They entertained a lot for George had many friends: the painters Burne-Jones, Edward Poynter, Leighton and Millais, writers like Swinburne and musicians like Arthur Sullivan. In 1864 their first child was born, a girl called Beatrix after George's favourite heroine from Thackeray, a writer whom he adored. From the very beginning Beatrix, or Trixie, was his favourite child. She, like the others who eventually arrived, had the entrée to his workroom, and while he peered myopically at his drawing-board she was allowed to climb unchecked over the furniture and to romp around him with her dolls and her toys. Trixie was, he declared, 'a beautiful babe'.

That same year also brought fulfilment of his ambition to join the regular staff of *Punch*. He now belonged to the most successful magazine of its kind, an institution in Victorian life as well as an exclusive social club noted for its weekly lunches, continued still, where the conversation, more ribald than witty, would never have been allowed to appear in the columns of that stately journal. The new member was a peculiarly exuberant figure who drank heartily, chain-smoked cigarettes and occasionally offended older colleagues with his irrepressible high spirits.

That was one side of him. The other side emerged in bouts of gloom when he recalled his youthful aspiration to be a great artist, the ever-present worry that one day, despite the current trappings of success, his right eye might suddenly fail, and that there might come a time when his drawings failed to satisfy Mark Lemon. To all appearances he became more Victorian than the Victorians and adopted the strictest views, particularly on moral conduct. Yet he could not forget the heritage of his dual upbringing in France and in England. Was he French? Was he English? He never resolved the problem.

In *Peter Ibbetson* he was to write: 'Indeed, bilingual boys – boys double-tongued from their very birth (especially in French and English) – enjoy certain rare privileges. It is not a bad thing for a schoolboy (since a schoolboy he must be) to hail from two mother-countries if he can, and revel now and then in the sweets of homesickness for that of his two mother-countries in which he does not happen to be . . .' True bilingualism is rare. Words are only symbols which represent deep and subtle concepts. At an obvious level, for example, the term *pain* means bread. What, though, the Frenchman understands by *pain* is something entirely different from what the Englishman takes for bread. Du Maurier knew the difference. '*Il était un p'tit navire*' meant as much to him, with all its inner resonances and associations, as 'Three Blind Mice'. 'Tommy make room for your uncle' was as deeply familiar to him as '*l'amant d'Amanda*'. Athos, Porthos and Aramis were heroes to be as intimately cherished as Sydney Carton, and Tartarin de Tarascon as Mr Micawber. He explained of the bilingual subject:

And for this strange enchantment to be well and thoroughly felt, both his languages must be native; not acquired, however perfectly. Every single word must have its roots deep down in a personal past so remote for him as to be almost unremembered; the very sound and printed aspect of each must be rich in childish memories of home; in all the countless, nameless, priceless associations that make it sweet and fresh and strong, and racy of the soil.

He enjoyed life and he relished the celebrity that his weekly drawing in *Punch* earned for him. It was splendid to know that people looked forward to it, that they talked about it at fashionable dinner tables, that they laughed at his witty captions and satirical gibes. There were, though, moments when his spirit faltered and his eye hurt. '*A quoi bon vivre? Ce n'est pas gai*,' he would mutter. What was the point of life? It could be very unamusing at times.

[ii]

L'Anglais Malgré Lui

In 1865 their first son, Guy Louis, was born. By the following year they had another daughter, Sylvia Jocelyn, and the house in Great Russell Street had become too small for a growing family. They moved to Kensington and were joined there by a third daughter, Marie-Louise, to be known as May. Kensington did not please and the du Mauriers finally came to rest in Hampstead.

George remembered Hampstead Heath from his London boyhood and loved the place. As he wrote in *Peter Ibbetson*, it was best viewed on a sunny morning in late October:

Half the leaves have fallen, so that one can see the fading glory of those that remain; yellow and brown and pale and hectic red, shining like golden guineas and bright copper coins against the rich, dark, business-like green of the trees that mean to flourish all the winter through, like the tall slanting pines near the Spaniards, and the old cedar trees, and hedges of yew and holly, for which the Hampstead gardens are famous.

Before us lies a sea of fern, gone a russet-brown from decay, in which are isles of dark green gorse, and little trees with little scarlet and orange and lemon-coloured leaflets fluttering down, and running after each other on the bright grass, under the brisk west wind which makes the willows rustle, and turn up the whites of their leaves in pious resignation to the coming change.

In those days Hampstead was a small but growing community perched on its hill away from the rest of London. Constable painted the landscape there, and so did Ford Madox Brown, attracted by the spacious prospect and rolling views.

Harrow-on-the-Hill, with its pointed spire, rises blue in the distance [went on du Maurier], and distant ridges, like receding waves, rise into blueness, one after the other, out of the low-lying mist; the last ridge bluely melting into space. In the midst of it all gleams the Welsh Harp lake, like a piece of sky that has become unstuck and tumbled into the landscape with its shiny side up.

On the other side, all London, with nothing but the gilded cross of St Paul's on a level with the eye; it lies at our feet, as Paris used to do from the heights of Passy, a sight to make true dreamers gaze and think and dream the more . . .

It was all rather like Montmartre, that proud little hamlet with its vineyard and windmill overlooking the capital and its inhabitants who would talk of 'going down to Paris' as if visiting a foreign town. Hampstead suited George very well. It preserved him from the racket of dinner parties and entertaining in central London, it gave him peace to work. He could be sure that those who made the wearisome climb to see him were genuinely anxious for his company. He hoped that his children would grow up, as he had, in surroundings of greenery and mysterious ponds. Emma liked Hampstead too. The air was purer, she had never cared much for society, and in Hampstead she could concentrate on raising her family.

They did not, however, lead a monastic life, and they had many friends in the area. The architect Gilbert Scott lived a few doors away in Church Row and a neighbour introduced the du Mauriers to George Eliot. They saw much of the novelist Walter Besant and of his old acquaintance Millais. Often George would visit Miss Kate Greenaway and take tea with her in the garden, where their talk was not of art or illustration but of matters horticultural. His closest intimates were the cleric Alfred Ainger and the Anglophile Henry James. Du Maurier knew much more about the French classical authors whom he read in his youth than about contemporary literature, and it is an amusing paradox that he should have been introduced to moderns like Maupassant and Zola by his American friend James.

The du Mauriers' fifth and last child, Gerald Hubert Edward Busson du Maurier, was born on 26th March, 1873, while they were living in the handsome Queen Anne building at 27, Church Row. Next year the family moved, yet again, to New Grove House where they stayed for some twenty years. This was an old place which, despite late eighteenth-century additions, had a Victorian aspect emphasised by stucco and ivy. It was large and rambling and contained a magnificent, well-lit studio. George worked there in the morning for several hours while the children roamed, scrambled, toddled and crawled around and sometimes over him. He chattered with them while Emma on occasion read aloud from a book. The noise and the romping failed to put him off, indeed helped him the better to work. Often he would use the family as models. They were readily available and cost him nothing. One of his *Punch* cartoons showed 'Mamma' (Emma) speaking to a line of five children neatly drawn up by order of descending height. 'What a din you are making, chicks! What *are* you playing at?' enquires Mamma. Trixie, the tallest and therefore the leader, replies in one of those typically verbose *Punch* captions: 'O, Mamma, we're playing at railway trains. *I'm* the engine and Guy's a first-class carriage, and Sylvia's a second-class carriage, and May's a third-class carriage, and Gerald, he's a third-class carriage, too – that is, he's really only a *truck*, you know, only you mustn't tell him so, as it would offend him!' Doubtless the playful cartoon raised a fond smile from many a Victorian parent, bland though it may seem today.

His morning's work done, George would go for his daily walk over the heath accompanied by the elder children and a large St Bernard dog which often appeared also in his cartoons. The rest of the day was spent in more drawing and occasional entertaining at home. Although he no longer sang much himself, he wanted to encourage musical talent in the children, arranged piano lessons for Trixie and had Guy taught to play the violin. Guy showed a talent for amateur theatricals which he usually stage-managed and produced. At a time when most Victorian parents believed that children should be seen and not heard, George took the contrary view and positively urged them to express themselves. He loved to hear their talk and to learn of their adventures. They were a lively brood, a shade spoilt perhaps, but delightful in their vivacity.

Trixie, the eldest, became a natural captain, determined and high-spirited. Guy was more quiet and methodical. Sylvia and May, their father noted with some anxiety, for he prized beauty above all else, had lost the enchanting looks of babyhood and were turning out rather plain at this stage. Gerald, the youngest, was rather a problem. As the most junior of the lot he was not always treated with kindness by the others. His mother noticed this and kept on the alert for signs of bullying or childish unkindness. Little Gerald turned into what Trixie contemptuously described as Mummie's 'ewe lamb', pronouncing it 'ewee'. The 'ewee lamb' was not handsome. His brown hair was lank, his upper lip disproportionately long, and his big eyes would cloud over with sadness at a moment's notice. Mummie worried about him and detected an alarming propensity to colds and sniffles. He soon learned to tremble at the suspicion of a sneeze or the hint of a chill. Behind the façade of delicate health, though, the 'ewee lamb' could be funny and exuberant. He liked to put on an act, to imitate people who called on them, to mimic voices and gestures, often with unkind but telling effect. 'Don't look at Gerald; he's showing off,' May would snort.

But Gerald knew that his father enjoyed his capers, that he was amused when the boy crept in and made faces behind the back of the unsuspecting model who posed for him. Gerald, too, would pose in return for a scale of fees that ranged from sixpence to ninepence. He was sure he did it much better than the professional models his father employed. When he was not capering about in the studio he would delve into the wardrobe of clothes that were kept for their use. Out came hats, cloaks, dress clothes, deerstalkers, knickerbockers, scarves, waistcoats. He put them on in front of the mirror, choosing each item with care, matching one against the other, and struck poses. The glass before him reflected a series of different characters: the man about town, the sporting gent, the cabbie, the retired colonel, the errand boy. Already, without knowing it, he showed every sign of the born actor. Once, later on, he dressed up and had himself ushered in as a stranger, an unknown boy come to ask the favour of a loan. His father, completely taken in, misled not so much by his poor sight as by Gerald's effective mumming, entertained the unwelcome visitor with effortful courtesy until the joke could be prolonged no further and his giggling son revealed himself. This charade was to be repeated several times, and on each occasion George rose innocently to the bait.

The summer holidays were spent in Folkestone, in Ramsgate, on the Isle of Wight and in Whitby. There were trips to Dieppe, Le Havre and Etretat. Du Maurier rarely penetrated further inland, and apart from a few months at Auteuil near Paris he preferred to leave France unexplored. During the Auteuil stay he had revisited Paris and found even more of his childhood landmarks obliterated. He did not choose to repeat the experience. Dieppe was good enough for him, Dieppe where Gerald bounded high on the beach playing tennis with a spectacular smash intended to impress the Frog children who gathered round and formed a wondering audience. Gerald watched them, surreptitiously, and studied the effect he made as he leaped gracefully into the air and delivered yet another stunning shot. Back at the hotel he amused the family with imitations of the execrable French spoken by English tourists abroad.

Sometimes the atmosphere clouded over. A doctor advised George du Maurier to work less and preserve his failing eyesight. The shock of this opinion induced a mood of hysteria followed by depression. With no savings put by and a large family to support he relied absolutely on the cartoons he sold to *Punch*. The memory of his early poverty-stricken days returned to harass him and, until the suspense was lifted by a more favourable verdict from another eye specialist, he wallowed in panic. To avoid tiring his eyes he now drew on a scale twice as large as he had done up to then so that the finished sketch had to be photographically reduced for block-making. Inevitably his technique became coarser and less detailed. He knew that his best creative period was over and that he must largely depend on old formulas to see him through. That, anyway, was better than blindness, and as a form of insurance he preserved, in a large box, all the original drawings he possibly could. 'These will make you a rich widow,' he liked to tell Emma.

Even so, the cartoons he drew satirising the Aesthetic Movement in the 1870s and 1880s have point and much wit. A notorious target in Gilbert's *Patience*, the Aesthetes were summed up by du Maurier in a character whom he baptised Mrs Cimabue Brown, thus absurdly juxtaposing a Florentine idol with the most common of English names. Mrs Brown won fame in the pages of *Punch*. So did 'Maudle', a monocled and long-maned aesthete who was to be seen advising the mother of a 'nice manly boy' to 'let him remain for ever content to *exist beautifully.*' Du Maurier's satires were close enough for Whistler to accuse Oscar Wilde of having found some of his ideas in them. The cartoonist's gift was for words also, as he had earlier shown in his mockery of the Pre-Raphaelites, when he featured verses by the aesthetic poet 'Jellaby Postlethwaite' accompanying Maudle's picture 'A love-agony':

> So an thou be, that faintest in such wise,
> With love-wan eyelids on love-wanton eyes,
> Fain of thyself! I faint, adoring thee,
> Fain of thy kisses, fainer of thy sighs,
> Yet fainest, love! An thou wert fain of me,
> So an thou be!

and so forth. The aesthetic delight in archaic language is cruelly, but accurately, pinned down.

As an outsider du Maurier observed English society with added sharpness. He did not like ugly people or canting parsons. He detested the new rich and the socially pretentious. The boredom of formal banquets and the agony of after-dinner entertainments gave him rewarding material. Children he loved, and his own family life with two boisterous sons and three lively daughters provided a constant source of ideas for drawings in which are clearly to be recognised the faces of Trixie, Guy, Sylvia, May, Gerald and, sometimes, his wife Emma. He loathed, above all, hypocrisy and sycophantic behaviour. Perhaps his most famous cartoon, one which added a new phrase to the English language, is entitled 'True Humility'. It shows a bishop entertaining a curate to breakfast. 'I'm afraid you've got a bad egg, Mr Jones,' says the right reverend host. 'Oh no, my lord, I assure you!' replies the curate. 'Parts of it are excellent!'

Unfortunately his children were growing up. When young they would cluster around the dinner table, all talking at once in French or English and cracking family jokes incomprehensible to others. Emma was the still centre, quiet, vague, a little dazed by the mercurial wit that bubbled around her and not really able to keep up with them but always ready to calm and console in emergencies. They teased her for her lack of quickness but adored her for her benevolence. Trixie was the first to leave the family circle. In 1884 she married the handsome and well-off Charles Hoyer Millar at St George's, Hanover Square. George was pleased by the match but sad at his girl's departure. 'I should have been content to go on just as we are for another twenty or thirty years,' he told a friend. On the way to the church she had grasped the reluctant father-in-law's arm and enquired earnestly: 'Papa, if one marries a good-looking man, does it necessarily mean one will have good-looking children?'

Guy had left school at Marlborough and joined the army where he was commissioned in the Royal Fusiliers. On his posting to India he revived his theatrical pursuits by organising shows for the soldiers. When he returned to Woolwich he stage-managed *The Forty Thieves*, recruited May to act as Morgiana and even found a small part for Gerald. It ran a week amid loud acclaim. The only drawback to Guy's early years in the army was lack of money. His pay was small and his father allowed him no more than a hundred pounds a year. George du Maurier was not a miser but he was oppressed by the dread of financial insecurity. He, moreover, did not realise that a junior officer in a crack regiment needed more than an art student in the Latin Quarter. But Guy, respectful and considerate, never dared raise the matter with 'The Governor', as he always called his father.

By the 1890s the noise of small children was rarely heard in New Grove House except when George's sister Isabella stayed there with her quartet of infants. She had married the English drama critic Clement Scott. For years he battled valiantly against all that was new or experimental in the theatre. Ibsen's *Ghosts* he described as 'a dull, undramatic, verbose, tedious, and utterly uninteresting play . . . It is a wretched, deplorable, loathsome history, as all must admit.' In private life, however, his taste for novelty was insatiable and led him to change his mistresses with remarkable speed. Isabella eventually left him to their company and found a happier existence with her youngest daughter. To Hampstead also came the children of George's brother Eugène, 'Gyggy', who had resigned from the army and was to end his life as a commercial traveller of sorts. He was an awkward fellow and, during his last illness, refused to see George. The reason may well have been an argument over money, for that was about the only topic which brought the impecunious Eugène into touch with his brother.

New Grove House became emptier still when Sylvia married

Arthur Llewelyn Davies, a handsome young barrister with a promising future. Only May and Gerald were left. The 'ewee lamb' was despatched to preparatory school and May alone stayed in the house to cheer up a bereft father who had begun to look on her as his favourite daughter. She returned his fondness with a devotion that was to brighten his last years. In the meantime Hampstead proved no longer bearable to him with its old family memories. The house was let and the du Mauriers moved down the hill to a succession of rented houses in Bayswater. Here George exhausted himself in a round of dinner parties and social engagements which he would never have undertaken in the quieter surroundings of Hampstead.

By now he was not only a famous member of the *Punch* team but also a popular writer, a guest to be welcomed in fashionable drawing-rooms, a 'lion' to be cultivated for the lustre of his presence. In 1891 he published a novel called *Peter Ibbetson*. His eyesight was so bad that he was obliged often to wear dark glasses when sketching. Worse, he had gone deaf in one ear. What should he do if at last *Punch* decided to drop a contributor who was deaf as well as blind? Earlier in his career he had written stories and even seen some of them published. His nimble mind was always full of ideas for plots and scenes. If drawing pictures was becoming more and more difficult, why should he not make use of this other talent he possessed to earn money and security? Once he began *Peter Ibbetson* he found the story came easily. Some of it he wrote in his own hand, the rest he dictated to Emma who scribbled it down and then made, lovingly, a fair copy. His voice rolled evenly on as the room grew bluer with cigarette smoke and the ash-tray filled with a mound of stubs.

Peter Ibbetson is a strange novel. It is presented as the autobiography of a convicted murderer who, found to be insane, has suddenly died after writing an account of his life. The story tells of his love affair with the 'Duchess of Towers' from whom circumstances keep him apart. They meet only in dreams where they live a perfect and ideally happy existence. The outside world does not exist, and the two lovers can move at will back and forward in time. They never grow old and their love does not fade. The murder of a villainous uncle brings the death sentence for Ibbetson, whereupon he goes insane and, for the rest of his life in the asylum, is only reunited with his beloved through the medium of dreams.

Like du Maurier's other novels, *Peter Ibbetson* is wordy and rambling. The style is digressive and spattered with French phrases. It reads like the casual talk of an unusually cultured man, though it is no less charming for all that. The plotting is haphazard and the framework clumsy. The characterisation is vague and often unsatisfactory. With all these faults against it, *Peter Ibbetson* remains a fascinating piece of work. What, it seems to ask, is reality and what is illusion? Where, the author hints, shall we find ideal happiness if not in dreams? Who shall know how racial and family memories are transmitted and how two minds can meet and commingle? The novel made a deep impression on young intellectuals of the time. Among them was the poet John Masefield. Du Maurier's discovery was, he wrote, 'a thing of romantic beauty, and the effect of it upon that generation was profound. Even now, after fifty years, I can think of no book which so startled and delighted the questing mind. Here was shewn something which made life more wonderful, more full of meaning, more glad with the power of sympathy.'

Some of the best passages in the book are those which recall the author's boyhood. These are the most spontaneous of all because here du Maurier was writing from direct experience. Others have a speculative appeal which explains the effect the novel had on Masefield and his contemporaries:

Nothing is lost – nothing. From the ineffable, high fleeting thought a Shakespeare can't find words to express, to the slightest sensation of an earthworm – nothing! Not a leaf's feeling of the light, not a loadstone's sense of the pole, not a single volcanic or electric thrill of the mother earth . . . After each individual's death the earth retains each individual clay to be used again and again; and, as far as I can see, it rains back each individual essence to the sun – or somewhere near it – like a precious waterdrop returned to the sea, where it mingles, after having been about and seen something of the world, and learned the use of five small wits – and remembering it all!

The author draws also on his musical knowledge and utilises a technical phenomenon to make a rare simile. He refers to the overtones of a musical note and speaks of the pianist who, when he strikes a low C, will at first hear nothing apart from the fundamental note.

But let him become *expectant* of certain other notes; for instance, of the C in the octave immediately above, then the G immediately above that, then the E higher still; he will hear them all in time as clearly as the note originally struck; and, finally, a shrill little ghostly and quite importunate B flat in the treble will pulsate so loudly in his ear, that he will never cease to hear it whenever that low C is sounded.

By just such a process, only with infinitely more pains (and in the end with what pleasure and surprise), will he grow aware in time of a dim, latent, antenatal experience that underlies his own personal experience of this life.

Judged artistically and philosophically, *Peter Ibbetson* is the best of du Maurier's three novels, although it did not enjoy an enthusiastic reception from the critics. He had, nonetheless, established himself as a writer and won admirers both among his own generation and younger folk. While he prepared himself for his next novel, which was to be called *Trilby*, he also had to think about the future of his youngest child Gerald. Irrepressible, cocky even, the boy was so amusing that his easy-going father could not bring himself to discipline him. If Gerald grew too outrageous in his escapades, George would simply shake his head and say: 'Wait till you come to forty year and see how you like it.' For a temperament such as Gerald's he could see that life held many disappointments in store.

The little victim played, however, all heedless of his doom, and, as a weekly boarder at Heath Mount School, complained bitterly of having to get up at a quarter past seven each morning, of scanty breakfasts, of the cramping formality. 'Prison life, I call it,' he grumbled to his mother. He caught colds and made a fuss about the gruel he was served and the Eno's Fruit Salt he was given. None of it in fact damped his spirits and he grew even cheekier and more facetious. He wrote home in one of the twice-weekly letters authority ruled he should produce:

We went to a lecture on Monday evening, and the money was given to the Sailors' Daughters' Home girls. The girls sang at the beginning, I think they must have done it to get rid of some of the people, if so, it was a jolly good dodge . . . Tell Sylvia and May I hope they are behaving well, and are neat and modest withal. Matnong Adu, as the Englishman said when he went to Paris, j'ai tant bezwang de tes leves.
Your loving son,
Gerald du Maurier
PS Don't forget apple pudding on Saturday night or you will ru the day.

The French Connection

In 1887, at the age of fourteen, he went to Harrow. There, thought his parents, the nonsense would be hammered out of him. (Though 'Mummie' continued to send him luscious hampers of grub and to advise warm clothing in the perpetual battle against colds – like May, poor little dear, he had a weak chest.) On his arrival the master said: 'Oh, are you any relation to the *Punch* chap?' and made him sit down while the other boys crowded round to inspect the child of fame. The master's irony was lost on him and he accepted the remark with naïve pride.

Despite this ambiguous introduction he soon evolved his own unique formula of coping with Harrow, which was to avoid work as much as possible and to play football and to swim at every opportunity. His charm, which he had early learned to manipulate with skill, eased him out of many a difficult situation, and his gift of mimicry transformed annoyance or dislike into sympathetic laughter. His position in class, though, remained obstinately low, and when parental reproaches were made he answered with pitiable explanations: he wasn't feeling well, he'd been sick, and 'I've also had a stinking cold, and felt awful, and that's what really accounts for me being nineteenth this week.'

A cold! At mention of this fell complaint Mummie instantly sent a vast hamper of roast duck and jams and cold tongue. The 'ewee lamb', said she to herself, desperately needed building up for the winter. And then his housemaster, anxious about the boy, would write to say that during the last term it appeared that 'frivolity was too much in the ascendant with him and conscience falling out of sight. I hope that this will pass away. He has again come out much lower than I should wish. But towards the latter part of the term I noticed an improvement in his behaviour, as though his face was set in the right direction, and I trust that he will yet grow to set a good example to the house.'

Whereupon Gerald entertained the boys in his house and did his uproarious imitation of Henry Irving, the famous limp and the corncrake voice all reproduced with unkind accuracy. When the family holidayed in Whitby, a favourite resort, he performed at a local concert. 'Master G. du Maurier,' reported a local newspaper, 'gave "The Whistling Coon", the ladies and gentlemen forming the chorus whistling the refrain. The young gentleman was vociferously applauded.' However much his parents disapproved of such foolery, it has to be noted that the young gentleman's accompanist at the piano on this occasion was his father, the musical George.

Perhaps the only person who might have curbed Gerald's reprehensible tendencies was Guy, the brother whom he admired for his good looks and whom he much respected. Sisters were all very well in their way, but there were things that could only be talked about with a brother. Guy could advise him on topics of which the girls were ignorant, could tell him how to behave in given situations, could show him the form. On the other hand Guy, too, had an unfortunate leaning towards the theatre. How was Gerald to be put on the right lines? His father decided he must become a solicitor, as he wrote to a friend, 'not from aptitude for it, but from want of aptitude for anything else (except play acting and music hall singing – which his mother won't hear of!)'.

A large sum of money was needed to set him up in the profession. *Peter Ibbetson*, although a respectable achievement, had not earned as much as the du Mauriers hoped, so George went off on a provincial lecture tour which, in those days, could be lucrative. From London to Wolverhampton, from Hull to Manchester, from Kirkby Lonsdale back to London again, the distinguished *Punch* contributor rattled along in third-class railway carriages with voluminous baggage that included the magic lantern slides he used to illustrate his talks on artists he had known. He gave eighteen such lectures around the country before retiring, exhausted, to the longed-for comfort of home. They were successful and made money, though by no means as much as his next novel which he completed in 1892 and which, to his surprise and a certain amount of discomfiture, turned him into a best-seller and an international celebrity.

The idea of *Trilby* had been with him for a long time. Thirty years previously, as a young man undecided between drawing and writing, he submitted to a magazine a tale on the theme of a talentless girl mesmerised into singing beautifully by a mysterious Jew. The manuscript disappeared. He now took up the story again and expanded it into a full-length novel. It was set in the Latin Quarter of his youth and featured three English art students. One of them falls in love with a ravishing young model called Trilby O'Ferrall and is only persuaded against marrying her by his pious mother. The girl slips into the hands of a sinister musician by the name of Svengali. He hypnotises her into becoming a great singer and the finest soprano in Europe. She can, though, only sing under the influence of his mesmeric power, and when, one evening at a sensational concert, he dies from a heart attack, her genius immediately deserts her. It returns, briefly, at the sight of his eyes peering at her from a photograph, after which she too expires, cut off in the fullness of her beauty.

The French Connection

As in *Peter Ibbetson*, the evocation of Paris at the time of du Maurier's youth, more particularly the Latin Quarter, is exquisitely done. What distinguishes *Trilby* from the earlier novel is his creation of two unforgettable characters. Trilby herself may well have been founded on a shop-girl with whom he and a fellow student once played about in amateur attempts at hypnotism. She is probably an amalgam of girls du Maurier knew at the time. Whatever her origin Trilby is a poignantly attractive woman, an artless charmer. Of vague Scottish ancestry, she speaks French with an accent which her creator, paraphrasing W. S. Gilbert's verdict on Beerbohm Tree's Hamlet, describes as 'funny without being vulgar'. Her grace is natural and is emphasised, if anything, by the incongruous military overcoat she always wears. She makes a vivid contrast with the figure who acquires a macabre ascendancy over her, the pianist Svengali.

His voice is a raven's croak, his beard and mane of black hair are greasy and tangled, his eyes flicker with an eerie light. He speaks fluent French in a glutinous German accent. As a student he had been the finest pianist at the Conservatoire, and even his numerous enemies will admit that his Chopin playing has a heavenly perfection. Yet he has always wanted to be a singer. Within his mind circulates a host of lovely melodies and glorious tunes which he cannot express, for his own voice is harsh and raucous. One day Trilby has a bad attack of neuralgia. He tells her to look him full in the eyes and waves his hands over her face and neck. Within a quarter of an hour the pain has vanished. Even so, she cannot move or open her mouth until he releases her from the hypnotic spell. In her gratitude she kisses his hand while he flashes his big brown teeth at her.

Svengali realises that he has found the ideal medium to free the music that lies within him. Trilby is all the more suitable in that she is tone-deaf, cannot even distinguish between treble and bass, and is therefore entirely reliant on his powers. For eight hours a day over three years he teaches her with the aid of his friend the violinist Gecko until, at a simple wave of his hand, she can produce a flood of exquisite sound. She sings the most ordinary nursery songs with a rich, fresh quality that makes them seem like the greatest masterpieces ever written. Her *vocalise* of Chopin's A-flat Impromptu has more beauty than even a Liszt or a Rubinstein could have given. The moment Svengali dies a sudden death in the middle of her London début her genius dies with him and the golden voice fades into a squawk.

Trilby is sprawling and awkwardly constructed. One soon tires of those hearty Musketeer-like figures Little Billee, Taffy and 'The

Laird'. The prim descriptions of student life in the Latin Quarter conceal, one cannot help feeling, many incidents which du Maurier, the respectable Victorian *père de famille*, deliberately chose to suppress when looking back on his youth and thereby introduced an element of falsity. On the other hand the novel is redeemed and lives still because it contains one character, Svengali, who is now a by-word in the language. He is a superbly villainous villain, and du Maurier, who had loathed Germans ever since the Franco-Prussian War, thought to give him the final touch of wickedness by endowing him with a Teutonic accent. Like Sherlock Holmes, Mr Micawber and Mr Toad, he transcends literature and belongs to the national heritage.

The novel captured the public's imagination as soon as it began to appear in serial form. Readers were charmed by the familiar style, the romance of the Latin Quarter, the pathos of the heroine and, above all, the black-hearted Svengali. If du Maurier's triumph had come earlier he would have been equal to it. Life is often very cruel. At the age of sixty he was old before his time, weary, frail and intimidated by the whirlwind success of *Trilby*. Money poured in, and praise and innumerable fan letters. His heart was giving trouble and his eyesight caused perpetual worry. He hated all the fuss and longed in vain for release from the demands of celebrity. It was distasteful to him that people should market Trilby shoes, Trilby songs and even Trilby kitchen ranges. All that survives today of the craze is the Trilby hat, so named from headgear worn in the inevitable stage version of the book.

Gerald shared none of his father's doubts about success. He was proud and very impressed, although he affected a careless manner. Would the Governor, he asked Mummie, think of putting electric light in the lumber-room now? He had left Harrow after three contented but undistinguished years and, instead of going into the law as intended, took a job in a shipping office. Regular hours and office routine, he soon decided, were not for him. There were much more amusing things to be done, and he rather fancied being a young man about town, staying with friends, going to dances and playing in amateur theatricals. In between there were family holidays and reunions with the sisters and with Guy, the latter still keen on the theatre despite his army career. One autumn Gerald appeared as William III in a charity production of a now forgotten play entitled *Lady Clancarty*. He made a good impression, at least on local newspaper critics, and his parents began to think that after all it might be a good idea if he went on the stage for a time. The experience would cure him of his folly.

George du Maurier's attitude toward his son's choice of career was ambiguous. In *Punch* he had commented satirically on the growing fashion for amateur theatricals and made jokes about the newly acquired respectability won by drama. Actors and actresses now were received and admired in aristocratic houses, not, of course, as equals, but as celebrities who shed glamour on the proceedings. George confided in his old friend Henry James and asked his opinion. If, James replied, the boy really wanted to go on the stage, he did not see how his parents could stop him.

'That's all very well, James,' answered du Maurier, 'but what would you say if you had a son who wanted to go into the Church?'

James lifted both hands in horror: 'My dear du Maurier, a father's curse!'

Where should Gerald begin? His father knew John Hare, later Sir John, the actor-manager who happened, despite his connection with the theatre, to be a gentleman. Since 1889 he had run the Garrick, a theatre which W. S. Gilbert built for him on a plot in the Charing Cross Road. During excavations an old river was discovered which, it appeared, had been flowing since Roman times. Gilbert is said to have remarked that he did not know whether to go on with the building or to let the fishing rights. Having made his statutory quip he continued the operation which resulted in a classic façade, an auditorium decorated in the Italian Renaissance mode and a seating capacity of eight hundred, which was just about right for the intimate, sentimental comedies Hare's admirers liked to see him play.

At the Garrick Hare built up a large clientèle for well-bred drama and genteel comedy. He followed the example of Sir Squire and Lady Bancroft, those earlier monarchs of the fashionable theatre, by dressing his productions with elegance and setting them in what looked like genuine rooms. The furniture was solid, the decoration was in the best of taste and the pictures were beautifully framed. The stockbrokers in his audience recognised with approval what might have been a drawing-room transported bodily from Park Lane or an entrance hall plucked from Belvoir Castle and set down with every lavish detail intact. Their ladies sighed with pleasure at rich drapes and luxurious curtains. Hare could also provide a nobleman's pleasure garden or an old vicarage with every honeysuckle neatly in place. His young heroes were clearly gentlemen and his *ingénues* had obviously emerged from the best finishing schools. He himself specialised in playing humorous old men. When he was young, and even middle-aged, his make-up and acting in such parts were admired for their ingenuity. Once he was past the age of fifty, sad to say, the trick seemed no longer so clever or so amusing.

He took Gerald on for a small part in *An Old Jew* which had a company of sixteen. Gerald was cast as Fritz, a waiter, and made his first professional appearance in this comedy at the Garrick on 6th January, 1894. The play had been written by Sydney Grundy, an advocate from Manchester who quitted the law when he discovered a gift for purveying comedies and melodramas which pleased West End theatregoers. His best-known play, a farce adapted from the French called *A Pair of Spectacles*, gave Hare one of his most famous parts, that of Benjamin Goldfinch, which he often played and as many times revived. Grundy's plays are now as dead as the author himself. He is only remembered, with some derision, for his righteous protest at Bernard Shaw's use of the word 'bloody' in *Pygmalion*. The 'incarnadine adverb' was 'poison' on Shaw's pen, he declared. One cannot help feeling that his annoyance was caused not so much by the word itself as by Shaw's dismissal of one of his plays as 'a mere contrivance for filling a theatre bill, and not, I am bound to say, a very apt contrivance even at that'.

Gerald gave satisfaction in his humble rôle. The famous name he bore invited attention and a critic noted that 'Mr du Maurier in a very few words showed that he had probably found his vocation, and that this was only the earnest of better things to come.' Gerald would have agreed with him. Acting was easy. He also found that it could be boring after the agreeable tension of a first night when the play had settled down and you went through your moves and cues in an established routine. It had not yet occurred to him that one of the severest tests an actor can face is to deliver the same speeches night after night with the same freshness and the same vivacity as at the first performance.

His mother, who at first had been strongly opposed to his going on the stage, now appeared resigned. His father was amused and raised no objection. George, in fact, had much to occupy himself at the moment. While still submerged in the flood of success unleashed by *Trilby* he had written another novel, *The Martian*, which he sincerely thought the best of them all. The hero Barty Josselin incarnates all those qualities which du Maurier saw as lacking in himself: Josselin is over six feet tall, aristocratic, glamorous, intellectual and immensely popular with women. Although there is a strong autobiographical element in the book, it is utilised in such a way as to project the idealised vision of du Maurier as he would have liked to be. This is linked with an unconvincing narrative line which supposes that Josselin has come under the influence of a being from the planet Mars. While the hero is asleep the Martian transmits to him ideas and messages which, in his waking hours, he dutifully carries out. Here again are themes from the earlier novels, that of communication through dreams as in *Peter Ibbetson*, and that of mesmeric possession as in *Trilby*. But *The Martian*, even more than the other two, is an *olla podrida* stuffed with theories and recurrent prejudices. It remained, notwithstanding, du Maurier's favourite among his novels, and he went to his grave believing it the finest thing he had ever done.

He planned yet another novel but was distracted by the continuing fuss over *Trilby* and by preparations for the stage version which Beerbohm Tree was to produce. The première in 1895 he was just about able to endure at the cost of badly shaken nerves. In summer the following year his right eye began to fail in earnest. His heart showed further signs of strain, his stomach was upset, his gums swelled from a bad tooth and he could only eat liquids. Asthma declared itself and there were no more cigarettes, no more of those little black cigars which helped to stimulate his work and ease the strain of creating.

Gerald came to his bedside, chatted lightly and mimicked fellow actors. He made his father laugh so much that, squinting with his good eye through a storm of coughing, he begged him to stop. What did Gerald really know of the complex man who was his father? Did he ever guess at the strange ideas and ambitions that circulated in the mind of the cartoonist, the writer, the failed great painter? Gerald's egotistical high spirits on the one hand, George's wry disillusionment on the other, formed a barrier between them even more impenetrable than that which traditionally separates father and son. All Gerald realised was that the dear old Governor was soon to leave him and he wished that in the past he had not taken so much for granted. '*Si c'est la mort, ce n'est pas gai,*' whispered George as he said goodbye.

He was sixty-four when he died on 8th October, 1896. The body, following his request, was cremated, something of a novelty at the time, and the ashes were buried at Hampstead Parish Church. Henry James, mourning deeply, attended the funeral with the family and most of the *Punch* staff, and du Maurier's friend Canon Ainger took the service. Everyone was miserable and spoke little except for Gerald, who, unable to contain himself, burst out: 'At all events we won't have to play rounders after lunch.'

On du Maurier's grave in the churchyard was inscribed the final couplet of a French poem he had translated as:

> A little trust that when we die
> We reap our sowing! And so – goodbye!

They are the lines with which he concluded *Trilby*.

CHAPTER II

THE ACTOR

[i]

The Author's Son

While George du Maurier's life moved to an end his son carried on a brisk stage apprenticeship under John Hare at the Garrick. During the 1894–95 season there Gerald appeared in six plays. After *An Old Jew* he acted in *Mrs Lessingham*, another forgotten melodrama which, according to Bernard Shaw, displayed the unfortunate heroine 'fainting with the shock of catching her husband embracing another lady on the summit of an eminence visible from seven counties' and 'dying by her own hand, after a prolonged scene of deepening despair, in a room like Maple's shop window'. One of the season's most successful attractions was a revival of *Money* by Bulwer Lytton, who, best-known for *The Last Days Of Pompeii*, also wrote dramas such as that popular hit *The Lady of Lyons*. Although first produced as long ago as 1840, *Money* had a long life and survived into the twentieth century as an ever-ready help for actor-managers in need of a reliable crowd puller. Then came yet another piece of Grundyism, *Slaves of The Ring*, which prompted the Shavian verdict already mentioned. For good measure, Shaw added, à propos of the first act: 'I can only say that my utter lack of any sort of relish for Mr Grundy's school of theatrical art must be my excuse if I fail, without some appearance of malice, adequately to convey my sense of the mathematic lifelessness and intricacy of his preliminaries.'

Soon afterwards Hare revived, once more, Grundy's *A Pair of Spectacles* and delighted his admirers with a loving impersonation of his most famous rôle. The only new play of the season was Pinero's *The Notorious Mrs Ebbsmith*. Pinero should not be underestimated. His stagecraft was considerable and he had the art of flavouring his entertainments with a dash of social message which, so the audience imagined, made them 'think'. That is one reason why his dramas now seem both stilted and unconvincing. On the other hand his gift for the mechanics of stage effect still shines brightly in farces like *The Magistrate* and *Dandy Dick* which today can provoke laughter with the same brio as they did when first performed. *The Notorious Mrs Ebbsmith*, however, was a think-piece and, as such, received with critical solemnity, except, inevitably, by Shaw. Playing alongside Gerald du Maurier was another young actor, C. Aubrey Smith. The latter had already established his persona as the tall, aristocratic, much moustached Briton who in Hollywood's heyday was to incarnate the spirit of Anglo-Saxonry. He was known to intimates as 'Round-the-Corner Smith' from his distinctive habit of bowling, for cricket was his passion. In years to come, like the true gentleman he was, he kept to himself his opinion of the writer fellow Evelyn Waugh who satirised him as 'Sir Ambrose Abercrombie', leader of the Hollywood cricket team, in that masterpiece *The Loved One*. As early as the 1890s his technique was the same as fifty years hence. Although in *The Notorious Mrs Ebbsmith* he played the rôle of a vicar, a critic summed him up well: 'There were better actors, but in his own sphere he had no equal. He acted in earnest the sort of part that many other actors play as a joke – the stern, tweedy, pipe-smoking squire type, solid and dependable as a rock.'

In all these plays du Maurier had little to do but did it well. Character parts were simple, and with the aid of dress and an amusing mannerism, a *tic nerveux* or a slight stutter or a cough, it wasn't hard to raise a laugh. Straight parts were more difficult, though, and he sometimes wondered how he would meet that challenge when it came. In the meantime he enjoyed himself. He liked the free-and-easy atmosphere backstage, the late nights, the card games, the companionship. His name, again, brought attention. 'Mr du Maurier,' wrote a critic, 'has done exceedingly good work at the Garrick, and, although he has not yet played any big part, he will be fully equipped with experience when the crucial moment in his career arrives.'

One of the leading players in Hare's company was Johnston Forbes-Robertson. By then in his mid-forties, he had achieved a reputation which grew as the years went by. His voice was resonant, his manner natural, his face Roman in its nobility. Generations of theatregoers acclaimed him as the finest Hamlet of the time. Shaw was to write *Caesar and Cleopatra* for him. When he became 'Sir' Johnston Forbes-Robertson no theatrical knight could have been more dignified or stately, and he was regarded as the successor to Henry Irving under whom he had learned his craft. Yet he disliked acting and would have much preferred to be an artist. He had, indeed, studied at the Royal Academy, but family circumstances dictated that he should earn a quicker living as an actor. 'Never at any time have I gone on the stage,' he once declared, 'without longing for the moment when the curtain would come down on the last act.'

After leaving Hare Forbes-Robertson set up as an actor-manager himself. He is said to have made more money out of *Hamlet* than any other producer. There were, however, times when, like all actor-managers who wish to stay in business, he was obliged to put on rubbish. Just as Martin-Harvey always fell back on *The Only Way* to refresh the box-office, so Forbes-Robertson looked to *The Passing of The Third Floor Back* when finances were low. This was a fantasy by the humorist Jerome K. Jerome who wrote it in a pious mood far removed from that of *Three Men In a Boat*. The play tells how a mysterious Christ-like person comes to lodge in a Bloomsbury boarding-house and affects the tenants in such a way that they are cleansed of their vices and turn into models of virtue. Edifying sermons were preached about the play, bishops lauded it and the public always rushed to see it in the belief that it represented a spiritual experience. Forbes-Robertson grew heartily sick of the thing. His stage-manager remembered being at his side one evening just before he made his first entrance as 'The Stranger'. Forbes-Robertson suddenly turned his eyes heavenward and declared: 'Chr-r-r-rist! Will they never let me give up this *bloody* part?' A moment later he was on stage, mystic, saintly, aureoled with goodness.

He discerned promise in the young du Maurier and engaged him for a provincial tour. 'Forbie', as Gerald came to know him, had no side and did not stand on his dignity. In his company even the horrors of theatrical digs and lumpy mattresses failed to depress. 'Tell Papa I am NOT drinking too much,' Gerald wrote home to Mummie. 'I'm enjoying it all very much, apart from the fleas and the bad eggs, but nevertheless I long for the bosom of my family.' In *The Profligate*, another of those smoothly machined dramas by Pinero, he played a waiter again and successfully performed some very tricky business which involved serving dinner throughout the whole of one act, removing the plates, bringing new ones in their stead and brushing the cloth. He managed it without breaking a single dish or obscuring the sight-lines. Food and drink, as everyone knows, are among the most difficult of props to handle on stage.

The other play in which he toured under Forbes-Robertson was

Diplomacy. It had been among the greatest triumphs achieved by the famous husband and wife management team of Sir Squire and Lady Bancroft who reigned over the London theatre for twenty successful years. During that time they introduced many reforms such as the use of practicable scenery and the payment of decent wages to their company. Their choice of plays was shrewd and their business judgment impeccable. *Diplomacy* was based on the French play *Dora* by Victorien Sardou, master of the 'well-made' piece which Shaw ridiculed as 'Sardoodledom'. Bancroft paid the very large sum of fifteen hundred pounds for the rights and set his adaptors, one of whom was the drama critic Clement Scott, to work on it under his close supervision. In terms of long runs *Diplomacy* came second only to the 'cup and saucer dramas' of Tom Robertson which formed the staple Bancroft repertory. As usual preparations for the new spectacle were long and painstaking. Many alternative titles were considered. One of them, only dropped when it appeared to have been used by someone else, was *The Mouse Trap*.

So prosperous were the Bancrofts that they were able to retire when in their mid-forties. If asked why he had left management at that early age, Sir Squire would reply that he had a hundred and eighty thousand reasons, each one of them deposited in the Bank of England. When he died in 1926 at the age of eighty-five his will showed that the joke was in earnest. As a widower he lived in Albany and each morning strolled along Piccadilly, top-hatted, frock-coated, monocled, white hair beautifully arranged. In old age he enjoyed attending the funerals of, and memorial services to, his contemporaries. A cremation ceremony, rather unusual for the time, aroused his professional curiosity. 'A most impressive occasion,' he remarked. 'And afterwards the relatives were kind enough to ask me to go behind.'

Bancroft took a paternal interest in du Maurier and later showed him much generosity. Gerald played the small part of 'Algy' in *Diplomacy* when it opened at Derby and he must have pleased the old man since a local newspaper account described his portrayal as 'every inch a gentleman'. Gerald was amused, but also relieved, by his reception, since 'Algy' was his first straight part and he had been unable to rely on character tricks. Much later, as an actor-manager himself, he was to revive *Diplomacy*.

He came back from the provinces and in the autumn of 1895 found an engagement with Herbert Beerbohm Tree. Tree, in his early forties, was already a leading actor-manager. He had built up his reputation at the Haymarket, the Bancrofts' old theatre, and was laying plans for the construction of Her Majesty's. His productions were lavish and realistic. Rabbits gambolled over the stage in rural scenes, water flowed, temples crashed and flames roared. He did everything on the grand scale. To one of his actors who was underplaying he observed: 'When an actor in my beautiful theatre carries on to the stage a single candle I tell the electrician to turn on two floodlights, two whole battens and twenty lamps in the footlights representing in all some six thousand candle power. That one candle is represented by six thousand. Remember that when you act here.'

As an actor Tree was unequal and wayward. Early on in a run he did not always know his lines and made up for the lack with brilliant improvisation. The performance he gave on the first night would often be entirely different from the one on the fifth. By the time he had the part safely memorised he would lose interest and lapse into boredom. 'I have not got technique,' he admitted. 'It is a dull thing; it enslaves the imagination.' A professional actor can give the same performance each night. Tree, who was an inspired amateur, could not. Yet at his best he easily outshone his more technically competent rivals.

His personality was as capricious as his acting. 'Never say a humorous thing to a man who does not possess humour,' he remarked. 'He will always use it in evidence against you.' At Victoria Station booking office he asked for some tickets. 'What station do you want?' enquired the clerk. 'What stations have you got?' answered Tree. With actors he was always a little uneasy. He apologised to one of them whom he had cut dead off-stage while preparing for his entrance: 'Forgive me. I didn't recognise you in my disguise.' Finding himself one day in a post office he greeted the clerk: 'I hear you sell stamps. May I see some?' The clerk produced a sheet which Tree inspected. He pointed to a stamp in the centre. 'I'll take that one.' Perhaps his neatest epigram was inspired by the titillating dresses of the chorus girls in *Chu Chin Chow*: 'More navel than millinery.'

His wife, the horse-faced Maud, also had a pretty wit that even he sometimes feared. To some extent it may have been self-defence, for in addition to his normal family he kept a second 'wife' and a brood of illegitimate children. 'Poor dear Herbert,' Maud used to say. 'All his affaires start with a compliment and end with a confinement.' When he spoke well of a fashionable doctor and said he had attended many of the greatest living Englishmen, she riposted: 'Dead, you mean.' A friend who told her, 'How charmingly you've done your hair, Maud,' was answered with: 'How sweet of you to call it *my* hair.'

She reserved her best witticisms for dear Herbert. Piqued that he should have chosen Ellen Terry and Madge Kendal, both mature figures, to appear with him in *The Merry Wives of Windsor*, she watched the three of them arm-in-arm at rehearsal and commented: 'Look at Herbert between two ancient lights!' It is not surprising that the Trees' daughter Viola should have inherited her parents' wit. She was to become a very close friend of Gerald du Maurier.

Tree's motive for engaging him may not have been entirely due to admiration of the young actor's skill. He was about to stage a version of *Trilby*, and there was an amusing chance for publicity if the author's own son were among the cast. Tree had seen a production of *Trilby* in New York, and, against the advice of his half-brother Max who was understandably horrified by the sensationalism of the thing, immediately negotiated the English rights. The novel was adapted by Paul Potter, an Englishman who chose to live in America by reason of some obscure incident in the distant past, and Tree set to work, as he always did with a new project, revising and altering and adding effective bits of business. He hurried down to Folkestone where the ailing George du Maurier was on holiday and obtained his agreement to all the changes he wanted. This was not difficult. Du Maurier was desperately tired, ready for the death that claimed him a year later, and anxious above all to be released from the importunate Tree.

At the very start, of course, Tree had seen a wonderful part for himself in Svengali and was keen to seize it. His instinct did not let him down. As Svengali he was to create a rôle even more famous than his macabre Fagin, his sweet-natured Colonel Newcome, his gruff Beethoven, and, in Shakespeare, his fantastical Malvolio and his majestic Richard II. The play, much amended and including scenes written by Tree, was first given in Manchester on tour and won immediate success. Dorothea Baird, later to be the first Mrs Darling in *Peter Pan*, moved the audience deeply with her natural playing of Trilby, though it was Tree who dominated, Tree as the demoniac Svengali, ugly, guttural-voiced and evil eyed. All the characters were dressed just as du Maurier had pictured them in his illustrations, but Tree's make-up set him apart as a creature of overwhelming villainy. The Manchester audience revelled in him.

So did those in London. Arrived at the Haymarket in October, *Trilby* was launched by a first night of splendour. Guests included the Prince of Wales, later Edward VII, and his consort. He remarked primly to George du Maurier, who had been dragged reluctantly forward, that the Princess was not keen on seeing Miss Baird with naked feet. Bernard Shaw, who had enjoyed the novel, was more penetrating and refused to be gammoned by Tree's bravura. 'I should no more dream of complimenting him on the Svengali business than Sir Henry Irving on *A Hero of Waterloo*,' he wrote, loosing off a shaft which was the deadliest in his quiver. Tree did not care. *Trilby* made more money than any of his other productions and ran for two hundred and sixty performances. It was revived again and again and served as an insurance for times when funds were low. He only had to announce a revival and crowds would flock to the box-office.

At a wage of four pounds a week Gerald played the minor part of Gontran, alias 'Zouzou', a corporal in the Zouaves and, one evening, saw for himself how skilfully the actor could rescue a difficult situation. Svengali was supposed to play the piano, an illusion created by Tree sitting at a dummy keyboard and fluttering his hands while an expert performed off-stage. On this occasion, absent-mindedly, Tree got up from the piano stool a few moments before the tune was over. The ghostly music went on as he paced about the stage. No one in the audience seemed to notice anything wrong, and Tree himself only realised when he glanced into the wings and met the horrified look of his stage manager. He pulled himself together, gestured haughtily at the piano, and said: 'See what Svengali can do!' as the last notes faded away.

In a letter home Gerald wrote:

You will be glad to hear that Tree is very pleased with my Zouzou; he says I am the life and soul of the *cancan* scene, and has put me right down in the front, and I have got the best girl to dance with too . . . lots of things are going to be altered now that the first night is over. I'm suggesting heaps myself and they are all going to be done. That's what comes of being the author's son! In fact when people want things altered they come to me and say, 'I wish you'd ask Tree,' etc, etc, and so I go up and say, 'Mr Tree, it would be much better for *you* if so-and-so did such-and-such a thing,' and he says, 'we'll see', and a few minutes later he says in a loud voice, 'An idea has just occurred to me,' and does what I've told him . . .

Whether or not Tree accepted so meekly the ideas put forward by a pushful, uncrushable and very junior member of his company is something that cannot now be verified. Probably he was amused by the young man's presumption and, for the sake of the family name, listened to his ideas with good humour. After *Trilby* ended its six-month run he cast du Maurier as Gadshill in his new production of *King Henry IV* (Part I). In the autumn of 1896 the company went on tour and then sailed for America. 'You mustn't be too depressed about my going away,' Gerald wrote to his lately widowed mother. 'Remember it's only for a short time and I will write very often. Of course, darling, you must miss Papa terribly; it's bad enough for all of *us*, but what it must be to you!' He was melancholy when the *St Louis* departed from Southampton and only perked up when he saw Mrs Tree and Viola casting bunches of violets in the wake of the vessel as Tree, in heroic pose, declared: 'Adieu, England!'

On the long voyage out Gerald recovered his spirits and diverted thoughts of sea-sickness by organising games and concerts. Tree looked on him as something of a court jester and enjoyed a news-sheet he concocted full of scandal about his fellow passengers. In America, where *Trilby* the novel was a famous best-seller, Gerald as the author's son became a welcome guest at receptions. Again he played in *King Henry IV* (Part I) and watched Tree's Hamlet, a performance which earlier had prompted W. S. Gilbert's wounding comment: 'My dear fellow, I never saw anything so funny in my life, and yet it was not in the least vulgar.' Other plays in the repertory included *Trilby* and *The Dancing Girl*. The last-named was by Henry Arthur Jones, a prominent dramatist of the time who nourished the curious belief, curious at least to Tree, that his lines should be spoken as he had written them. At rehearsals when Tree made some particularly outrageous alteration, Jones would roar: 'No! No!! No!!!' 'Don't repeat yourself,' Tree would murmur. They usually ended up shaking fists at one another and exchanging solicitors' letters. Finally there was *The Seats of The Mighty*, a dramatisation based on a popular novel. Tree had great hopes of it, though it failed when he put it on in New York. Unabashed, he doctored the piece extensively and staged it again in other American cities. Still it failed and still he persevered, believing it to be the perfect opener for Her Majesty's Theatre, that ambitious undertaking nursed so long and, with only a few months to go, on the point of completion. Criticism of the play left him outwardly unmoved. 'I am bearing it all,' he wrote to Maud, 'with a fortitude which I cannot help admiring.'

A few days later he told her: 'I dare say you have heard that Gerald du Maurier and Miss Sylva are engaged to be married – I hear Miss Sylva's mother objects – so I shall write to her all about it and appease her mind.' Marguerite Sylva, known as Maggie, was a young French actress in the company who for some time had interested Gerald. A little homesick, anxious for distraction, he gradually persuaded himself that he was in love with her and asked her to marry him. A newspaper report that he had attended a White House reception with his 'fiancée' Miss Sylva astonished his mother and family back home who had heard nothing of the affair. Brother Guy immediately despatched a stern telegram: 'May I contradict report of your engagement?' His mother reproached him sharply.

> You know, Mummie darling [he answered], I put you before everyone and always shall, and if you could only speak to her for five minutes all your unhappiness would vanish. The only fault you can possibly find is that she is French in appearance, in voice, in everything. Why in Heaven's name she has fallen in love with me, nobody knows . . . Anyway, it's no use talking any more about it. I love her and you must too . . . She *is* younger than I am, though you say she doesn't look it, and what's more she has a beautiful voice and speaks three languages and is devoted to me . . .

The loving couple had their small tiffs. Gerald did not like New York. Maggie did, and spoke of settling there. Her mother, unmoved by Tree's kindly intercession, threatened to disown her if she persisted in this foolish union with a penniless actor. Mrs du Maurier also remained implacable. Within a short time the engagement was broken off, and, although he did not admit it, Gerald felt rather pleased to be free once more.

He came back to England with Tree and the company prepared for the grand opening of Her Majesty's Theatre on 28th April, 1897. The building was ready at last, a domed edifice of Portland stone and red granite with its own royal warrant and attendants habited in liveries which recalled those of Buckingham Palace. The auditorium followed the style of Louis XIV and the act drop reproduced the pattern of a Gobelin tapestry. An excellent orchestra hid discreetly behind palm leaves. Programmes were free, as were cloakrooms, and playgoers were welcomed as guests rather than customers. Tree was delighted with his new creation and showed it off to everyone he came across. After lunch at the Garrick Club he took Sir Squire Bancroft to admire the Renaissance-style façade. Sir Squire, white hair glinting in the sunshine, put up his eye-glass and stared long and carefully. 'Well?' said Tree impatiently. In his sonorous tone the lately knighted actor replied, 'A great many windows to clean.'

Tree opened his beautiful theatre, as he had always stubbornly intended, with *The Seats of The Mighty*. Before the play he gave an address and, as Bernard Shaw wrote, 'told us that he would never disgrace the name the theatre bore; and his air as he spoke was that of a man who, on the brink of forgery, arson, and bigamy, was saved by the feeling that the owner of Her Majesty's Theatre must not do such things'. The Poet Laureate supplied a piece of occasional verse which Maud recited without conviction, Clara Butt sang the National Anthem, and the curtain rose on a drama which the audience, including yet again the Prince of Wales, sat through with earnest politeness. Bernard Shaw devoted the whole of his notice to praise of 'the handsomest theatre in London', and ended: 'The proceedings terminated with a play . . .' Gerald acted the part of Lieutenant Ferney and at least saw his name mentioned in Shaw's article. When all the bouquets and congratulations were over, Tree went out to the cabmen's shelter in Piccadilly where he stayed until six in the morning drinking coffee and playing dominoes with the cabbies.

The Seats of The Mighty, as unsuccessful in London as it had been in America, did not last more than a few months, and by July it was replaced with *The Silver Key*, an adaptation of Dumas by the hard-working Sydney Grundy. 'Why on earth cannot Mr Grundy let well alone?' groaned Shaw. As Chamillac, Gerald played in lace and jabot, a rare excursion into period dress. He acted too in *The Red Lamp* and in *A Man's Shadow*, a police court drama adapted from the French. Next year he was in *Julius Caesar* and *The Musketeers*, another Grundy adaptation of Dumas. The season ended with *Ragged Robin* which had been translated from the French by that charming and industrious figure Louis-Napoleon Parker. Born in France, he was the composer of many cantatas and songs, having been for nineteen years a music teacher at Sherborne School. Then he turned to the stage and wrote or adapted upwards of sixty plays as well as producing numerous pageants in towns throughout the country. At rehearsals his anxious person was always accompanied by a walking-stick to which he had fixed the ear trumpet he used as a hearing-aid. Of Tree, with whom he often worked on crowd scenes, he observed: 'The most lovable man I have ever met; the most aggravating man, too.'

In between these appearances Gerald convinced himself that he had fallen in love again. This time his target was the American actress Ethel Barrymore, sister of John and Lionel, whose performance on the London stage reminded Max Beerbohm 'of many various things – of a bird, a fairy, a child, a terrier, a flower, what-not; but of a woman, never . . . Perhaps she can best be summed up as a Pierrot.' She was nineteen years old and had a tough character, as Gerald's mother instantly perceived. Mrs du Maurier, with a sigh, gradually nerved herself to accept this new folly and in time prepared for a marriage. Ethel found Gerald not at all good-looking but was captivated by his wit and gaiety. A New York paper commented: 'Mr du Maurier impressed most of those who beheld him as being scarcely ripe. His physique was frail to the point of attenuation, his legs looked for all the world like a couple of sectional gas-pipes with abrupt bony projections midway between the floor and their jointure to the trunk.' But Ethel, 'in all the radiance of her young loveliness, will be far and away the spectacular feature of the wedding'.

It did not take place. Ethel suddenly decided she must go home and, in a flood of tears, was escorted to her train by Gerald. The young lady had taken fright when Mrs du Maurier, reconciled at last to her 'ewee lamb's' departure from the family, began to heap upon her lavish advice about the proper care of Gerald, what he should wear, what he should eat, how to help him avoid catching cold. Yet although the affair died away Gerald had been much more closely involved with Ethel than he was with Miss Sylva. In private life friends called her by her second name of Daphne. That was the name he later gave to one of his daughters. Something of the old feeling lingered on.

[ii]

The Admirable Crichton and Romance

The pang Miss Barrymore caused him was soothed by an offer of the most important rôle that had yet come his way. Pinero's new play *Trelawny of The 'Wells'*, due for production in January 1898, was to be done at the Court Theatre and Tree 'lent' him to the management for the part of Ferdinand Gadd. The fragrant little comedy with a theatrical setting looked back nostalgically to an earlier age of crinolines and peg-top trousers. During rehearsals 'Pin', as the dramatist was known, haunted the auditorium, hands clasped behind his back, watching and listening intently as he prowled around the stalls and jerked his bald dome forward when he had a remark to make. He wore an impeccable black morning coat, a carefully arranged tie, pepper-and-salt trousers and a short boxy overcoat that suggested, together with large bowler hat and wash-leather gloves, the racecourse. His manner was polite, genial and thoughtful. At that time he had reached the height of his fame and was to be knighted a few years later. Then began the long decline until the 1930s when he drifted out of touch completely. To a friend who asked why he no longer wrote plays in his old age he sadly replied: 'Because today there are no more rules to break.'

The leading lady was Irene Vanbrugh, née Barnes, sister of Kenneth who became the first principal of RADA, or Royal Academy of Dramatic Art. She later married Dion Boucicault who also appeared in *Trelawny of The 'Wells'*. The part of Rose Trelawny was her first big rôle and she delighted in privileges new to her, not least of which was being allotted a special armchair on stage at the reading of the play. From her experience she judged du Maurier as Ferdinand Gadd and decided that his own sense of humour tended to falsify 'the character of an actor of the old school full of pomposity and completely without humour. Gerald appreciated this lack but in his portrayal his own gift resulted in his giving a false value instead of the lack of that quality in Ferdinand, thus missing a side of the character which had been in Pinero's conception.' Bernard Shaw thought otherwise and laid the blame on Pinero, remarking that

> when we come to Ferdinand Gadd, the leading juvenile of *The 'Wells'*, we find Mr Gerald du Maurier in a difficulty. At his age his only chance of doing anything with the part is to suggest Sir Henry Irving in embryo. But Mr Pinero has not written it that way: he has left Ferdinand Gadd in the old groove as completely as Mr Crummles was. The result is that the part falls between two stools.

After *Trelawny of The 'Wells'*, which ran for a hundred and thirty-five performances, Gerald went back to Tree and made his last appearance at Her Majesty's in *Carnac Sahib*, yet another offering by the prolific Henry Arthur Jones and yet another occasion for those jousts between dramatist and actor-manager which turned rehearsals into a battlefield. The plot, a fragile affair concerning two army officers in love with a married flirt, was set against a colourful Indian background on which Tree lavished all his gift for exotic stage-pictures. He failed to impress the incomparable Max who had by then succeeded Shaw on the *Saturday Review*.

> As it is [complained the new critic], there is practically no play at all. There are gorgeous spectacles, a great many characters, a great deal of noise. One sees Anglo-India, just as at the Lyceum one sees the French Revolution. It is an interesting place to see.

But one cannot really get up any personal interest in the characters of a play which is scarcely more dramatic than was the Indian Exhibition at Earl's Court.

It sounds, in other words, like any of Tree's grandiloquent productions.

In 1900, at the age of twenty-seven, Gerald left Tree and joined Mrs Patrick Campbell's company at the Royalty Theatre which she had boldly taken under her management. The Royalty, in Dean Street, Soho, exists no longer. Before it closed in 1938 to be replaced with an office block, it housed some memorable productions, among them Mrs Pat's seasons of 1901 and 1902. She had assembled a strong company which included the thirty-two-year-old George Arliss. He was a well-known and versatile West End actor fated to become a star in America and especially in Hollywood. During the 1930s he was one of the highest-paid film actors of the time and enjoyed regal sway over the studios where, at half-past four each day, work automatically stopped so that his valet might serve him afternoon tea. His large vulturine nose, high cheekbones and precise diction conferred a dignity and presence which enabled him to play with conviction in film biographies of Richelieu, Voltaire, the Duke of Wellington, Rothschild and Disraeli. Indeed, a generation of cinemagoers grew up believing that most famous men in history had all resembled George Arliss. Forgotten though he may be now, he exerted influence in unexpected quarters. Laurence Olivier much admired him and, as late as the 1970s, modelled his interpretation of Shylock on Arliss as Disraeli. Towards the end of his career he heard that he had been chosen for a knighthood. So excited was he that he threw a grand party before the official announcement could be made. The King, extremely cross, dropped his name from the list as punishment for such bad form. Still, even a knighthood would have added little to his notably majestic style. A clubman once asked a barman for a 'George Arliss sherry'. The barman looked puzzled. 'Old, pale and dry,' explained the customer.

If Tree had been a difficult and autocratic employer, du Maurier was to find Mrs Patrick Campbell an even more trying one. With no formal training for the stage and only a magnificent natural talent, she conquered London as the second Mrs Tanqueray, as Mrs Ebbsmith, as Magda, as Lady Macbeth and as Mélisande. Early marriage to an obscure army officer who died soon afterwards left her with two small children and no money, so she went on the stage to earn her living. Witty, perverse, domineering, she could be unbearable and yet, at the same time, a commanding actress praised by Sarah Bernhardt with whom she appeared in *Pelléas et Mélisande*. Money was hers, and glory and the respect of fashionable society which meant a lot to her, but she in time threw it all away. Some strange demon impelled her to sacrifice everything for the sake of stinging witticisms that earned her the nickname of 'the Pat-Cat'. As the first Eliza Doolittle in *Pygmalion* she reduced her partner Tree to sobs and drove Bernard Shaw into fits of exasperation. Even when old and penniless she never resisted the temptation of making epigrams which hurt and scared off those who loved her and sought only to help. In Hollywood where she spent some of her miserable old age she could not remember her lines before the camera and, at the end of the day, still failed to deliver them.

'What's the time, dear,' she asked her impatient director.

'Five o'clock.'

'No, in London, dear.'

'It's eight hours ahead there. That would make it one a.m.'

'As late as that? No wonder I'm so tired.'

Sweeping into a friend's dressing-room at a first night she would trumpet: 'Darling, how insincere people are! You know, you have the most awful failure on your hands.' This was the sort of thing her friends came to expect of Stella Patrick Campbell. On only one thing was she truly vulnerable. In a contemporary issue of *The Green Room Book* she included among her recreations 'an extraordinary fondness for animals'. This accounted for the procession of small yapping dogs, usually Pekes, which she enfolded in her bosom and which covered her expensive dresses with a perennial harvest of dribble and hair. A New York taxi-driver complained to her once about a puddle on the floor. 'Who's responsible for this?' he snarled.

'*I* am!' said Mrs Pat, gathering up her pet and stepping haughtily out of the vehicle.

When she first saw du Maurier her reaction was characteristic. 'Oh,' she exclaimed, looking at his gaunt features and spindly frame, 'how can I act with a dreadful, ugly face like that?' Despite this unfavourable reception she thought she could detect something of promise in the twenty-seven-year-old actor and she engaged him for her new season. One of his early roles was in *The Fantasticks*, an adaptation of Rostand's *Les Romanesques*. The play has never wholly succeeded in its occasional revivals this century over here because it is so exclusively French and does not travel well. The poetry, as always with the author of *Cyrano de Bergerac*, is delicate, fine

as a spider's web and quite untranslatable. The plot has echoes
of *Romeo and Juliet*, although in this case the respective fathers of
hero and heroine only pretend to be enemies in order to bring the
lovers together. The atmosphere is one of Watteauesque elegance.
It was, thought Max Beerbohm, 'the prettiest and wittiest little play
in the town', although he found Mrs Campbell rather too intense
and George Arliss not refined enough in a play which, he admitted,
was very hard to cast well since it belonged to a kind never written
in this country. 'Mr Gerald du Maurier,' he added, 'as the Bravo,
did his best to be fantastic, but did not succeed in being more than
boisterous.' Another critic showed greater enthusiasm.

> No one was light enough, quick enough, extravagant enough –
> with one exception, Mr Gerald du Maurier [he wrote]. He
> alone seemed to catch the spirit of the piece, and to understand
> what was wanted. He acted with infinite humour, dash, and
> grace. How much there is in heredity and parentage! Mr du
> Maurier is French in family, and had a delightful humorist as
> father.

An important event of the 1900 season was Mrs Campbell's production of a play by the notorious Frank Harris. His venture into
the theatre, like his activity elsewhere, reminded Max Beerbohm
of a bull in a china shop, and he showed a breezy contempt for
dramatic convention by inserting soliloquies and placing climaxes
where they were least expected. And how was Gerald in all this?
He, 'as the lover, need not have been quite so deeply sunk in
melancholy calm. He might have managed a bright smile or two,
now and again. He might have gesticulated, just a little. His
immobility distressed me. Restraint is an admirable thing in acting,
but it should not be the kind of restraint that is enforced by a strait
waistcoat.'

This was perceptive. It shows that already Gerald had begun to
evolve his own distinctive style. As a reaction against the flamboyant
manner of Irving and Tree he was looking for something quieter,
more realistic. He was learning to discipline his natural exuberance
and to aim at understatement. Though sensing the need for restraint
he could not as yet suggest it effectively. Restraint is only successful
if there is something to restrain. There must be the unmistakable
hint of power in reserve, power that may burst forth suddenly, like
the snapping of a taut wire. He still lacked the means to create this
impression.

That he had reached such a point in his artistic development is largely due to Mrs Pat. She recognised in him someone like herself who, never having been to drama school, possessed a natural gift. It needed bringing out and training. For all her wilfulness and eccentricity she was an artist who appreciated talent in others. She took him in hand, polished his diction, taught him how to project. Her tuition was informal and coloured with tart witticisms that penetrated beneath the skin and made him wriggle. There were moments when he loathed her and others when he adored her. She could be a tyrant and then, within moments, the sweetest of companions. Even in a play totally unsuited to him like *Pelléas et Mélisande* she was able to conjure a good performance out of him. 'I have taught a clown to play Pelléas,' she declared.

Off-stage, too, she groomed him. He no longer sought to dominate the company in which he found himself and he subdued his urge to shine as a solo performer. Now he listened to what other people said. He was not, he realised, the only pebble on the beach. A new depth became apparent in him, his charm grew less unruly and more sympathetic. He was flattered by Mrs Pat's concern for him, and so was his mother who succumbed to her impeccably polite manner. There were pleasant little dinners *tête-à-tête* with 'Mrs Campbell', as he called her at first. Soon she became 'Stella'. He drove her up to Hampstead and showed her the place where he lived as a boy. 'And I am being very good,' wrote the 'ewee-lamb' to Mrs du Maurier, 'not sitting up late or drinking too much, so don't alarm yourself.'

'Clown', Mrs Pat would call him, and 'Mr Walk-About', as she strove to shake him out of his easy-going approach and to encourage the more positive aspect of his talent. She drilled him to play opposite her in those vehicles she had made her own, *The Notorious Mrs Ebbsmith* and *The Second Mrs Tanqueray*, and he responded with characterisations that had a little more steel to them, a little more sharpness. They went on tour and Gerald wrote to his mother from Leeds:

I have just been out shopping with Mrs Campbell. I've never seen such a person for buying old furniture and things. My knowledge is getting vast on such subjects as Dutch and French antiques. Afterwards I played golf, and she walked round and sat about, it did her tons of good, and she's never been so well . . . There is to be a supper-party to the company this week, and Mrs Campbell says I am to do all my tricks!

She did, on occasion, relax the discipline and give him his head.

But not for long. 'My success as yet in the part is not pronounced, but I mean to do better in about a week,' he wrote soon afterwards. 'It's such awfully nervous work and so impossible a part to be natural in. I think acting is the most difficult and heart-breaking work, but splendid for the inside. I'm trying hard all the time, and Mrs Campbell is untiring with me.'

At the end of 1901 she took the company to America. George Arliss travelled with her and stayed on to lay the basis there of a distinguished career. Gerald remained in England, wiser, certainly maturer, than he had been when he first came under the spell of Mrs Pat two years earlier. She played in his life the part of Balzac's *femme de trente ans*, the older woman who, experienced but still youthful, dominates the junior partner and teaches him the bittersweet lesson he must learn. She left him thoughtful and with a sense of regret he had never known before that moments of happiness are fleeting and never to be recaptured.

He played a lot of golf – it had become a passion with him and was to fascinate him for the rest of his life – and bridge which he adored, sitting up late at the Green Room Club and the Garrick where he was already a popular member. His quick tongue and teasing mimicry gave no offence because they were accompanied, at least in public, by an engaging warmth and sociability. The targets of his good-natured mockery shrugged their shoulders and declared that Gerald up to mischief was quite priceless, a regular card.

As a rising star he had no difficulty in finding new engagements and early in 1902 he was at the Prince of Wales as the Honourable Archie Vyse in *A Country Mouse*. It involved a beautiful girl who comes up from the country and finds many admirers in London high society. Gerald was required to lounge around as an elegant *jeune premier*, invariably wearing tails or morning dress which showed off his slim figure, and to express his admiration for the heroine with such remarks as, 'By Jove, I wish you could pour out tea for me every day.' True, there were moments of crisper dialogue, as when the heroine politely congratulates an elderly Duke on being a good croquet player. Archie, who sees him as a rival, says: 'He ought to be. He's had lots of practice.' Duke: 'Not lately.' Archie: 'No, I mean all those years before I was born.' Generally, however, the main interest of the play resided in the *toilettes* worn by the ladies: evening gowns of black and white satin, Empire frocks with silver net, dinner dresses of pink muslin.

A Country Mouse, later transferred to the Criterion, its natural home, was typical of the plays then most fashionable. The cast invariably included a Duke, or at least a minor member of the aristocracy, and the settings were laid in gentlemen's country residences or town houses. With a plot little more than anecdotal and dialogue resolutely flippant, such plays satisfied an audience which delighted in glimpses of high life and enjoyed seeing the upper classes portrayed on stage while the lower orders provided comic relief as servants. Arthur Law, its now forgotten author, provided many successful after-dinner entertainments of this nature. Gerald played his part with ease and spread an effortless glamour over the stage. He felt a certain relief at lapsing into his old ways, and, after all, the rôle presented no challenge to him. It was pleasant to know that Mrs Pat was not at his back, urging him, dragooning him, pestering him.

Yet a malaise persisted. Mrs Pat had instilled in him a vague longing, he could not define for what, and night after night, as he loped smoothly over the Criterion stage and spoke the feathery dialogue with exquisite point, a sense of boredom invaded him. His next part, although it did not make serious demands on him, at least cast him in a better play. At the Duke of York's he was offered yet another aristocrat, the Honourable Ernest Woolley, in J. M. Barrie's *The Admirable Crichton*. He asked for, and received, a weekly salary of twenty-five pounds. The salary, as it turned out, was not so important, for the play, which explored human relationships at a level far deeper than that of *A Country Mouse*, brought him closer acquaintance with an author whose effect on various members of the du Maurier family was to be at once eerie and beneficial. *The Admirable Crichton* also introduced Gerald to his future wife.

Barrie first made his name with *The Little Minister*, a novel which he turned into a play that was to earn him some eighty thousand pounds and to inaugurate his career as the most prosperous dramatist of the age. His modest childhood in Kirriemuir as the ninth child of a poor weaver had given him material which he exploited skilfully for the rest of his life. *Margaret Ogilvy*, a moving tribute to his mother, indicates one of the greatest influences on him. *A Window in Thrums* brought together sketches and stories which typify his unique blend of sentimentality and nostalgia. A few months before the première of *The Admirable Crichton* he had won triumph with *Quality Street*, a play in which he showed his gift as a master of stagecraft and displayed an irony worthy of Jane Austen. Today he is often dismissed as a mere sentimentalist. This is too sweeping a verdict. Sentimentalist he was, but with an undercurrent of pessimism and a dark, cynical view of men and women.

The theme of *The Admirable Crichton* is summed up by the eponymous hero, a butler, in conversation with one of his superiors.

'My lady,' he says, 'I am the son of a butler and a lady's maid – perhaps the happiest of all combinations; and to me the most beautiful thing in the world is a haughty, aristocratic English house, with everyone kept in his place. Though I were equal to your ladyship, where would be the pleasure to me? It would be counterbalanced by the pain of feeling that Thomas and John were equal to me.'

'But,' replies Lady Catherine, 'Father says if we were to return to nature — '

'If we did, my lady,' says Crichton, 'the first thing we should do would be to elect a head. Circumstances might alter cases; the same person might not be master; the same persons might not be servants. I can't say as to that, nor should we have the deciding of it. Nature would decide for us.'

His employer is the pompous Lord Loam who prides himself on his 'democratic' views and, in support of them, gives his servants a tea party each month in his own gracious drawing-room. Barrie portrays the scene and all its dreadfulness with brilliant wit. Lord Loam and his family, accompanied by Crichton and the servants, go off for a cruise in his yacht. They are shipwrecked on a desert island. The family proves hopeless in this emergency and it is, of course, the admirable Crichton who takes charge and organises them, puts a roof over their head and even conjures up a supply of electricity. Two years later the castaways are rescued by a passing ship and, back in London, the social order is restored.

Most of the survivors conveniently forget Crichton's leadership, although Lady Mary does not. 'You are the best man among us,' she tells Crichton.

'On an island, my lady, perhaps; but in England, no,' he blandly replies.

'Then there is something wrong with England,' she rejoins.

'My lady, not even from you can I listen to a word against England.'

The part of Crichton in this Shavian piece was taken by H. B. Irving, the eldest son of Henry. Originally trained for the law, he soon deserted it for the stage, although in between playing Hamlet and his father's old rôles he kept up his interest by writing a biography of Judge Jeffreys and studies of French criminals. His wife was Dorothea Baird whom we have already met as Trilby.

Another familiar face was Irene Vanbrugh, whose husband Dion Boucicault produced. Du Maurier as the Hon Ernest Woolley had the part of Lord Loam's vapid and selfish nephew. He opened the play with an exchange that shows Barrie at the top of his ironic form.

ERNEST: I perceive, from the tea-cups, Crichton, that the great function is to take place here.
CRICHTON   (*with a respectful sigh*): Yes, sir.
ERNEST   (*chuckling heartlessly*): The servants' hall coming up to have tea in the drawing-room! (*With terrible sarcasm*) No wonder you look happy, Crichton.
CRICHTON   (*under the knife*): No, sir.
ERNEST: Do you know, Crichton, I think that with an effort you might look even happier. (*Crichton smiles wanly.*) You don't approve of his lordship's compelling his servants to be his equals – once a month?
CRICHTON: It is not for me, sir, to disapprove of his lordship's radical views.

This delightful little scene had more wit and body than anything Gerald had played before, even in Pinero. As the opening of the play, which is never an easy task, it presented a challenge. He rose to it well. His best scene came in Act II where the family are settling down under Crichton's leadership. The fatuous Ernest, blithe and uncomprehending, continues to make silly witticisms that annoy everyone. What, Lord Loam asks Crichton, are they to do with him? Crichton suggests dousing his head in a bucket of cold spring water. It will be done, he adds, in the privacy of the wood and not before the ladies. He rolls up his sleeves, instructs Ernest to bring the bucket, and retires. At this point Barrie's stage direction for Ernest reads: *He then lifts the bucket and follows Crichton to the nearest spring.* These simple words became, at Gerald's inspiration, an excellent piece of business. He picked up the bucket with a reluctant hand, took a few uncertain steps, dawdled, hesitated, in short made crossing the stage into something as momentous as Hannibal's crossing of the Alps. His dejected expression and wilting frame turned the incident into a moment of high comedy which first-nighters remembered for a long time.

That first night, as always, prickled with crises. At eleven on the evening of the dress rehearsal the stagehands went on strike in protest at the complications of elaborate sets which included not only the obligatory nobleman's drawing-room but also a bamboo forest and a well-equipped log hut for the desert island scenes. When they refused Boucicault's pleas to return he called on the heads of stage staff at Drury Lane and other theatres. Although not quite so triumphant as *Quality Street*, its predecessor, *The Admirable Crichton* had an initial run of three hundred and twenty-eight performances. It was, said Max Beerbohm, a welcome play and 'quite the best thing that has happened, in my time, to the British stage'. Another excitement came later when Charles Frohman, the American impresario who presented the play, shipped the company and scenery over to Paris for a single night's performance. H. B. Irving arrived early and spent the day at the Palais de Justice and in the police courts adding to his criminal expertise. Much applause was earned that evening, and the stage effects all went smoothly, including an imitation fire simulated by an electric motor agitating strips of red silk under a cauldron to give an impression of flames. At the end of the second act the sets were already being struck to catch a train at three in the morning. 'And,' reported one observer, 'boulevardiers fancied the Honourable Ernest very much.' Gerald, as the very English, very Wodehousian Ernest, had done well in the land of his father.

The part of Lady Agatha in *The Admirable Crichton* was filled by a twenty-one-year-old actress called Muriel Beaumont. Gerald had met her, briefly, some months previously at a function where he did his imitations of famous actors and other party pieces. She remembered them, and him, and spoke unaffectedly of her amusement. During their scenes together as young lovers on a desert island he projected his adoration of her with more than professional warmth. She was very pretty, had round eyes, a trim little nose and simple manners. Her mother, one of sixteen children, was a daughter of the then Duke of Portland's agent. Her father, a solicitor, was said to have fallen in love with her mother when she was only twelve years old, his first present to her being that of a doll. After they married they had five children of whom the eldest was Comyns Beaumont, later a well-known journalist. Muriel was their second child. While she was still a girl Mr Beaumont lost all his money and life became difficult. Obliged to earn a living when she was only seventeen, she made her first appearance on the stage in Barrie's *The Little Minister* and thereafter played *ingénue* rôles in trifles with names like *Frocks and Frills*. Despite this early baptism of theatre she remained innocent and unspoilt. She had read *Trilby* and was interested to know more about the author and his family. She was content to let Gerald do all the talking and listened to him in flattering silence. This, for him, was only one of her many virtues.

She took him home to Battersea where her parents lived. Her father, a strict man who had not much liked the idea of her going on the stage, was polite but reserved. Then he, too, melted in the sunshine of Gerald's cheerful presence. Mrs Beaumont, intuitively, sympathised with the two young people who had begun as lovers in the theatre and were now lovers in real life. Gerald and Muriel went to a dance, and, while the music played and couples whirled, they sat in a quiet spot and he asked her to marry him. She said she would and prepared for the exacting test which awaited her at Portman Mansions where Mrs du Maurier now lived.

Gerald's mother was sceptical. She had been through this sort of episode twice before and cherished no particular hope of a third occasion. Guy du Maurier was away on active service so she gathered her daughters around her to welcome Miss Beaumont. The girl who appeared in her home that evening gave no suggestion of being an actress. Slim, neatly dressed, brown-haired, she looked like any well-brought-up young woman of good family. She cannot, though, have been quite as innocent as she seemed, for her handling of Gerald's mother testified to a guile that few would have suspected. After greeting the assembled company she went forward and made a remark which instantly charmed Mrs du Maurier into acquiescence and could not have been better designed to win her approval. 'I'm in such a way about Gerald,' she said with an anxious look, 'he is starting one of his horrid colds.'

Their engagement lasted six weeks and they were married on 11th April, 1903, at St Peter's Church, Cranley Gardens, Kensington. The honeymooners travelled to Whitby, scene of many happy outings in Gerald's childhood, and he escorted his bride on nostalgic rambles across the shore, up on the cliffs and over the moors. Back in London they resumed their parts in *The Admirable Crichton* and, when it came off in August, they took a small three-roomed cottage at Walton-on-Thames with a garden whose parsley and Japanese Iris and roses Gerald affected to assess with expert judgment. By September they were installed in a house at No. 5, Chester Place, Regent's Park, and Muriel was busy selecting curtains, wallpaper and servants. It is, these days, difficult to envisage how an actor earning around twenty-five pounds a week could afford to maintain an establishment with cook and maid in one of the most fashionable areas of London. Yet he did, because houses could then be rented easily and a maid's annual wage amounted to less than his weekly salary.

The house lay not far from Mrs du Maurier's flat. Communication between Chester Place and Baker Street was full and frequent, since by now Muriel had won her spurs as a member of the family. The house was also convenient for the theatre and Gerald had time to dine before leaving at twenty past seven and making the short journey that delivered him at the evening performance. He hoped Muriel would not find her evenings too dull without him.

Soon after moving to Chester Place he was at Wyndham's Theatre in a minor Barrie play, *Little Mary*, which, if not so pronounced a success as *The Admirable Crichton*, at least gave him a billing second only to that of his old mentor, John Hare, and showed how quickly he was establishing his reputation. The cast also included A. E. Matthews. He, at the age of thirty-four, played a schoolboy, one of the many unlikely rôles that distinguished a career which seemed to last for ever. It ended only in the 1960s with his apotheosis as a grand old man of the theatre notoriously incapable of remembering his lines and gagging outrageously to cover up the deficiency which his fans loved to expect of him. Gerald, as Hare's son in the play, gave, said Max Beerbohm, 'a study of a young Englishman which is all the more amusing because it has been made with a touch of French malice and is instinct with French finesse'.

His new wife, after setting up the household in Chester Place with enthusiastic aid from Mrs du Maurier senior, continued a stage career under her maiden name of Muriel Beaumont. In 1904 she was at the Garrick in a new play and, the following year, appeared as Nerissa in *The Merchant of Venice*. Somehow, between these engagements, she arranged to give birth to the first du Maurier child on 1st March, 1904, a daughter whom they called Angela. Everyone was delighted, especially Gerald, whose only regret was that his father, ever keen for a granddaughter while his children were all producing sons, had not survived to welcome the new arrival. Gerald wrote an ecstatic poem of greeting which ended:

> I don't know why I love you so.
> Ah! yes, I do:
> It is because you're part of me
> And part of one,
> The only one,
> The heart and very life of me.
> Still! there is you
> And well you know
> How happily we both contrive
> To love each other and to live
> With you, my dear.

Alas, the happy father was kept apart from Angela for some time by an attack of diphtheria which confined him to bed upstairs. A cat, he thought, had passed on the germ. Angela was, of course, the cleverest and most beautiful baby the world had ever seen. At the age of two she was taken to a luncheon party where she saw her father propose the loyal toast: 'The King!' She piped up quickly: 'God B'ess him.' Grandpa and Grandma Beaumont were enchanted with her. So was her spinster aunt 'Billy' who became Gerald's secretary and, during his subsequent management of Wyndham's Theatre, had her own office in the building where she typed his letters and organised his life. He was especially attached to his mother-in-law Grandma Beaumont. Towards the end of her life, and of his, he wrote to her: 'Everything in the world that matters to me – I owe to you. If my three daughters grow up nearly as nice women as your and your dear old man's have, I shall not have lived in vain. We all love you very much – you know that, don't you?'

After fatherhood and diphtheria he returned to the stage in *Cynthia*, by Hubert Henry Davies, with his one-time love Ethel Barrymore. It closed rather speedily, and in September he was back at the Duke of York's in *Merely Mary Ann*. This was a minor piece by Israel Zangwill, author of that small classic *Children of The Ghetto*. Keen Zionist, son of a Russian refugee, he had put none of his political opinions into *Merely Mary Ann* which turned out to be a light romance with a Cinderella flavour. Mary Ann is a country girl who slaves as a maid of all work in a south London boarding-house which recalls *The Passing of The Third Floor Back*. One of the lodgers is an earnest composer who falls in love with her despite the class barrier that separates them. 'And I do understand why it's impossible for you to marry me – I'm not good enough for you, sir,' says the humble maid. 'No, Mary Ann; I'm not good enough for *you*,' he answers nobly. Despite which they drift apart. Then, by a coincidence easy to imagine, Mary Ann inherits a million pounds from her long-lost brother. Six years later, the composer meanwhile having won fame with his symphonies and concertos, they meet again and are happily married. Although, as Sacha Guitry once remarked, comedies that end in a marriage are usually the first act of a drama.

No cynical reflection of this nature taints *Merely Mary Ann* which would have needed the genius of a Barrie to make its whimsy credible. The part of the composer was taken by Henry Ainley, a young actor so unusually handsome as to deserve the epithet beautiful. Having left the bank where he worked as an accountant and having trained under George Alexander and Frank Benson, he soon was a leading matinée idol, although he tired of the label and distressed his female admirers by preferring to think of himself as a character actor. Gerald played his friend, another composer who, with a commercial gift for turning out popular songs, has carefully avoided writing the ambitious works that the high-minded hero insists on attempting. While Ainley as the struggling composer wore a huge Lavallière bow tie and crushed felt hat, Gerald's character, altogether more prosperous and chic, enabled him to don his familiar trappings, even in the seedy lodging-house, of top hat and white tie. The programme, with its advertisements for Kleinert's dress shields, Rowland's Macassar Oil, the London Corset Company ('Every Corset made in Paris'), and those hallowed costumiers' names familiar to generations of theatregoers, B. J. Simmons, L. & H. Nathan, W. Clarkson, contained a thread of editorial which trickled its way between the commercial announcements. 'During his stage career,' it noted, 'Mr du Maurier's lines have been cast in singularly pleasant places, and he has had the good fortune to be associated with many lengthy runs.' *Merely Mary Ann*, which died after a hundred and eleven performances, was not among them. Within a few weeks Gerald was to be involved in a play which became one of the most successful and legendary in the English theatre.

[iii]

Peter Pan, Raffles and the Lost Boys

On 7th January, 1901, he had acted in a private performance of a little pantomime entitled *The Greedy Dwarf*. This 'Entirely Amazing Moral Tale', which was given only once, featured Gerald's sister Sylvia as 'The Principal Boy' and the novelist A. E. W. Mason as 'Sleepyhead'. Gerald was the malevolent dwarf 'Allahakbarrie' who opened the play, threatening and sinister in a ghostly spotlight. The audience consisted of excited children wearing their party clothes, and after the climax in 'The Horrible Home of The Greedy Dwarf' they relieved the tension by gorging themselves on ice-cream and cakes. The author was, inevitably, J. M. Barrie, who himself took the rôle of 'Cowardy Custard', a schoolboy with a moustache and a corn-coloured wig. When challenged to a fight he cravenly put off the action by removing, one after another, twelve waistcoats. His wife acted 'Brownie' and his pet dog was cast as 'Chang'. Some of the children, said an observer, found Barrie 'almost as terrifying as the Dwarf'.

The Greedy Dwarf received its only performance at 133, Gloucester Road, Kensington, the home of Mr and Mrs Barrie. They had been married for seven years. Mrs Barrie, the actress Mary Ansell, met her husband while appearing in his early play *Walker, London*, and was attracted by his humour and his intelligence. There is little doubt that she genuinely loved him at first. Barrie, for his part, liked to imagine that he was in love with her. More than a lover, however, he was a professional writer who only came to life when putting words on paper. For such a man, everyone and everything around him is regarded as a source of copy. An experience, whatever its nature, is weighed and assessed only in so far as it provides raw material for his art. Even while their courtship proceeded Barrie was making detailed notes for a novel he thought of writing about it. 'I would write an article, I think, on my mother's coffin,' he once remarked, and that is more or less what he did in *Margaret Ogilvy*, a touching homage to his mother, the only woman he ever loved with passion.

As a young man he had written an article called 'My Ghastly Dream'. The dream, the horrid nightmare, is that he has been married and borne away by some cruel woman dressed in a bridal veil. The article, meant to be humorous, revealed nonetheless a macabre fear. The morning after his engagement to Mary Ansell he noted that it was 'a startling thing to waken up and remember you're tied for life'. Yet Mary Ansell became the wife of this dour little man who, though sometimes witty and amusing, was more often silent, forbidding, grim-faced, ambiguous and for ever scribbling in his notebooks. His wife soon turned for the affection she craved to animals, especially dogs, and the St Bernard her husband gave her as a wedding present was the first in a long line of adored pets. Ironically enough, Barrie was as attached to Porthos the dog as she was. 'I only loved clever men,' wrote his wife years later. 'And clever men, it seems to me, are made up of reserves. It is out of their reserves they bring their clever things.' Dogs, she found, were never complicated as men were complicated.

Both husband and wife longed for children. Barrie's frustrated paternity is the key to his bizarre character. It governed all his thoughts, all his actions, all his writing. Eight years after *The Greedy Dwarf* he was cuckolded by the writer Gilbert Cannan and the uneasy union ended in divorce. Why had they never produced children? Nobody knows, although close acquaintances made plenty of guesses. The most ribald, on the analogy of Peter Pan the boy who wouldn't grow up, nicknamed Barrie 'the boy who couldn't go up'.

Not far from Gloucester Road is Kensington Gardens where Barrie and his wife took Porthos for walks. Shrouded in an outsize overcoat, bowler-hatted, coughing from his eternal pipe, the diminutive writer was liable to be dwarfed when Porthos reared up on his hind legs. Barrie's dark little eyes, ringed with black shadows, watched attentively and in silence the children and their nannies who paraded there. Two, in particular, caught his interest. They were brothers, George and Jack, five and four years old respectively, and very handsome fellows. He talked to them a lot, entranced them by wriggling his ears and telling them tales of pirates and shipwrecks and fairies. Soon afterwards he found himself at a large dinner party next to a very beautiful young woman. She, he learned, was Mrs Arthur Llewelyn Davies, the sister of Gerald du Maurier and daughter of George. He told her he had named Porthos after the dog in *Peter Ibbetson*. Her youngest, Peter, she revealed, had his name from the novel's title. There were two other sons, she added, called George, after her father, and Jack. He realised he had met the mother of his two little friends in Kensington Gardens.

Barrie gradually came to know the family. George remained his favourite and was the subject of many passages in the notebooks. The boy inspired the central character David in Barrie's novel *The Little White Bird*. There is a curious passage in it about 'a tremendous adventure' when the boy's mother allows David/George to spend a night with the narrator, a lonely old bachelor. 'Then I placed my hand carelessly on his shoulder,' runs the account, 'like one a trifle bored by the dull routine of putting my little boys to bed, and conducted him to the night nursery, which had lately been my private chamber.' The boy puts out his legs for the narrator to relieve him of his boots. 'I took them off with all the coolness of an old hand, and then I placed him on my knee and removed his blouse. This was a delightful experience, but I think I remained wonderfully calm until I came somewhat too suddenly to his little braces, which agitated me profoundly. I cannot proceed in public with the disrobing of David.'

David is put to bed but cannot sleep. He insists on holding the narrator's hand and asks if he may come into his host's bed.

For the rest of the night he lay on me and across me, and sometimes his feet were at the bottom of the bed and sometimes on the pillow, but he always retained possession of my finger, and occasionally he woke me to say that he was sleeping with me. I had not a good night. I lay thinking.

Of this little boy, who in the midst of his play while I undressed him, had suddenly buried his head on my knees . . .

Of David's dripping little form in the bath, and how when I essayed to catch him he had slipped from my arms like a trout.

One needs a tough stomach to put up with Barrie in this mood. No writer today would publish such an account without inviting accusations of paedophilia and worse. Yet Barrie, in the manner of Lewis Carroll and his nude photographs of little girls, was consciously innocent. His snapshots of the tiny lads frolicking bare-bottomed on the beach, the cowboy and Indian adventures he made up for them, the coy letters he wrote and the amateur dramatics he organised, were a means to enjoy the pleasures of fatherhood with none of the pains. In Sylvia du Maurier's children he discovered an ideal outlet for the frustration which obsessed him.

George, Jack and Peter were soon joined by two more brothers, Michael and Nico. Their father, Arthur Llewelyn Davies, was not altogether enchanted at Barrie's growing intimacy with the family. This now extended to shared holidays when Barrie organised elaborate games for the boys which involved pirates and shipwrecks and walking the plank. Inspired by his own favourite childhood reading, *The Coral Island*, Barrie had a little book printed and illustrated with holiday snapshots which he called *The Boy Castaways of Black Lake Island*. The copy which he presented to Arthur Davies vanished: it was lost, Davies claimed, unconvincingly, in a railway carriage.

The adventures in Kensington Gardens and the piratical exploits on holiday encouraged Barrie's completion of a 'fairy play' which he decided to call *Peter Pan*. It was enthusiastically accepted by his friend the American impresario Charles Frohman, who did not for a moment flinch at the technical demands of a spectacle in which the hero was to be played by a girl who flew through the air and in which a crocodile swallowed an alarm clock. Nina Boucicault, whose brother directed, took the rôle of Peter Pan. The girl Wendy was played by Hilda Trevelyan, and Dorothea Baird, some years earlier a famous 'Trilby', acted as Mrs Darling. Barrie had at first thought of Seymour Hicks for Captain Hook. Eventually Gerald du Maurier, now a close friend through his sister Sylvia, was asked to undertake the part. He, in fact, doubled up as Mr Darling also. There has been speculation that Barrie might have intended some deep psychological comment by using the same actor to impersonate

both the villainous Hook and the benevolent Mr Darling. Was this
a device to illustrate the good and the evil which co-exist in all of
us? It was not. Gerald, with his actor's egoism, saw a magnificent
part in Hook but was greedy as well to show off his virtuosity by
playing Mr Darling.

The artist William Nicholson designed some of the costumes.
The clothes of the 'lost boys' were modelled on those worn by
Gerald's nephews when Barrie first came across them in Kensington
Gardens: berets, square-necked blouses, linen breeches. Barrie was
insistent that Captain Hook should be a genuinely terrifying figure
and not something comic out of Gilbert and Sullivan. Nicholson
designed for him a towering wig made of purple chenille and
arranged to look like squirming snakes. Gerald's wife Muriel protested that it was unsuitable. He agreed with her, rejected it, and
went on, says Nicholson's biographer, 'looking like a cross between
Charles II and a fourteen-year-old schoolgirl'. In any case, the
play, thought Gerald, would probably run for only a short time,
it was such an unusual combination of pantomime and extravaganza.

First given on 27th December, 1904, at the Duke of York's
Theatre, *Peter Pan* seemed initially to bear out his pessimism. It
played, or such was his impression, to thin houses during the first
week, although box-office returns showed that from the start ticket
sales were good and soon became excellent. Critics described *Peter
Pan* as true, natural, touching, original and 'a spree'. Some, as to this
day, remained unmoved and declined to answer Peter's question, 'Do
you believe in fairies?' Among them was the writer Anthony Hope,
who, surrounded by a mass of uproarious children, sighed, 'Oh,
for an hour of Herod!' Max Beerbohm, feline, ambiguous, wrote
nothing about the actual performance and concentrated instead on
the author and the play.

> Mr Barrie is not that rare creature, a man of genius [he decided].
> He is something even more rare – a child who, by some divine
> grace, can express through an artistic medium the childishness
> that is within him. Mr Barrie has never grown up. He is still
> a child, absolutely. But some fairy once waved a wand over
> him, and changed him from a dear little boy into a dear little
> girl.

Gerald in the early days enjoyed himself very much. To mask a
longish pause when scenery was being changed he devised a little

'front' episode where he was carried on stage in a sedan-chair. Out stepped the living image of Sir Henry Irving. It strutted and declaimed for a few moments and then popped back into the sedan-chair whence emerged, almost immediately, Herbert Beerbohm Tree. In this way, like a conjuror producing tricks, Gerald masqueraded as Charles Wyndham, George Alexander and other ornaments of the London stage. It was a rare occasion when he exercised in public those gifts of mimicry which he usually restricted to private entertainments.

His portrayal of the father, said the critic W. A. Darlington, was done 'with his accustomed lightness of style', but his Captain Hook 'ranks as one of the great comic creations of our time'. The most vivid account of his acting was written by his daughter Daphne. Although she had not even been born when he first played the part in 1904, she was to see him in revivals and to appreciate why he had made it particularly his own.

> How he was hated, with his flourish, his poses, his dreaded diabolical smile! That ashen face, those blood-red lips, the long, dark, greasy curls; the sardonic laugh, the maniacal scream, the appalling courtesy of his gestures; and that above all most terrible of moments when he descended the stairs and with slow, merciless cunning poured the poison into Peter's glass. There was no peace in those days until the monster was destroyed, and the fight upon the pirate ship was a fight to the death. Gerald *was* Hook; he was no dummy dressed from Simmons' in a Clarkson wig, ranting and roaring about the stage, a grotesque figure whom the modern child finds a little comic. He was a tragic and rather ghastly creation who knew no peace, and whose soul was in torment; a dark shadow; a sinister dream; a bogey of fear who lives perpetually in the grey recesses of every small boy's mind . . . and, because he had imagination and a spark of genius, Gerald made him alive.

Whether his Captain Hook was a great comic creation, as Darlington saw it, or a frightening embodiment of the macabre as Daphne believed, Gerald was more closely involved in the elaboration of the part than in any other he ever played. While the play was still being completed he had many new ideas to offer for the character and inspired Barrie to make numerous revisions. Once, however, the thing was done and Hook become a finished, rounded portrayal tested out and projected against an audience, he began to lose interest. Early in the run A. E. Matthews took over as Mr Darling, a rôle thankfully relinquished by its creator. Long before *Peter Pan* closed on 1st April, 1905, Gerald was thoroughly bored with Hook. He wearied, besides, of playing two long performances each day to a theatre full of noisy children. 'There is only one thing I'd rather not be doing,' he snapped in a moment of annoyance, 'and that's sweeping the floors of a mortuary at a shilling a week.'

As soon as *Peter Pan* ended his taste for novelty was gratified by the leading rôle in a curtain-raiser Barrie wrote for a new piece called *Alice-Sit-By-The-Fire*. The curtain-raiser, entitled *Pantaloon*, offered a welcome chance for versatility since he had to play the elderly performer, rheumatic, on crutches, lost in dreams of the past, whose daughter Columbine elopes with Harlequin and leaves him to his cheerless poverty . . . until they return and show him a tiny grandchild who toddles forward and delights him by slapping his leg with a property red-hot poker in the old tradition. This little fantasy, exquisitely poised on a knife-edge between bathos and true feeling, prepared the way for *Alice-Sit-By-The-Fire* in which the star was Ellen Terry assisted by C. Aubrey Smith as a haughty Colonel. The grand old lady of the English theatre had, as always, great trouble in remembering her lines. At rehearsals Barrie lost his temper with her. 'It doesn't matter what you say, dear lady,' he cried, 'but for God's sake say something!' During the run she spent much time furtively looking for the cues which she had hidden under her handkerchief. 'If the audience noticed anything, I am sure they thought it was I who was wrong,' remarked Smith later. Some time afterwards she went on tour with the court scene from *The Merchant of Venice*. One evening, about to launch Portia's famous speech 'The quality of mercy is not strain'd,' she dried up completely. She gave up the struggle and advanced to the footlights. 'I'm a very silly old woman,' she announced, 'and I cannot remember what I have to say.' In unison the audience chanted the lines and applauded when she beamed her thanks. She remained word-perfect for the rest of the scene.

In 1906 Gerald was among the huge cast assembled at Drury Lane for the Ellen Terry Jubilee. Three hundred of the country's leading actors and actresses paid tribute to her in an evening of plays and recitations and musical offerings including a scene from *Trial By Jury* which featured W. S. Gilbert himself. All the famous names were there: Wyndham, Alexander, Mrs Patrick Campbell, Beerbohm Tree, Seymour Hicks and Caruso. Had a bomb dropped on the theatre that night the London stage would have been robbed of its best and brightest performers. For her own contribution, Ellen Terry played a scene from *Much Ado About Nothing*. It was not, one would have thought, a very tactful choice of title for the occasion.

That Gerald should appear at such an event on an equal footing with the distinguished company showed that he had established himself in his own right. *Peter Pan*, duly revived each Christmas, had already made him something of an institution. This was succeeded by a few unimportant plays until, in the year of the Ellen Terry Jubilee, *Raffles* gave him his first big characteristic success.

It was not a very good play. The novel by E. W. Hornung, a relative of Conan Doyle, was a best-seller which to a certain extent echoed the Sherlock Holmes saga in its basic relationship between a clever hero and his admiring but not very intelligent friend. The difference is that the central figure happens to be a gentleman, an Old Harrovian who, from his rooms in Albany, operates as an amateur cracksman, not so much for the money as for the thrill of the game. Accompanied by his friend 'Bunny', an adoring chum ever since their Harrow days together, he spends a weekend at the stately home of an Earl. Some daring burglaries have lately taken place in the neighbourhood and the Earl has engaged a famous American detective who bets Raffles that he will get possession of a stolen diamond necklace within twenty-four hours. Also present are the Earl's niece to provide the love interest and a woman guest who knows Raffles of old and suspects his complicity in a sensational robbery some years ago. All these elements are skilfully blended so that Raffles wins his bet, secures the necklace and makes his escape, pistols ablaze, after hiding in a grandfather clock.

This may sound a little mild, but in 1906 *Raffles* struck audiences as an exciting novelty. They were pleasurably startled by the notion of an Old Harrovian, a gentleman and a cricketer, who was also an accomplished crook. The piece was adapted by the novel's author and by Eugène Presbery, an American play doctor, although there is no doubt that Gerald had a very big hand in shaping the climaxes and pointing the dialogue. In print it reads badly. On the stage it moved with exhilarating speed. *Raffles* enabled Gerald to perfect the technique which gradually superseded the grandiose manner of the old actor-managers who until then had dominated the theatre. As Gerald once said to a friend: 'I couldn't do some of the plays – realistic plays, like *Raffles* – in that declamatory style which everybody had been using since David Garrick. I had to find another way.'

The 'other way' he found was deceptively simple and more closely allied to the style of everyday life. It is, however, more difficult to project realism than it is to put on a Shakespearean wig and defy the heavens. If you do not succeed, the audience finds you dull. If you do, they take your 'naturalness' for granted and cannot really accept that you are acting. You are, they say, just being yourself. Behind Gerald's apparent spontaneity lay careful and painstaking thought. He would rehearse, alone and for hours in front of a long mirror, such small items of business as lighting a cigarette or mixing a drink, studying each move and paring it down until he achieved the economy he sought. The one element he did conserve from his Edwardian predecessors was audibility. However intimate the scene, however low-key the playing, his voice could always be heard in every corner of the theatre. His diction remained clear and perfectly enunciated. This was something his many imitators tended to ignore, and he has been blamed, unjustly, for that curse of the modern theatre, actors who cannot easily be heard.

The revolution in English acting may, therefore, be said to date from *Raffles*. Without melodrama or flamboyant poses, Gerald was able to imply the tension beneath the surface that builds up gradually into release. There was an episode where, after much strain, he succeeded in wresting a gun from one of his adversaries. A critic, moved by the sheer force of emotion he showed, wrote: 'Such acting leaves an impress on the memory as of some scene that has been lived through. To play such a scene as this, slowly but surely working to a tremendous emotional climax, with few words and the difficulty of an assumed calmness which needs much subtlety, is the achievement of a tragedian of uncommon quality.'

With only a break at Christmas for his ritual appearance as Captain Hook and in August for a short Scottish holiday, *Raffles* continued its successful run and closed after three hundred and fifty-one performances. Muriel was expecting another baby, and, the house in Chester Place proving too small, the du Mauriers took another, larger home at 24, Cumberland Terrace not far away. It was grander, had a basement, and stood in a little courtyard which you entered through an elegant archway. The rent was a hundred and fifty pounds a year but Gerald was confident, he told his mother, that he could manage it. From Albany Street, which runs along the back, came the clop and jingle of Life Guards trotting on the way to their barracks.

The year after, *Raffles* found him in another long run with *Brewster's Millions* at the Hicks Theatre in Shaftesbury Avenue. Now known as the Globe, the theatre was then a year old and one of a pair, the other being the Aldwych, put up by the energetic Seymour Hicks, who, not content with writing and producing dozens of plays in which to star himself, also liked to have his own roof over his head when he did so. Somewhere up among the granite facings he carved the initials of his wife Ellaline Terriss as a sentimental gesture to one with whom in public he carried on a famous love affair, though in private he never missed an opportunity for dalliance elsewhere.

Brewster's Millions was an American play founded on an idea which is irresistible. The central character, an impoverished Montgomery Brewster, is to inherit a fortune of six million pounds. To qualify for it, however, he must first spend another sum of half a million. The task is not so easy as it sounds. Investments in dubious companies turn out to be highly profitable and bets on spavined racehorses produce winners, although at the end, after unwillingly enriching himself, he does succeed in getting rid of the cash. Everyone would enjoy such a problem and everyone has ideas about how to spend money, with the result that the formula of the play has had a long life. One of the more successful films based on it had Jack Buchanan playing a debonair hero in the mould of du Maurier. As late as the 1950s a musical version called *Zip Goes A Million* starred the Lancashire comic George Formby on his first and last appearance in the West End and ran for over five hundred performances.

Gerald, again, had a personal triumph. Although the play was a comedy, he brought to it a mixture of thoughtfulness and gaiety which impressed audiences. Said a critic with more enthusiasm than grammar:

> Once more the point of the evening was the fine work of Gerald du Maurier, who, if he did not improve on Raffles, continued the same amazing promise, and on whose shoulders rested the chief weight of the acting. He conveyed the passing joy and despair of the character with extraordinary skill, without any exaggeration or any apparent trick. Coming so soon after his wonderful impersonation of Raffles, it confirmed his reputation as the cleverest comedian on the English stage.

Professional triumph was chequered by domestic tragedy. Only ten days or so before the curtain rose on *Brewster's Millions* Gerald heard that his brother-in-law Arthur Llewelyn Davies had died after months of lingering agony. An abscess in his face turned out to be a sarcoma and an operation was performed. His palate, teeth, a cheekbone and half the upper jaw were removed. The bandages were taken off a week later and Gerald went to visit him in the evening. Appalled by the mutilation of her handsome husband's features, Sylvia wept on Gerald's shoulder. 'They've spoilt my darling's face,' she cried.

An artificial jaw was fitted, although Arthur could still only communicate with those around him by writing notes on paper. The tumour began to spread and he relied on ever-increasing doses of morphia to deaden the pain. Barrie now came into his own. Every other activity was set aside in order to help Arthur, Sylvia and 'the lost boys' whom he had immortalised in *Peter Pan*. He went on errands, haunted the sick-room and cheerfully paid the large medical expenses. Arthur up to then had not been very fond of the quaint little man whom he saw as an intruder in the family circle. Now, moved by Barrie's generosity, his touching desire to help, his tactful charm, he regarded him as a saviour. Having earlier in a moment of pique deliberately mislaid his copy of *The Boy Castaways of Black Lake Island*, he asked for the other surviving copy and pored eagerly over it in his hospital bed, recapturing through Barrie's snapshots the image of his five handsome sons.

The odd *ménage à trois* persisted until Arthur's death with Barrie distributing his allegiance equally between husband and wife. Arthur did not leave much money and Sylvia would have had great trouble in supporting her family had it not been for Barrie, whom she called 'the best friend in the whole world'. The success of *Peter Pan* and of his other plays had made him rich, and he did not hesitate to pour out his wealth on Sylvia and the boys. He helped her buy a new home, paid for the boys' education at prep school and Eton, and even, in moments of private fantasy, thought of marrying her, for his own marriage was to all intents and purposes over. But, ever the professional writer, he went on doggedly filling his notebooks. Arthur's deathbed was a rich source, and, while the sick man lay dying beside him, he jotted down the idea on which he later based his play *Dear Brutus*.

Sylvia lived only for another three years, her youthful beauty matured by suffering. She became frail and listless. In her will she made Barrie a trustee, knowing that he would 'do everything in his power to help our boys – to advise, to comfort, to sympathise in all their joys and sorrows'. Inoperable cancer was diagnosed and she died in 1910 at forty-four, the same age as Arthur at his death. Barrie received the news wild-eyed and tearful. Yet even so there remained to him the consolation of the boys and the pleasure of watching them grow up. For Gerald there was no such comfort. He had lost his favourite sister, the gentlest of them and the sweetest. What was the point of such needless, undeserved suffering? Why should good, kindly people have to go through ordeals like this? He was not a religious man and he never found the answer to his agonised questions.

CHAPTER III

THE ACTOR-MANAGER

[i]

'The fun men have, Sybil!'
Lady Tree on boiler scraping.
(At rehearsals of *What Every Woman Knows*)

The year 1907, a Chekhovian mixture of light and shadow, brought the death of Arthur Davies, but also marked the happy arrival of a second du Maurier daughter. She was christened Daphne and made her appearance in the large nursery that had been prepared for her at 24, Cumberland Terrace. Early the following year her mother and father both played in a revival of *The Admirable Crichton*. They took the parts they acted in the original production and, as they spoke the familiar dialogue that had so many personal associations for them, lived again a sentimental episode they often loved to recall. After this Muriel's ventures on the stage dwindled until, in 1910, she retired from the theatre. Running the home of a famous actor and bringing up her children absorbed her. She had no wish to rival her husband.

In the autumn of 1908 came another Barrie play called *What Every Woman Knows*. And what, according to Barrie, did every woman know? Despite living in a world apparently ruled by the opposite sex, she knew that men were vain and foolish. She knew they were easily swayed by trifles. She knew they needed a strong hand to guide them and to fashion their careers. *What Every Woman Knows* contains some of Barrie's neatest epigrams. When asked to define the elusive quality of charm, the heroine replies: 'Oh, it's – it's a sort of bloom on a woman. If you have it, you don't need to have anything else; and if you don't have it, it doesn't much matter what else you have. Some women, the few, have charm for all; and most have charm for one. But some have charm for none.' The atmosphere is very Scottish and very wry. Says one of the characters: 'You've forgotten the grandest

67

moral attribute of a Scotsman, Maggie, that he'll do nothing which might damage his career.' And later in the play Maggie observes: 'However careful a man is, his wife always finds out his failings.'

Gerald played the leading male character whom it would be over-generous to describe as the 'hero'. He is John Shand, a brainy but penniless student intended for the ministry. A local Scottish family who revere education offer to finance his studies with a grant of three hundred pounds on condition that, five years hence, he will marry their daughter Maggie should such be her wish. He graduates brilliantly, enters politics, wins a sensational by-election and is soon perceived as a rising hope for his party. Remembering the bargain he struck, he weds Maggie as agreed, despite her gentle remonstrance that she may not be right for him. 'The woman never rises with the man,' she says. 'I'll drag you down, John.' She reminds him that up to now he has worked so hard that he has missed all the fun men of his age usually enjoy. 'I never was one for fun,' he answers. 'I cannot call to mind, Maggie, ever having laughed in my life.' He goes on: 'I remember reading of someone that said it needed a surgical operation to get a joke into a Scotsman's head . . . What beats me, Maggie, is how you could insert a joke with an operation.' At which point Barrie's stage direction reads: *He considers this and gives it up.*

Maggie continues to write his speeches and to ply him with effective retorts for hecklers. He ascends to the upper reaches of politics and moves in circles where he meets and becomes infatuated with a lady of title. Rather than oppose the affair outright, Maggie shrewdly encourages it up to a point since she knows that her rival has neither the brains nor the patience to help him with his career. At a crucial moment when he has to make the speech that will assure his future, Maggie comes to the rescue with a script containing all the clever little touches his colleagues had learned to expect of him (or her). She wins him back and he begins to realise her true worth. 'It's nothing unusual I've done, John,' she tells him. 'Every man who is high up loves to think that he has done it all himself; and the wife smiles, and lets it go at that. It's our only joke. Every woman knows that. Oh, John, if only you could laugh at me.' As the curtain begins to descend his face takes on a strange expression. For the first time in his existence he is laughing.

Maggie was played by Hilda Trevelyan, the original Wendy of *Peter Pan*, who portrayed exquisitely the subtle, teasing, very feminine quality of the part. Maggie's pawky brother was Edmund Gwenn, a specialist in sly humour and already set up on a long career which eventually took him to Hollywood where he acted many character parts, usually as an elderly gentleman of twinkle-eyed benevolence touched with a hint of mystery, if not the sinister. The juiciest of the supporting rôles went to Maud Tree, not yet 'Lady', who was to survive her husband by some twenty years until 1937. In youth rather plain, in maturity and old age she acquired a stateliness which made up for her equine features. Until her death at the age of seventy-eight she went on acting and even appeared in films. *What Every Woman Knows* gave her every opportunity as a dominating French countess, and she took it with gusto, even to the extent of enlarging the part. There is a passage in Act II where the characters discuss John Shand's early life. It is revealed that as a student he was obliged to earn money by working in an iron-cementer's business. An iron cementer? she enquires, out of her depth. 'They scrape boilers,' someone explains to her. 'I see,' she says. 'The fun men have, Sybil!' The last sentence was an impromptu addition she made at the dress rehearsal. Barrie liked it so much that he kept it in the printed edition of the play.

The rôle of John Shand presented Gerald with difficulties. The man is a humourless bore, and to depict such a character without boring the audience is a major problem. He must bore, yes, but not in such a way as to put people off. Gerald solved the dilemma by, as it were, standing outside the character and allowing the humour to develop unconsciously around him. His skill in suggesting spontaneity was never more closely tested, yet he managed to tread unerringly the fine line between comedy and priggishness. It had been an effort, as he confessed to his mother, and for the first time in his career he had been forced to think very hard.

It's all over [he told her after the first night], and we're none of us sorry. It was a highly strung, nervous business, and no good to one's internal arrangements. If Angela and Daphne look like following in their parents' footsteps, I shall put them in a convent. It was the biggest success Barrie has had, and you should have heard the applause. I'm told I played my bit well, and everyone was pleased all round, but what an effort it has been. There must be some happy medium in life between a rainy day in the country, with no immediate occupation, and the first night of a long and difficult part.

Success it undoubtedly was, although on the last day of the run, its three hundred and eighty-fifth performance in July 1909, Barrie received news that finally shattered his ailing marriage. He learned that his wife had been having an affair with the writer Gilbert Cannan. Divorce in those days meant scandal and public appearances in the witness-box. Barrie solaced himself in the only way he knew how: that of writing, and, as the long ordeal dragged on, he composed his one-act play *The Twelve Pound Look* which has for its theme the man who is a worldly success but who, in his private life, is a failure. At last, however, the ugly episode of solicitors' meetings and cross-examinations was over, and he, now free, could devote himself wholeheartedly to bringing up Gerald's nephews, those lovely boys George and Jack and Peter and Michael and Nico, each one of whom he loved as the sons he had never had.

He also found time to help Gerald with advice on a new play which had special importance for the du Maurier family. It was written by Gerald's brother Guy, now a Major in the 20th Mounted Infantry and soon to be a Lieutenant-Colonel. For his achievements in South Africa, where he was currently stationed, he had won the DSO. In appearance he closely resembled Gerald except for the addition of a neatly clipped moustache and steel-grey hair. He had the same sense of humour, too, and often disconcerted his father George du Maurier by teasing him. His skit on *Trilby*, which poked fun at George's habit of larding his prose with sentences in French, began:

> *Act I. The Studio*
> J'ai
> Tu as
> Il a
> Nous avons
> Vous avez
> Ils ont.

The last act of the skit took place in Trafalgar Square and featured Trilby singing on top of Nelson's monument while Svengali conducts her from below. At Svengali's death she falls off her perch. Guy showed his script to the rest of the family and, hearing their titters, George asked what was going on. The sacrilege was displayed to him. 'Quite unfunny,' said 'The Governor' icily.

Guy never, despite being a professional soldier, lost his love of the stage. On leave he often spoke with family and friends about the growth of German militarism and the possibility of a European war. What, he thought, if the enemy suddenly invaded during a Bank Holiday weekend at a moment when the whole country was relaxed and unsuspecting? (Indeed, years later Mussolini chose to invade Abyssinia at the start of a weekend knowing that British government ministers would be concerned with more important things like hunting and shooting.) Guy put his idea on paper and found it developing into a play. Before going back to South Africa at the end of his next leave he gave the manuscript to Gerald for an opinion. Gerald read it and was instantly enthusiastic. 'This,' he declared, 'is the real stuff at last. I knew Guy had it in him, and it was bound to come out. He wasn't born Papa's son for nothing.'

The action of Guy's play is set in the home of the Brown family, Myrtle Villa, at Wickham in Essex. It is Boxing Day and they talk frivolities while playing diabolo and puzzling over newspaper competitions. They are unconcerned with international politics and mock the arguments of a family friend who, alarmed at the way things are going, has just enrolled in the newly formed Territorial Army. Suddenly a foreign Captain and his Lieutenant burst in to announce that the invasion has begun and that Myrtle Villa is now an outpost in the battle raging between their forces and English troops. In the course of the play the enemy is dislodged and the house recaptured. Bullets fly, the roof starts to burn and the English retire. Mr Brown, the father of the family, stays on to defend his home with a rifle and picks off one of the enemy. They storm the place and take him prisoner. The Captain orders him to be shot in turn.

'Do we stay here, sir?' asks the Captain's aide-de-camp.

'Yes,' he replies, 'here, in what the late owner called "An Englishman's Home".'

'For how long, sir?' comes the enquiry as the curtain falls.

Gerald and Barrie together went through the play, strengthening the situations and revising here and there the dialogue. The biggest change they made was to the ending. In the last act Guy predicted victory for the invaders from 'Nearland', the pseudonym of Germany. For box-office reasons Barrie and Gerald decided that Britain should win. A title was still needed and Gerald proposed *An Englishman's Home*. He then went to see Frank Curzon, a leading impresario with whom he was soon to be closely associated, and booked Wyndham's Theatre for the production. The opening night was billed for 27th January, 1909. The author was described, anonymously, as 'A Patriot', yet another of Gerald's shrewd touches.

The weather was bad that evening. Fog crept through the streets and drifted on to the stage. A medium-sized audience contained none of the fashionable people who usually came to first nights. At the end of the performance, however, there were loud cheers and many curtain calls. Next morning, it is reported, a flood of young men hastened to enlist at the Territorial Army offices. Crude and obvious though it was, *An Englishman's Home* captured the public imagination and brought full houses. The Secretary of State for War described it as excellent propaganda. Lord Roberts, ex-Commander-in-Chief of the army, sent his personal congratulations to Guy. The author was the last person to know of his success. At the first night the audience thought Barrie had written the play and directed their applause at him while he retreated, embarrassed, into the shadow of the box where he had come to view the result of his friend Gerald's work. *An Englishman's Home* obsessed the country and Guy was famous. On his visits to London he found himself a celebrity and a lion of the drawing-rooms. He did not enjoy fame. Although he was a contented married man, women continued to fall in love with his handsome, dashing person. One of them was Mabel Terry-Lewis, a member of that vast Terry clan which for generations has permeated the theatre. She had acted with Gerald but nonetheless took a patrician view of the stage. Her nephew John Gielgud said to her when she told him about Guy: 'But surely you must have been in love with Gerald?'

'In love?' she replied scornfully. 'With an *actor*?'

The sensation made by the play and its political overtones caused Max Beerbohm sly misgivings. Although, he said, Guy may have rendered admirable service to his country, he would also have encouraged those thousands of people scribbling away up and down the land hoping to make a fortune out of a play on the lines of *An Englishman's Home*. Most, he thought, would have taken as their theme the peril of islanders unarmed. Others would be dividing their favours between 'Old Age Pensions, Education, Aeroplanes, the licensing of Public Houses, and other burning topics.'

Gerald was entirely innocent of political convictions and viewed *An Englishman's Home* simply as an excellent piece of theatre. It was the first time he had directed a new play, and the result was peculiarly satisfying, even more so, perhaps, than if he had taken the leading part. As director he was able to shape the total presentation and give it his personal authority. He enjoyed coaching his actors and actresses. Moreover, as an accomplished player and mimic himself, he was able to demonstrate exactly what he wanted of them. To Guy he wrote:

As you may imagine, it has been an anxious time for your little brother, but he has been rewarded by the thought that he has worked a little surprise on one who could make a fortune writing for the stage if he were not so monstrously indifferent, unambitious, or, shall we say, lazy? Well, good luck, *mon brave*. The Governor would have said, 'All of which is very amusing!'

The excitement caused by *An Englishman's Home* died down as suddenly as it had flared. Since Gerald was still acting in *What Every Woman Knows* the cast, unobserved by his watchful eye, began to improvise and to add bits of business he did not know about. After a respectable run the play came to an abrupt conclusion, although many must have recalled its warning five years later in 1914.

By contrast Gerald was playing the lead a few months later in a new thriller without the slightest political implications. Entitled *Arsène Lupin*, it was a dramatisation of the popular French novel by Maurice Leblanc who went on to write a series of tales about the hero, '*le gentleman-cambrioleur*', or gentleman-burglar. They are witty and still readable. In one of his adventures, for example, Lupin does battle with an English detective whose identity is transparently disguised by the name of 'Herlock Sholmès'. The play was adapted for the stage by Leblanc with the assistance of Francis de Croisset, an old hand at boulevard comedies, and together they produced an entertaining blend of humour, excitement and romance. For the debonair Lupin is a Gallic Raffles, though a Raffles unencumbered by Bunny and preferring women to cricket.

Lupin, masquerading as the Duc de Charmerace, gets himself engaged to the daughter of a millionaire whom he has, in the past, robbed of many precious things. He now intends to relieve his prospective father-in-law of the most valuable pictures in his collection. The plot resolves itself into a contest between Lupin and the great detective Guerchard who has sworn to arrest him after ten years of cat-and-mouse manoeuvres. It ends with Lupin's dramatic escape in which he impudently disguises himself as Guerchard and, helped by a bomb and a secret lift, makes off in the detective's own horseless carriage. 'Oh, hang it!' screams Guerchard, peering out of the window. 'He's doing a bunk in my motor-car!'

Suave, imperturbable yet lightning-swift in action, Gerald made an effortless hero. As the Duc de Charmerace he sported a moustache and hunting gear of impeccable pedigree. As Arsène Lupin he dazzled in white tie and tails. As Guerchard, his most startling quick-change transformation, he was indistinguishable from the stocky, heavily moustached original. Max Beerbohm enjoyed what he called this 'antinomian drama' and poked gentle fun at the enthusiasm of a respectable audience which, paradoxically, revelled in the triumph of a villain and cheered the discomfiture of the law.

> If the audience were composed entirely of members of the criminal classes, its behaviour would seem natural enough [he mused]. But I have no reason to suppose that the audiences at the Duke of York's are below the average level of respectability that one finds in other theatres. It is a strange thing, this lack of *esprit de corps* among the virtuous . . . However, the mischief is done, and we may congratulate Mr Gerald du Maurier on a part in which there is excellent scope for his peculiar dexterity of grace of style, and for his inventive humour.

Playing the dapper Arsène Lupin was a bit of fun Gerald relished, although it did not give him the fulfilment he had from directing *An Englishman's Home*. Neither did *Alias Jimmy Valentine*, the play that followed *Arsène Lupin*. It was an American importation, and this time he played yet another suave crook with a genius for safe-breaking. At the age of thirty-seven he had made his name in a succession of light rôles which, apart from the Barrie plays, were carried off with the help of a natural talent and charm polished by unobtrusive technique. It is true that he worked hard to obtain the effect of spontaneous ease and that the relaxed manner was only achieved through hours of careful practice. Yet he was the victim of his own success, judges of acting sometimes dismissed him as a lightweight, and he wryly spoke of himself as a dinner-jacket comedian. It was time for him to do something more substantial. The experience of directing Guy's play had given him a taste for organisation and management. Why should he not go into partnership with Frank Curzon, the impresario who joined him to present *An Englishman's Home*?

Curzon liked and appreciated du Maurier. Both men had a shrewd idea of what the public wanted and what an audience would find attractive. Curzon was a bluff, burly figure who looked like a gentleman farmer. It was appropriate that he should have been born near Aintree, for his judgment of horses proved as accurate as his judgment of plays. An excellent shot and a first-class rider to hounds, he loved a gamble, both on the racecourse and in the theatre. His brother was Mallaby-Deeley, a giant in the tailoring and hotel trade with whom he shared an acute business sense. Early in life he changed his name to the more aristocratic Curzon, became a not very effective actor and worked for a time under Frank Benson. He soon realised that his talent lay in management and put what little money he had into a musical comedy called *A Chinese Honeymoon*. It ran, in London and the provinces, for years and made his fortune. Within a short time he had eight London theatres under his control. Gradually he whittled them down to the Prince of Wales's and Wyndham's. Although he still put on musical comedies, some of them by a young writer called Frederick Lonsdale whom he generously subsidised through hard-up periods, he more often exercised his flair by teaming up box-office names such as Charles Hawtrey and Marie Tempest. He died in 1929 at the age of fifty-nine and left over a hundred and eighty thousand pounds, much the same as that other clever entrepreneur Sir Squire Bancroft. For all his theatrical success, perhaps the achievement that delighted him most was winning the Derby with a horse named Call Boy.

Up to 1910 Gerald was an actor earning a fixed salary. Although this had grown in proportion to his fame, it gave him no responsibility or interest in the financial side of affairs. He had asked Charles Frohman, the impresario of *Peter Pan*, whether they might go into partnership, but Frohman could not help as he would have liked because he had no theatre. Curzon did. He offered an agreement by which Gerald was to receive a salary of three thousand pounds a year and, even more important, a twenty-five per cent share of the profits.

I have got to settle soon about my future and it's rather a knotty proposition . . . [Gerald wrote to his mother]. Curzon would merely supply the money, and give advice when I asked for it. It would mean finishing first the run of *Alias Jimmy Valentine*, which is playing to enormous business. I know of a play I could start with, and perhaps Barrie would let me have one later on. What about it, old lady? I have the du Maurier timidity and unventuresomeness, but I feel that the time has come.

The birth of another daughter called Jeanne now meant that there were three children to support. He had an expensive establishment in Cumberland Terrace and domestic staff to keep up. He might lose a lot of money. On the other hand he might make a great deal. He decided to accept Frank Curzon's offer.

Wyndham's Theatre in the Charing Cross Road had been put up in 1899 by the actor Charles Wyndham and his leading lady Mary Moore who later became his wife. It was small and intimate with accommodation for seven hundred and sixty people. The proscenium had a cream and gold border, the decorations were vaguely Louis

XVI, and the ceiling, lit by the sparkle of a crystal pendant, displayed copies of luxuriant Boucher paintings. Here was the perfect setting for Gerald's confidential style. It remained so for the next fifteen years.

His choice of opening play at Wyndham's fell on *Nobody's Daughter*. The author, who wrote under the name of 'George Paston', was a clergyman's offspring, a spinster with a prolific record of plays which included titles such as *The Pharisee's Wife, Feed The Brute* and *Dinner While You Wait*. She had, it is clear, a talent for choosing 'daring' if not robust subjects that she treated demurely enough to titillate West End audiences without going over the edge. *Nobody's Daughter* cleverly applied this formula. A Colonel and a lady, now both happily married to other spouses, have in their youth had an imprudent love affair which gave birth to a daughter. The girl is brought up as a ward, the true parents remaining in the background. Unfortunately, not knowing that she is of gentle birth, she falls in love with a working-class mechanic. Worse still, her mother's husband discovers the shameful secret. 'How many more lies have you lived? How many more lovers have you had?' he rages. 'How many more children . . . a fake friend, a false wife, the very earth doesn't seem firm under my feet.' The blend of snobbery and illegitimacy was developed with the skill of a writer who, it should be remembered, had also confected those audacious novels *A Modern Amazon* and *A Bread and Butter Miss*.

Gerald played the indignant husband and refined what might have been in other hands a barnstorming display into a study of quiet grievousness. When he said to his wife: 'If you'd trusted me as I trusted you, you wouldn't have found me hard. You might have had your child and me,' he spoke the lines softly, almost threw them away, and, by understatement, gave them a telling power. One of the supporting players was the twenty-four-year-old Ronald Squire who made his first appearance on the London stage in *Nobody's Daughter*. Today he is remembered as the elderly *raisonneur*, the cynical clubman in scores of light comedies where his polished delivery and nonchalant manner were an assurance that even if the lines were poor they would be spoken to give an illusion of wit. His armoury included a shy smile, a gurgling chuckle, a bald pate that seemed to blush with enjoyment at each mischievous riposte, a voice that rumbled engagingly from the depths, a mouth that curved upwards in rich amusement, and an eye that hinted malice. In 1910 he still had his hair, flat as if painted on the skull, and a complexion unlined by the years. Already, though, he possessed the casual technique which

Gerald with Alexandra Carlisle in *Arsène Lupin* (1909).

ABOVE: Gerald's father, the artist
George du Maurier, in 1896 — caricature by
'Spy'. ABOVE RIGHT: Muriel, his wife, soon
after their marriage in 1903. RIGHT: With
his daughters Daphne, Angela and Jeanne
round about 1912. BELOW: Cannon
Hall, Hampstead, Gerald's home from
1916 until his death in 1934.

Wyndham's, Gerald's beloved theatre, at about the time he began his reign there as actor-manager in 1910. His first production, *Nobody's Daughter,* with Rosalie Toller and Lilian Braithwaite also had Ronald Squire (left) making one of his earliest West End appearances.

Gerald as *Raffles* (1906), one of his early 'thick-ear' melodramas.

Friends and patrons. ABOVE LEFT: Sir Johnston Forbes-Robertson, 'the noblest Roman of them all,' who encouraged Gerald's early promise. RIGHT: Maud and Herbert Beerbohm-Tree with whom Gerald served a none too arduous apprenticeship. BELOW LEFT: Mrs Patrick Campbell who taught Gerald about life and love. RIGHT: Viola Tree, Gerald's lifelong, and long-suffering, friend.

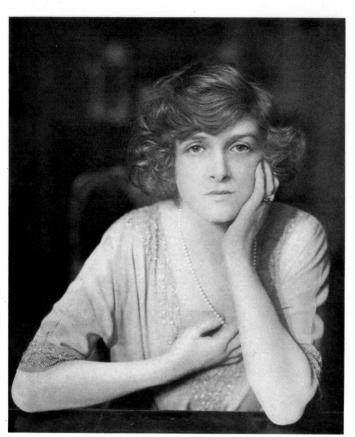

Gladys Cooper, 'discovered' by Gerald in 1913 and soon a star in her own right.

Although *Peter Pan* was the most famous of the Barrie plays featuring Gerald, *Dear Brutus* inspired his finest performance — George Stampa's caricature of the 1924 revival shows Gerald as the failed artist and Faith Celli as his 'dream' daughter.

Interference (1927). A tense moment during Gerald's tour de force: the ten-minute scene played entirely in dumb show.

Gerald and Gertrude Lawrence, his last leading lady, in *Behold, We Live* (1932), a piece of acting that deeply impressed the young Charles Laughton.

acquaintance with Gerald was to perfect. He was the son of a Colonel in the 93rd Argyll and Sutherland Highlanders and was born Ronald Squirl, a name he changed to Squire as soon as possible. His first stage rôle was in a provincial production of *An Englishman's Home*, and his association with Gerald, at first professional, turned into a close family friendship. Angela du Maurier remembered seeing him at Debenham and Freebody's one afternoon engaged in the task of buying knickers for his little daughter. The suave man about town, the witty hero of the drawing-room, was pathetically out of his depth. He greeted Angela with a sigh of relief and happily abdicated a responsibility which he found more trying than any first night.

He also played opposite Gerald in *Mr Jarvis*, one of the few failures during that early period of management. It was a costume affair set in the period of Charles II and did not appeal. Gerald quickly returned to the formula of *Nobody's Daughter* and mounted the sort of play his customers preferred, a domestic drama called *Passers By* of a type which the veteran boulevard playwright Abel Hermant once defined as 'respectable but a little bit naughty and with a dash of feeling'. Again we have the illegitimate child born of a youthful liaison between a man and a woman long since gone on their different ways. For the sake of variation the child was a small boy, a sweet cherub in a little Lord Fauntleroy velvet suit who won the hearts of all the ladies in the audience. As if this competition were not enough, Gerald at one point had to imitate Harry Lauder and sing a song in the attempt to entertain him. This he did with fascinating aplomb. The settings were luxurious: glossy furniture, solid oak panelling, thick curtains, for Wyndham's could turn out a baronial hall or a picturesque cottage garden with convincing facility. The play's author, Haddon Chambers, is long forgotten and few people remember now that he coined the phrase 'the long arm of coincidence'. It was something he called on frequently when he ran into difficulties with a plot. In private he was a man of considerable wit and enjoyed exchanging repartee with Frederick Lonsdale, whose daughter remembers him as 'looking like a polished but, nevertheless, repellent frog'. Gerald often joined them for night-long sessions over brandy and cigars. Once, incautiously, he spoke with malice of Chambers's current lover. The dramatist made no immediate reply, but, later in the evening, mentioned a dinner given to a famous American impresario by actors and actresses. After the toast had been offered to the guest of honour he was found to be asleep. Nudged awake, he replied: 'Ladies and gentlemen, any man who paints his face is a son of a bitch,' and fell asleep again. Gerald was silenced. But not for long. The conversation turned to the law on pen-names. Chambers argued there was nothing to stop a man calling himself what he liked. 'I could call myself Christ if I chose,' he declared. 'You do, you do,' murmured Gerald asperously.

More plays on the Haddon Chambers model followed. They filled the theatre reasonably well, had a fair box-office record and vanished once they served their purpose, which was to exhibit Gerald's easy command of an audience and to enthral lady spectators with fashions that ranged from dresses in pale blue satin meteor to squirrel ties, from Persian embroidery to hats in gold lace and red ostrich feathers. It was not until 1913, at the age of forty, that he staged one of his greatest successes. This, surprisingly, was not a new play but a work already thirty-five years old. When he announced his plan to revive *Diplomacy*, the Bancrofts' venerable triumph, everyone thought he had gone ever so slightly mad. Sir Squire himself, who owned the rights in the play, was however one of the few who believed him to be sane.

Opinion about Gerald's aberration hardened when it was learned that he had cast a young actress called Gladys Cooper for the leading rôle of Dora made famous by the legendary Madge Kendal. The beautiful but inexperienced young girl had played small parts up to then with charm and delicacy, but no one save Gerald thought she was capable of much more. Having seen her acting on stage he happened to meet her at a charity dance in the Albert Hall and had a sudden idea. 'We've been trying to think of someone for the leading woman's part in *Diplomacy*,' he told her, 'and I believe you could do it.' She was thrilled, for she had seen him in *Raffles* and, like many other girls, fallen in love with him at a distance, as witness the photograph of him which she carried around with her. Later the feeling cooled though her professional respect did not change. At the time, though, she admitted it was no use pretending that 'I wasn't as much carried away as any of the other young women who worshipped him.'

She had been a Gaiety Girl in those popular musical comedies *The Dollar Princess, Our Miss Gibbs* and the like. There she learned everything that drama schools were later to teach: elocution, singing, dancing, movement and fencing. From Daly's and the Gaiety Theatre she moved over to the legitimate stage where for years she was resigned to ecstatic praise for her beauty rather than her acting talent. A beauty she was, a postcard queen whose pictures sold by the thousand. Her grandson Sheridan Morley reports that between 1905 and 1920 she posed for over four hundred of them. One Sunday

Gerald invited her down to Hertfordshire where he had taken a house for the summer. He drove with Angela to the station and told her to go and meet Miss Cooper. How, enquired the tiny girl, would she recognise her? 'Just pick out the prettiest face you see,' he replied. Among the mass of travellers she discerned 'a very lovely person in a blue hat which matched her eyes'. The task was easy.

His decision to cast her in *Diplomacy* was not so bizarre as it might have seemed. (He did not tell her that the actress originally chosen had withdrawn because of pregnancy.) In directing the ancient melodrama he could either attempt to reproduce the Bancroft production of decades ago or work out an entirely new approach. The first alternative was absurd. The second, which he adopted, offered promise of excitement. He compounded his apparent idiocy by engaging as the hero another untried performer whose handsomeness, almost as striking as Henry Ainley's, was the male equivalent of Miss Cooper's beauty. The youth was called Owen Nares, later a prominent matinée idol and actor-manager himself. At the end of long rehearsals he and Gladys Cooper were ordered to stay on while the company departed. Terrified, the pair went through their big scene in a theatre empty except for Gerald and old Sir Squire watching intently from the stalls. When they finished there was a long silence. What had they done wrong? The two men came up slowly from the gloom of the auditorium. They had, they said, been moved to tears and unable to face them immediately. 'I think,' said Gladys Cooper, 'that was one of the most marvellous moments of my life.'

After the first performance in March 1913, *The Times*, describing Gladys Cooper as hitherto 'a dainty player of dainty parts', went on to remark that 'last night the opportunity came to her of showing something bigger and she took that opportunity splendidly.' In the climax of Act II, where the heroine bangs at the door and screams the name of her lover 'Julian, Julian, Julian', before collapsing in a faint, she proved that she could act as well as look beautiful. Gerald was delighted with her, and also with Owen Nares as Julian. His unconventional treatment of the old play had succeeded completely, and he did not mind that his own playing was described by a critic as 'somewhat light'. *Diplomacy* enjoyed a run of four hundred and fifty-five performances, which is over a hundred more than it had when the Bancrofts originally produced it. The play was revived yet again in 1924 with Gladys Cooper and Owen Nares repeating their success. Its run was almost as long. Critics were baffled and, as they do today, reproached managers for reviving old-fashioned plays instead of presenting new ones.

Why *Diplomacy* has been successful I do not know [complained one of them], except that the conduct of the plot is exciting, and it gives many opportunities for broad and emotional acting. Essentially it is an old-fashioned play, and its drama is quite machine-made. It must be remembered, however, that its revival appealed to many middle-aged playgoers who naturally desired to see it once again. That would not account, of course, for such a long run, but doubtless it was a factor in its success. Also there is a reaction in favour of melodrama, or, perhaps, one should say, in favour of exciting, picturesque plays.

Gerald was the last person to attempt an analysis of why his instinct had been justified. He, with his ten per cent of the profits, and Gladys Cooper, who at forty pounds a week was earning a very good salary for the time, were happy to go on playing until the box-office told them to stop.

With *Diplomacy* Gerald developed still further the talent for direction which he showed in *An Englishman's Home*. Since he had only a small part in it he could give his full attention to other members of the cast. Although *Diplomacy* was not a modern work it gave him what he looked for in a play: strong scenes, meaty plot and wealth of action. Shavian drama was not for him and he disliked too much talk. What he sought was constant movement, the excitement of things happening. The audience must be kept in a state of anticipation. He believed, as Tristan Bernard would have said, that they liked to be surprised, but to be surprised by something they were already expecting. There was no room for experimental drama or innovation at Wyndham's. Patrons wanted a smooth and satisfying evening's entertainment, well staged and nicely dressed. Gerald, who described himself as the 'lowest of the lowbrows', gave them what they liked, and, as a result, the plays with which he was identified, except for those of Barrie, are now entirely forgotten.

Even though they may have been unworthy of the gift he lavished on them, they were staged with flair and elegance. He was a perfect director. His method was first of all to act each character himself and then let the cast get on with it. 'Don't force it, don't be self-conscious,' his daughter Daphne remembered him saying at rehearsals. 'Do what you generally do any day of your life when you come into a room. Bite your nails, yawn, lie down on a sofa and read a book – do anything or nothing, but don't look dramatically at the audience and speak with one eye on the right-hand box. If you must look in front of you, stare right at the back of the pit as though nobody was there.' All this was entirely different from the technique of an Irving or a Tree who embraced the audience with a rolling eye and used scripts in which the direction APPLAUSE was written at points where the actor believed he could win a round of claps.

When the cast had begun to feel their way into the rôles and started to build their characters Gerald would nudge them along with tact. Brilliant, he would say, it's coming on just as I expected. Why not, though, do such and such, or emphasise the second word rather than the first? Flattered by his appreciation, stimulated by his sympathy, the cast responded well to his diplomatic treatment. No feelings were hurt and confidence bloomed. As an excellent mimic himself he could hit off their unnecessary mannerisms with such good humour that no one felt hurt.

He had his own way of handling love scenes, which are always difficult and invite either exaggeration or woodenness. If an actor overdid the passion, says Daphne, he would murmur: 'Must you kiss her as though you were having steak and onions for lunch? It may be what you feel, but it's damned unattractive from the front row of the stalls. Can't you just say, "I love you," and yawn, and light a cigarette and walk away?' This was what he did himself, though no one could do it quite like him. They had not, as he had, spent hours before the looking-glass rehearsing the simplest of gestures.

On the other hand he deplored shyness. 'Be playful, be like puppies, be fond of one another,' he suggested, 'but don't go to the extremes, either one way or the other. Strike some sort of medium between afternoon tea in a cathedral town and supper in a flat in Paris, for God's sake!' He would have agreed with Sacha Guitry, his nearest French counterpart, that:

To act is to tell lies with the aim of deceiving. Everything around one should tell lies. The good actor should say 'I love you' with greater conviction to an actress he doesn't love than to one whom he does. And he should convince the audience that he is eating on stage when in reality he is not. The refinement of refinements is to *appear* to be in love with an actress whom one does really love – it's like eating a genuine chicken while making believe it's cardboard.

In the year of *Diplomacy* he reached his fortieth birthday. He always remembered his father saying to him when he was young and carefree, 'Wait till you come to forty year.' Well, he had come to it and nothing much seemed to have gone wrong. There had been sorrows, of course, like the deaths of Sylvia and her husband, but on the whole fate was treating him very kindly. He had a happy family and his own theatre where he ruled with benevolence a company who adored him. He was at the top of his profession. Perhaps his father, ill and prematurely old, had been pessimistic? Sir Squire Bancroft, who had known George and been his friend, said: 'Poor du Maurier, I wish he had lived to see how his son Gerald adorns the stage he so greatly loved himself.'

[ii]

Dear Brutus

In 1914 Gerald took *Diplomacy* to Windsor Castle for a Command Performance. Royal recognition followed public acknowledgment of him as a leading theatrical figure. Honorary posts began to multiply. He was elected President of the Actors' Orphanage Fund which had been established in 1896 by the wife of the man who inaugurated the *Stage* newspaper and by his own aunt, wife to the drama critic Clement Scott. The fund had in its care some fifty orphans of theatrical folk and undertook their schooling and job training. These 'destitute children', as the Fund's deed called them, were housed in a large seventeenth-century mansion at Langley Place, Buckinghamshire. A yearly income of three thousand pounds was enough to provide for the children, much of it coming from the Theatrical Garden Party which the Fund held annually at Kew or in the Chelsea Royal Botanical Gardens. Gerald entered on his duties with vigour and turned the Garden Party into a glittering event. The men in top hats and the ladies in glamorous dresses gave it the appearance of Ascot, and in the afternoon Queen Alexandra and her daughters added royal chic. Members of the public crowded in to mingle with the famous and to patronise a coconut shy operated by C. Aubrey Smith, a lucky dip run by Ellen Terry, a greasy pig competition organised by Herbert Beerbohm Tree and other sideshows where their money was taken by George Alexander or Lady Tree or Lady Bancroft. At one of the most popular stalls you could buy an autographed postcard or, for a somewhat higher price, a kiss from Gladys Cooper. Takings flourished wondrously.

Gerald was never busier. That year he put on and starred in two new plays at Wyndham's. They made no great stir but sold enough tickets to bring him a fair percentage of the takings. He also took part in charity performances, one of them, to help King George's Pension Fund for Actors, becoming a regular event. At Christmas, without a new piece on the stocks, he exhumed *Raffles* and was gratified by a run much longer than either of his productions during those twelve months. Life was full. He usually had breakfast in bed with Muriel, or 'Mo' as he affectionately nicknamed his wife, and got up at mid-morning to choose his suit for the day and his shoes from the two dozen pairs that were always arranged, gleaming and neatly treed, on a stand in his dressing-room. If there was a rehearsal he would leave home at half-past ten so as to arrive punctually at Wyndham's by eleven. Besides directing and acting there were meetings to be held with his partner Frank Curzon, new plays to be scrutinised, new ideas to be discussed, letters to be written. His business manager, Tom Vaughan, a shrewd and cautious administrator, went over the box-office returns with him, examined the bar takings and settled the day-to-day problems of running a fashionable London theatre. In time Vaughan's prudence extended beyond Wyndham's and was called on to guide the du Maurier finances.

Should there be no matinée that afternoon Gerald was free, after lunch at the Garrick, to play golf. This, with cards, had become an obsessive recreation for him and indeed for many of his friends in the theatre. He already was a lively animator of the Peter Pan Golf Club, founded by J. M. Barrie to encourage the 'health and morals' of the Peter Pan touring company, and presented it with trophies. Early on he signed up as a keen member of the Stage Golfing Society which began in 1903 on the understanding that its adherents 'should be expected to play like gentlemen', and as its eventual President he donated the first Cup. Soon afterwards the Stage Ladies' Golfing Society was formed under the presidency of Mo who proved just as enthusiastic as her husband in pursuing the game. Long and strenuous hours in the open air kept his figure trim and aided the muscular co-ordination an actor needs for graceful movement. His prestige helped add respectability to a profession hitherto more noted for drunkenness than for healthy sport. As, however, a convivial guest at parties, he was a trifle unnerved to find himself being commended by temperance bodies and thoughtful vicars.

Usually home at Cumberland Terrace by six thirty after an exuberant afternoon's golf, he would bound up the stairs to the nursery. His three little girls awaited him and looked forward to the performance he never failed to entertain them with: a choice bit of clowning, an uproarious imitation of a family friend, or a comic turn that made them gasp with laughter and amused them so much that they could not get to sleep for hours and were the despair of Nanny. Sometimes they would have had some childish quarrel that led to hair pulling and scratching. He would intervene and rig himself up like a judge. The girls were arraigned before him and their evidence cross-examined. By the time the verdict was reached peace had been restored and the dispute forgotten. More seriously, he impressed on them the importance of good manners. He would introduce them to pieces of furniture in the room pretending they were guests and showing them how to shake hands. Angela never forgot his terrible and genuine annoyance when, presented to his business manager Tom Vaughan, she innocently proffered her left hand.

Then he would have an early dinner, preferably the cold meat, underdone, which was his favourite, and some lettuce. After that he allowed himself a quick snooze, what people of his generation called 'shut-eye', in his study or the morning-room. He arrived at Wyndham's in good time to make up and dress, for, impulsive and wayward in private life though he may have been, in professional matters he was disciplined and correct. He made his entrance with that distinctive walk of his, abrupt and inimitable, and spoke his lines in the familiar voice, staccato but unemphatic. By now he had forgotten his aversion to long runs. He possessed the technique to deal with them, to give an air of freshness even though heartily sick of the dialogue, and in any case, as a manager, he welcomed them since they were good business. When the curtain fell for the last time he took off his make-up, bathed and put on street clothes. Admirers who wished an audience of him sent in their visiting cards which his dresser handed over on a tray. An amusing form of snobbery dictated whom he should receive and whom not. Without bothering to read them he ran his fingers over the cards like a blind man deciphering Braille. Those that were merely printed, and therefore belonging to people who were not quite right, he threw away. Only those that were embossed, and thus acceptable, qualified for an audience of him.

He did not relish holidays. The first few days of a stay in the country were agreeable enough and he would even set out, tweeded and carrying binoculars, the girls following at the rear, on bird-watching expeditions. Suddenly boredom would set in. He felt lonely and ached to be back again in the fever and fret of London. 'I'm a Cockney,' Daphne used to hear him say. 'It's no use getting away from it. A day or two in the country is all very well, but not for ever; it's too slack. I find trees depressing after a while, and I can't relax.

It's no good, one is either born like that or one isn't. It's something in the blood.' His nerves perpetually strung to the highest pitch, his temperament always on edge for new challenges, new excitements, he could not relax and hated to be alone. He needed people around him, and hustle and conversation. Seaside holidays were no good, either. At Dinard one summer his visits to the casino were spoilt by the insufferably dull atmosphere of the place. Dieppe was a little better, but only because its casino had a livelier ambience and, to Mo's dismay, he spent all his time there gambling instead of breathing the healthy sea air.

After the theatre he enjoyed most of all an evening, which usually became an early morning, with his favoured cronies. Chief of them was Frederick Lonsdale. Gerald appeared in only one of his plays, *The Last of Mrs Cheyney*, and that towards the end of his life. It was his friend Ronald Squire who is most closely associated with Lonsdale and is regarded as the interpreter *par excellence* of those polished comedies. Yet Gerald was perhaps Lonsdale's closest friend despite his teasing description of him as a 'muck writer'. This was probably a reference to the musical comedies which the dramatist wrote in his early career – hits like *The Maid of the Mountains*, *The Balkan Princess* and *The King of Cadonia* which earned lots of money. It is, though, not easy to construct a good libretto, and Freddy had the knack. He also possessed an acrid wit. Hailed by a stranger who said, 'Aren't you Freddy Lonsdale?' he quickly summed him up and replied, 'No. Not tonight.' One New Year's Eve, having quarrelled with a fellow member of the Garrick, he was persuaded by Seymour Hicks to make up and to wish his enemy a happy New Year. Freddy walked over to the man in question and snapped: 'I wish you a happy New Year. But only one.'

He had fair hair, sharp blue eyes and a ruddy complexion. Born Frederick Leonard, in Jersey, the son of a tobacconist, he mysteriously acquired an Old Etonian manner and what was then known as an upper-crust accent. After emigrating to the mainland he was unable for some years to revisit his birthplace because a debt contracted in youth carried the penalty of instant arrest the moment he landed there. Other debts plagued his early years, and when he complained to a friend about all the money he owed he was advised to put creditors off the scent by changing his name. As he happened to be passing through Lonsdale Street at the time he adopted the suggestion there and then. His financial problems did not improve with marriage, though they failed to crush his spirit. He and his wife were out one day when he saw a pretty girl who took his fancy approaching them. Mrs Lonsdale was asked to walk on the other side of the road. 'I don't want her to know I'm married to you,' he explained. She did as she was told. As a father, too, he had his limits. He would obligingly crawl out of bed to make a bottle for a child crying in the night. If she persisted, though, he would grunt: 'Can't the bloody fool see I'm getting it?'

While in the army he had stumbled on a gift for writing plays. A sketch that lampooned his Commanding Officer at a regimental entertainment amused everyone but its subject, and Freddy next day was confined to barracks. The General's wife, however, was extremely diverted, and afterwards, when he fell ill, she visited him in hospital and told him he had genuine talent. If she got him out of the army, she said, would he promise to write plays? She used her influence and obtained a medical discharge for him. Years later he told the story to Gerald who was charmed and insisted on meeting her. Gerald invited her to lunch with Freddy and himself. After a joyous meal she went out and, on her way through the hall, looked at the hat-stand and remarked: 'Oh, what a lovely umbrella!' The moment she had gone Gerald rang the airport and chartered an aeroplane to take the umbrella to her home in Norfolk. On walking into the house hours later she was astonished by the sight of the umbrella awaiting her.

Freddy kept his promise to her. From comedies he graduated to straight plays. Gerald's wife Mo appeared in one of the latter with A. E. Matthews. It was called *The Early Worm* and already showed signs of the mature Lonsdale in the final exchange between heiress and impoverished Duke: 'You are not marrying me for my money?'

'No. But I'm awfully glad you've got it.'

Freddy loved dukes and has been accused of snobbery. This is not quite fair. The poor, and those who need to work for a living, do not have the time to be witty and epigrammatical. So Freddy, like Racine who peopled his dramas with kings and queens exclusively, found his characters among people who had ample leisure to indulge their wit and their emotions.

He was largely innocent of education and, reading few books, was content to glance at perhaps one a year. Neither could he sit through a play by anyone other than himself. This doubtless helped him to preserve his originality, for his touch is unique and, in his lifetime, the only other dramatists he was compared with are Congreve and Sheridan. His special talent was to use an obvious, even hackneyed theme, and to spin it out the length of three acts by means of deft and unexpected twists. He illustrates perfectly the dictum that the playwright need not be a literary man. As Somerset Maugham once remarked, a dramatist can succeed with no more than the intellectual equipment of an average bartender. *Aren't We All?*, *On Approval* and especially *The Last of Mrs Cheyney* are masterly examples of plotting. The dialogue, while containing few conscious epigrams of the Wildean type, depends for wit on less blatant methods. A speech taken in isolation may not seem very humorous. The Lonsdale wit arises from what is said before and after. In this context a simple phrase like 'Good morning' or 'How do you do?' can make a hugely entertaining effect.

Boredom was what Lonsdale feared most. It led him to set up home apart from his wife and children, although he retained an affection for them, and to travel ceaselessly without purpose or destination. If he felt an attack of boredom coming on he might reserve a last-minute passage to New York and then, on arrival, turn round and immediately sail back again. He was obsessed with Baudelaire's perpetual urge to escape *'n'importe où hors de ce monde'*. Until the end of his restless life he never found the goal he was seeking. The Garrick Club was the only place where he felt at home, though only too often a fellow member would disappoint him by turning out to be 'one of the bloodiest bores in the world'. He wrote his plays not because he had an urgent need to express himself but because he liked exercising his craft – which might just as well have been woodwork or the making of jigsaw puzzles – and because he needed a great deal of money to keep up his expensive way of life. Decked out in his white scarf and the white socks he affected long before they became fashionable, he took all his meals in luxury restaurants. Head waiters became pliant when subjected to his formidable mixture of charm and haughtiness.

'Taste this, my dear fellow,' he demanded of a maître d'hôtel.

'What is wrong with it, sir?'

'Prussic acid. Do you imagine the chef bears me some grudge?'

Years afterward, escorted to the best table in the room, he would be told confidentially: 'No prussic acid today, sir.'

He did not always succeed in keeping at bay the loneliness and melancholy that festered behind his outward nonchalance. Gerald was one of the few people who understood this, for he, too, was afflicted in the same way. He could not rest and craved incessant activity, anything, be it launching a new play or gambling, or a violent bout of tennis, as long as his nerves were kept at full stretch and there was no time to brood. When the stimulus had gone and the effort been made he looked round feverishly for new excitement. Freddy, he knew, was like him, and the similarity of temperament drew them together. The only holidays Gerald really enjoyed were those he spent visiting Freddy's home in Birchington. He would bring his family with him and put up at one of the two hotels. Others followed his example, and for a time the little Kentish watering-place became a fashionable resort where Gladys Cooper entertained at weekends, Ivor Novello sunbathed on the beach and P. G. Wodehouse wrote some of his novels. While Mo and the three girls played on the sands Gerald and Freddy sat together at home talking and drinking. Long into the night they gossiped. From time to time the two men flicked playing cards into the well of a large gramophone and made bets on how they would fall.

Late one evening Freddy walked upstairs to rouse his wife who had long since gone to bed. 'Could you come?' he said. 'Gerald wants to go home and there's a horse leaning over the front gate. Gerald doesn't like horses.' Mrs Lonsdale, ever helpful, got up and shooed the animal away. As an extra precaution she proposed that Gerald leave through the back garden. She then fell thankfully back into bed. Soon afterwards Freddy came in once more. 'I'm most awfully sorry to bother you,' he explained, 'but that horse is leaning over the back gate now.'

Freddy's daughter Frances remembered with lifelong horror the games Gerald and her father devised in an attempt to fight boredom. There were three du Maurier girls and three Lonsdales, and if any of the children had committed some small offence a court of law was organised with each allocated a part as the accused, prosecuting and defending counsel, and witness. The du Maurier girls were used to such games, having already played them at home, but the Lonsdales were not and they hated the idea. Gerald, moreover, confused them with his mockery and sophisticated jokes. On another occasion a tennis match was arranged between pairs of girls who were led to believe that bets of a hundred pounds depended on the result. Confidence was undermined and feelings hurt by the quips of the two men who stood by laughing and joking. To Mrs Lonsdale's reproaches for their callous behaviour, Freddy answered: 'They must learn to have a sense of humour.' 'As a result,' says Frances Lonsdale, 'we are all deeply touchy, desperately without humour in personal relationships to this day.'

Soon there was to be little excuse for humour, black or otherwise, since in August 1914, came the declaration of war. Gerald, at the time, was rehearsing a new play for Wyndham's called *The Outcast* and opened with it a month later. The author was Hubert Henry

Davies who had begun his career as a journalist in America but soon found his niche as a purveyor of polite comedies for the carriage trade at Wyndham's, the Haymarket and the Criterion. He died at the age of only forty-eight, and there is a youthfulness about his work that Max Beerbohm gently touched on:

> Mr Davies himself is by way of being an infant dramatist; but he is not such an infant that he needs anyone else to keep the public keenly alive to the fact of his infancy: he knows how to work the reminders himself. In case his rare instinct for dramatic craftsmanship, and his flashes of very real and delightful humour, should cause the audience to forget how wonderfully young he is, he takes care that his knowledge of life shall seem to be that of a child on a rocking-horse. The scene of the play must needs be a boudoir, peopled by adults; but nothing there shall happen that could conceivably happen anywhere but upstairs in the nursery.

The Outcast was not a play for wartime and it closed by December.

A few weeks later, in 1915, Gerald's mother died. She was seventy-four, plagued by a weary heart and disquieted by news of war. An operation was advised though she did not survive, and her children wondered guiltily to themselves whether, had they not insisted 'for her own good' on having it, she might have stayed with them a little longer. The 'old cup of tea' had been a devoted mother and grandmother, a centre of calm and security for a family often made wretched by the hard world outside. She had seen her son-in-law and her daughters Sylvia, and latterly Trixie, die young, and had lived out the tragedies with fortitude. Every scrap of paper her two sons wrote her was carefully stored, from prep-school scribbles to the long letters Guy sent her on his postings abroad. Gerald had written less since he was close at hand, but his scrawls were also preserved, together with receipts for old bills paid long, long ago. Her boys sat at her bed as she died on the very day of her wedding anniversary. They buried her in the graveyard of Hampstead Parish Church beside George du Maurier whom she had married fifty-one years previously.

February came, and March, chill and dismal. One evening, as Gerald made up in his dressing-room at Wyndham's, a telegram arrived. He opened it to learn that Guy had been killed in France. While he was evacuating his battalion from the front line a shell exploded nearby. There was just enough time left for him to murmur a few words before he died. Light-hearted, humorous, though taking his profession very seriously, he had been due, it was said, for promotion to Brigadier-General the next day. Gerald remembered their last meeting on the eve of Guy's return to active service in France. 'Take this,' Guy said, slipping from his little finger the signet ring he wore. 'One never knows, and it was always meant for you.' One never knows, thought Gerald.

Only a few days afterward, on 15th March, Gerald's nephew George, eldest of the 'lost boys', now a Second Lieutenant in the Rifle Brigade, was shot through the head. His comrades buried him in a Flanders field and put violets on the grave. In what was to be the last letter he received from his adoring guardian Barrie, George had read of his Uncle Guy's death.

> He certainly had the du Maurier charm at its best – the light heart with the sad smile, and it might be the sad heart with the bright smile [wrote Barrie]. There was always something pathetic about him to me. He had lots of stern stuff in him, and yet always the mournful smile of one who could pretend that life was gay but knew it wasn't. One of the most attractive personalities I have ever known.

'*A quoi bon vivre? Ce n'est pas gai!*' George du Maurier used to say. What was the point of life? It wasn't very amusing. As a boy full of vigour and confidence, Gerald had not known what he meant. At best he assumed that George's semi-blindness and the disappointment of his artistic ambition had prejudiced his attitude. How otherwise could a man be so gloomy about life and its joyful expectations? Even in his twenties and thirties, when success came rushing to meet him and blotted out his trifling failures, Gerald remained exuberantly untouched by his father's dark view. Now, at the age of forty-two, he was beginning to understand. In a few short weeks he had lost his mother, his only brother and a cherished nephew. Emma du Maurier was frail and old, and her death, sad though it was, belonged to the unchangeable order of things. Guy, however, was in his prime, mature enough to have established himself in his profession but still with many years left for greater achievements, while George Davies, at the age of twenty-one, had been cut off before his promise could flower. In France they were only a few miles apart, surrounded in muddy trenches by rotting corpses, the stink of decomposing flesh heavy on the air. Although Guy had been hardened in battle and won the DSO, he did not lose his sensitiveness. During the Boer War a man was killed next to him, and the shock is said to have turned his hair white. If men like Guy were to be destroyed, their talent wasted, their gift squandered, what was the reason, Gerald asked? Oppressed by futility, puzzled by the random horror of life, he began to question his own existence. For the first time he wondered if putting make-up on your face and speaking words other men had written was a decent way to earn a living. Beside the tragedy of Guy the theatre, with its fake emotions and limelit poses, seemed a very tawdry thing.

Then he remembered that he was not only an actor but a manager as well, an employer with responsibilities to the staff of his theatre, and that if he did not find a play for Wyndham's soon they would all be out of work. He tried to forget his sorrow in reading scripts, choosing a cast, ordering scenery and costumes, arranging rehearsals, plotting moves. When the dreadful spring of 1915 had relented into summer he produced *Gamblers All*, a typical Wyndham's offering by a dramatist, daughter of the man who wrote that pertinacious Edwardian success *Jim the Penman*. The heroine, Lady Langworthy, has a taste for illegal gambling which her stockbroker husband deplores. When he refuses to help with her heavy losses at the tables she is forced into the power of a money-lender. Debtors close in and her brother forges a bill. Happily, the money-lender falls in love with the improvident lady and, in a noble gesture, clears up the matter of the forgery and reconciles her with her husband. The moral is, according to one of the characters: 'It's such a mistake to deceive your husband – unnecessarily.'

As sometimes happens, the cast was more interesting than the play. Gerald acted the part of the brother, a charming light-headed fellow easily led into misdemeanours for the best of reasons. With the twitch of an eyebrow, the tap of a cigarette on his silver case, he implied gallantry, fraternal kindness and misguided heroism. Lady Langworthy was Madge Titheradge, a very experienced actress known to her familiars as 'Midge'. She had small features, dark eyes and a husky voice that sounded comic or tragic at will. Both on and off stage, says John Gielgud, she could be very emotional and was apt to faint with excitement. She did this at curtain fall in a play with Marie Tempest but smartly recovered when she saw that the formidable star was preparing to hit her with the walking-stick she carried as a prop. The part of the money-lender was taken by Lewis Waller. Few people remember him now, but in those days he was an enormously popular star whose virile good looks inspired hysteria among young women. They worshipped him as today their descendants adore pop musicians, and they formed themselves into what was known as the

KOWB or 'Keen on Waller Brigade'. For over half an hour they would applaud him at the final curtain of *The Three Musketeers* and other dashing melodramas, though he preferred Shakespeare which he spoke, especially as Henry V, in a voice like a silver trumpet. Box-office reasons impelled him to put on the costume dramas which his fans demanded. On the night of Queen Victoria's death he entered a friend's dressing-room, stricken with grief, and burst into sobs. 'She's dead, Bill, she's dead!' he spluttered through his tears. His friend tried to console him but he refused to be comforted in his sorrow. 'It's the receipts, Bill, the receipts,' he wept. 'The receipts are bound to drop.' He was right and they did.

Gamblers All did not last long and was taken off in August. The play seemed to have a curse on it, for the author died soon after its run began. It was also the last time Lewis Waller appeared on stage, for he died too, a few months later, at the age of fifty-five. He was distantly related to Gerald through the latter's French aunt who had been wife to the drama critic Clement Scott. On her death Scott married Waller's sister-in-law. Genealogists may well have the correct term to describe such a remote relationship. Madge Titheradge was said to have loved Waller, and so was Lady Tree. It is further said that both these rivals were observed at his funeral clad in deepest black. No one has recorded Mrs Waller's thoughts on the occasion.

A week after the run of *Gamblers All* ended Gerald re-opened his theatre with a play that gave him one of his finest triumphs as well as demonstrating his versatility. In *The Ware Case* he showed a gift for bravura acting entirely different from his usual quiet manner. The play had been written by George Pleydell, otherwise George Pleydell Bancroft, the son of Gerald's old friend Sir Squire. Educated at Eton and Oxford, Pleydell was called to the Bar, although in youth he acted with Sir George Alexander, and in later years ran the newly founded Academy of Dramatic Art, not yet Royal, before settling down as Clerk of the Assize on the Midland Circuit. He also wrote plays on the 'well-made' Sardou principle that would naturally attract a precise and tidy legal brain. Max Beerbohm saw him as a modern Casabianca:

The wreck of the good ship *Sardou*, whence all but he have fled, sinks lower and lower beneath the surface, but he, that lonely, gallant boy, stands on the burning deck with head erect and arms folded, never flinching. Though the flames envelop him and the waters compass him about, he persists, pale but undaunted, on the 'well-made' timbers of that dear old craft which he was taught to honour. He is a little hero.

The Ware Case, based on a novel he had written, offered a novelty in that it had a court-room setting, the Old Bailey, in fact. It appears to be the first time that a playwright has taken full advantage of the natural drama arising from a hard-fought legal case, and although the idea has been used again several times *The Ware Case* inaugurated a fashion. Gerald played Hubert Ware, the selfish and amoral but strangely appealing central figure who is accused of murdering his brother-in-law. Throughout the development of the play, as Ware struggled desperately for his life, Gerald managed to suggest that despite the man's callousness he had something attractive about him, something that made his story ring true. When the verdict of not guilty was delivered the audience found themselves agreeing. Here, they thought, was a character who, with all the circumstances against him and regardless of an obvious flaw in his personality, could not have committed a ruthless murder. They were unprepared for the climax, a dazzling *coup de théâtre* which began with the cleared man returning home to acclamation from crowds in the street outside. His nerve snaps after the terrible strain he has been under and an expression of bitterness transforms his face. He turns to the window and shouts: 'You bloody fools, I did it!' He kills himself with poison and collapses dead on the floor.

Gerald directed with restraint and economy. Not for a moment did the pace falter, and tension was built up in a series of finely graded steps. His own performance had a compelling power that drove the audience to believe he was innocent despite their misgiving, and when the dénouement came it burst upon them with the shock of a thunderclap. In *The Ware Case* he was not just a matinée idol but an actor who, through his command of those who saw and heard him, was able to convince them of something they were reluctant to believe.

As his next play Barrie gave him *A Kiss For Cinderella*, a piece of whimsy far removed from the grim drama of *The Ware Case*. It is, one cannot help feeling, Barrie at his most repellent. An excited speech from one of the characters is accompanied by the direction: *He contemplates a letter to* The Times. When Cinderella is asked the following riddle by the Prince: 'On the night of the first Zeppelin raids, what was it that everyone rushed to save first?' she wins the prize with her answer: 'There's just one thing all true Britons would be anxious about . . . Their love letters.' The play opens in wartime London. Cinderella, the little charwoman, is visited by a policeman who suspects her of harbouring German spies. She enlightens him by pointing at the boxes which are nailed against a wall. Each contains a small child: one the orphan of a sailor, two representing the French and Belgian allies, and the fourth a little German girl. Cinderella explains that she is doing her bit in the war by looking after them. The gruff policeman begins to soften. In the next act, a gorgeous Dream Palace which Daphne du Maurier recalled as 'an incredible *mélange* of Edmond Dulac and Watteau and *Alice in Wonderland*', Cinderella meets her Prince who is revealed as the policeman transformed. The last act comes back to earth in a hospital where the patriotic Cinderella is nursing wounded soldiers. The galumphing constable proposes marriage and offers a pair of glass slippers – 'It's a policeman's idea of an engagement ring,' he explains – which fit her, she delightedly squeals, 'like two kisses'.

However faded *A Kiss For Cinderella* may appear today, it was welcomed by a London sated with battle and wartime horrors. Cinderella was Hilda Trevelyan, the first Wendy, and Gerald doubled the roles of 'Our Policeman' and 'The Prince', switching easily from the clumsy copper to the elegant hero. He was to revive *A Kiss For Cinderella* a number of times, especially at Christmas, its most appropriate season, when the Dream Palace enthralled an audience packed with small children. It had music by Ernest Bucalossi, suggestive and reminiscent as good stage music usually is. A slow waltz in the manner of Delibes accompanied the Prince's despairing call for Cinderella when she vanished at midnight, and as the rival Beauties lined up for inspection there floated a melody that predicted the Noël Coward of *Bitter Sweet*. The marriage of Cinderella and her Prince occurred while the orchestra droned a solemn motif that sounded almost, but not quite, like Mendelssohn's *Wedding March*, and the fun ended with King, Queen and courtiers all embarking on a syncopated shuffle in two-step time. It was the sort of workmanlike stuff to be expected from a craftsman who, before he died in 1933, had written many best-selling parlour pieces, among them an enduring *Grasshoppers' Dance* for which the only possible epithet is 'dainty'.

As the war blundered on and names like Ypres, Artois and Verdun turned into words of mourning, Gerald was caught up more and more in charity performances and gala matinées. At Drury Lane in April 1916, he played a Barrie one-acter for the benefit of women munition workers. Lily Elsie was at his side in this little spoof called *Shakespeare's Legacy* which an uncharitable reviewer described as 'poor fooling'. Barrie doubtless agreed with him since he did not include it in the collected edition of his works, although the audience found Gerald and the star of *The Merry Widow* a glamorous change from assembling shells at the factory bench.

A more spectacular occasion was the Shakespeare Tercentenary performance at the same theatre a month later. King, Queen and royal family watched a star cast take part in *Julius Caesar* prefaced with musical interludes conducted by Henry Wood, Thomas Beecham and Edward German. Frank Benson had the name part, Henry Ainley played Antony, and all the other rôles down to the smallest were filled by distinguished names. Gerald walked on as the First Citizen among a crowd that included everyone in the London theatre. Afterwards there was a pageant of tableaux from eight of the major plays. Amid scenery used for that year's pantomime groups of performers swept up, took their bow and went off under the absent-minded gaze of Ellen Terry dressed up to represent the spirit of Comedy while beside her stood the spirit of Tragedy, an ancient and bad-tempered actress called Geneviève Ward still muttering angrily because she had been obliged to share a dressing-room with the upstart Ellen. Down in the auditorium a zealous army of gracious ladies sold programmes and, with helpful intent, often ushered patrons into the wrong seats. Mo was one of them, and, together with mingled baronesses and viscountesses, so were Alice Delysia, Gertie Millar and the Lady Diana Manners who later flowered into Diana Cooper. During the interval Frank Benson was called to the royal box where King George V prepared to knight him. No sword was available and a property article was hastily acquired from Simmonds, the theatrical costumiers round the corner, so that the veteran actor could be dubbed in seemly manner.

Gerald also contributed to wartime propaganda. In 1917, at the inspiration of Lord Beaverbrook then in charge of such matters, he made an early, if not his first, appearance before the cameras. The film, entitled *Everybody's Business*, exhorted the populace to be sparing and economical in their use of food. It was blessedly short and featured Matheson Lang as Gerald's collaborator in an appeal for patriotic austerity. Another film he embarked on at the same time was intended to raise money for the newly established Academy of Dramatic Art. Irene Vanbrugh and Forbes-Robertson decided it should be a version of Charles Reade's old play *Masks and Faces* with Vanbrugh herself as the heroine Peg Woffington. It was, after many difficulties, completed, and must now have a rare documentary value, for one of the scenes showed the Academy Council in session with Barrie, Alexander, Pinero, Bernard Shaw,

Bancroft and others sitting demurely round a table. Gerald caused problems by going down with measles halfway through. The rest of his scenes were shot when, in Irene Vanbrugh's words, he was 'his radiant self again'.

Restored to the theatre after this brief skirmish with a medium which he never really enjoyed or appreciated, he directed at Wyndham's, in April 1917, a play ever to be associated with him by virtue of his subtle performance. It was Barrie's *Dear Brutus*, a penetrating study in the vanity of human wishes and disappointed hope. There is not much Barriesque whimsy here, and the little he allows himself is touched with grimness, as when he writes of Lob's garden: 'The moonshine stealing about among the flowers, to give them their last instructions, has left a smile upon them, but it is a smile with a menace in it for the dwellers in darkness.' The title comes from Shakespeare:

> The fault, dear Brutus, is not in our stars
> But in ourselves, that we are underlings.

A group of people have been invited for a week as guests in the country house of a mysterious little man called Lob. It is Midsummer Eve, a time when strange things happen, when an enchanted wood materialises outside and vanishes at daybreak. The theme of the play is announced early on when the butler is found to have stolen some of the guests' rings and he laments: 'When I was young, Ma'am, I was offered a clerkship in the City. If I had taken it there wouldn't be a more honest man alive today. I would give the world to be able to begin over again.' The guests themselves are not without faults. One of the husbands is having an affair with another woman, and, each time they reach a particularly memorable stage of their romance, he gives his wife a present to salve his conscience. She, of course, knows the reason for his unwonted generosity, and muses to herself: 'Poor old Jack. A woman like that!' Another guest is the failed artist Harry Dearth, shaky, watery-eyed, alcoholic. Perhaps, he tells his wife, their marriage would have succeeded and he might have fulfilled his artistic ambitions if they had children? 'Three things, they say, come not back to men nor women – the spoken word, the past life, and the neglected opportunity,' he says. 'Wonder if we should make any more of them, Alice, if they did come back to us?' And there is also the guest who, having assembled massive notes for a great historical work, can somehow never steel himself to begin writing it. 'I have often thought,' he remarks, 'that if I had a second chance I should be a useful man instead of just a nice lazy one.' The window curtain is drawn back to reveal an endless wood that has suddenly grown up outside splashed with moonlight and blackness. Lob addresses the gathering: 'They say that in the wood you get what nearly everybody here is longing for – a second chance.' Fearful, hesitant, his guests step out among the lowering trees.

The first of them to have his life again is the butler. We learn that he took the City clerkship he was offered, worked his way up and is now a rich tycoon married to the aristocratic lady who in Act I led the complaints against his ring stealing. The philanderer's mistress has become his wife, but, still unsatisfied, he longs for the lover to whom he had previously been married. Harry Dearth has found the daughter he wanted and thinks he is happy. Things that are too beautiful, she warns him, can't last, and to be very happy is so near to being very sad. What, she asks him unexpectedly, is a 'might-have-been'? He tells her: 'They are ghosts, Margaret. I dare say I "might have been" a great swell of a painter, instead of just this uncommonly happy nobody. Or again, I "might have been" a worthless idle waster of a fellow . . . Who knows? Some little kink might have set me off on the wrong road.' But, he decides, 'Fame is rot. Daughters are the thing.' His wife, meanwhile, has married the man she loved but quarrelled with before becoming Mrs Dearth. As a result she is poor and miserable. Even Dearth's contentment does not last because what he feared comes to pass: Margaret grows up and, inevitably, his little girl is lost to him.

Everyone returns to the house and gradually realises that the second chance has made no difference to life. Although the butler acquired great wealth he remains what he was and acts as he always did: the pilferer of rings became a financial swindler on a grand scale as he fought his way to the top. Others have found the partners they wanted but know that even if their desires have been fulfilled they bungle them through making the same mistakes. The would-be author has still frittered his time away and never got down to writing the great book he envisages. Dearth comes back from the wood and his eyes soon turn watery again, his hand shaky, himself and all his dreams revealed as another 'might-have-been'. As for his wife, even though their marriage was unsatisfactory, she has found the bitter proof that in any case she would always choose 'the wrong man, good man or bad man, but the wrong man for her'. The philanderer sums up what they have all learned: 'Fate is something outside us. What really plays the dickens with us is something in ourselves. Something that makes us go on doing the same sort of fool things, however many chances we get.' They all prepare to leave while their strange host Lob tends flowers in the garden where last night the wood suddenly appeared. Is there, then, no hope? Barrie's message may not be entirely cheerless, as the final exchange between butler and guest seems to hint: 'A strange experiment, Matey; does it ever have any permanent effect?'

'So far as I know, not often, Miss; but, I believe, once in a while.'

Some years later John Gielgud revived *Dear Brutus* with himself in Gerald's rôle and confessed: 'I kept remembering how marvellous du Maurier had been as the painter Dearth. I could not touch him in the part.' Gerald at first dressed himself up with a beard and grey hair which made him look uncommonly like his father. Others in the cast persuaded him to drop the idea because audiences, they argued, would prefer to see their idol with a clean-shaven face. Yet, says Daphne, there was still a touch of George du Maurier in the portrayal, the way he sang in French, the attitude before the easel, the banter he exchanged with his daughter. Added to this was the sympathy Gerald felt for the character. Himself the acme of success with a golden reputation and a happy family, he looked at what Barrie had drawn and reflected that, but for the smallest change of circumstance, the slightest adjustment of character, he too might have been another Dearth, bitter, frustrated. In no other rôle did he probe so deep within himself or so ruthlessly to picture the desolation of failure. Daphne at the age of ten came to see the play and was so affected that she had to be led out in tears.

The supreme moment in Gerald's performance came when he realised that he had lost his dream daughter and broke into a sob. 'Daughters are the thing,' he earlier exulted with Margaret, 'daughters are the thing,' an opinion Gerald as father might have echoed. *Dear Brutus* also contained many of Barrie's personal regrets: an unsuccessful marriage, a longing for his own children, a nostalgia for what might have been. Despite the sadness of its theme the play ran for as many days as there are in the year. The plot is beautifully constructed, the ideas are introduced and developed with unerring stagecraft, and the psychology of the characters is faultlessly drawn. One remembers, for example, the pleasant but useless husband who has long forgotten his first wife except only that she was a bit lame. He has so got into the habit of looking out footstools for her that he mechanically does the same for his second wife. She, taking it for kindness, has over twenty-five years evolved a friendly limp. Then there is the philanderer exuding masculine pomposity and telling his lover that he cannot understand why his wife distrusts him: 'I think she has some sort of idea now that when I give her anything nice it means that you have been nice to me. She has rather a suspicious nature, Mabel; she never used to have it, but it seems to be growing on her. I wonder why, I wonder why?' The combination of Barrie's dramatic genius with inspired acting by Gerald and by Faith Celli as the elusive daughter brought full houses at Wyndham's for many months.

Of the four big successes Gerald produced at Wyndham's between 1914 and 1918 three had subjects that avoided the war entirely. *The Ware Case* was melodrama, *A Kiss For Cinderella* pure fantasy, and *Dear Brutus* a timeless study in human nature. Only in *London Pride* did he bring wartime events to the stage and, incidentally, present an unexpected side of his acting skills. The hero of *London Pride* was Cuthbert Tunks, a Cockney costermonger who joins the army and slips off without permission to see his girlfriend. On the way he finds many adventures which include the rescue of a mate whom he carries on his back during heavy fire. Instead of being charged with desertion, a capital offence, he returns as a much-decorated hero to be acclaimed by all Whitechapel. Gerald played Cuthbert and once again proved that he could, when necessary, create types other than those who frequent the drawing-rooms of Mayfair. His Cockney accent was ripe, his manner bouncy and irrepressible, his laughter broad. Like Old Bill, the popular cartoon soldier who had recently been brought to life in a stage adaptation, Cuthbert symbolised all those rough virtues of a London which defied Kaiser Bill with sturdy humour. At a time when the outcome of the war seemed tragically obscure, *London Pride* offered hope and laughter and fresh confidence. It was a thing of the moment, a play which, like *An Englishman's Home* though in a different way, struck a topical chord and would not bear revival.

By way of a tranquil postscript to the blatant flag-wagging of *London Pride* Gerald concluded his wartime productions with a monochrome piece from Barrie called *A Well-Remembered Voice*. The idea for it had been prompted by the death of George, eldest among the 'lost boys'. In his last letter to him Barrie wrote how he wished more and more 'you were a girl of twenty-one instead of a boy, so that I could say the things to you that are now always in my heart. For four years I have been waiting for you to become twenty-one and a little more so that we could get closer and closer to each other, without any words needed.' In *Dear Brutus*, too, he had touched on the problem of relationships between father and son. Sons, declares Harry Dearth, are 'not a patch on daughters.

99

The awful thing about a son is that never, never – at least, from the day he goes to school – can you tell him that you rather like him. By the time he is ten you can't even take him on your knee. Sons are not worth having, Margaret.' No, says Dearth, for that reason daughters are the thing. On the other hand, wondered Barrie, was it true, as the general belief had it, that mothers were closer to their sons than fathers?

In *A Well-Remembered Voice* a mother who has lost her son at the war tries to get in touch with him at spiritualist séances. Her unbelieving husband keeps himself apart and reads his newspaper in a quiet corner. She cannot really understand his behaviour and says: 'I suppose it is just that a son is so much more to a mother than a father.' Graceful, pious, intelligent, devotedly she preserves everything that had belonged to her dead boy and lays out his fishing rods as if they were sacred objects. At the séance a spirit is called but can get no further than rapping out the letters F and A. 'Is the word Father?' enquires the mother. The séance is given up and the father is left alone with his newspaper. Through the darkness of the room a well-remembered voice says: 'Father.' No figure can be seen and only the voice is heard. Why, enquires the husband, did he not contact his mother? 'We can only come to one,' he is told. But, the father replies: 'It was your mother who was everything to you. It can't be you if you have forgotten that. I used to feel so out of it; but, of course, you didn't know.' The son answers: 'I didn't know it till now, Father; but heaps of things that I didn't know once are clear to me now. I didn't know that you were the one who would miss me most; but I know now.'

So they go on, reminiscing about the old times, schooldays, cricket, fishing. When the father shows signs of going deeper the son lightly changes the conversation, mentions a schoolmate they used to call KCMG, 'kindly call me God', or laughs about the day he sat on his father's palette. In a more serious vein he explains that death is a veil, like a mist. 'But when one has been at the Front for a bit, you can't think how thin the veil seems to get; just one layer of it. I suppose it seems thin to you out there because one step takes you through it.' Then he cracks another joke and the sound of laughter brings his mother in. She, of course, cannot see him and is puzzled though reassured when her husband, prompted by the invisible son, says it was a joke he read in his newspaper. On her exit she is replaced by Laura, the boy's sweetheart who cannot see him either or speak directly to him. In an adroitly dialogued episode Barrie nonetheless conjures up their vanished romance. Finally the two men are left alone. Using the same unemphatic manner he has employed all through, the boy says: 'Pretty awful things, these partings. Father, don't feel hurt though I dodge the goodbye business when I leave you.' Understated and ever restrained, the one-act play argues a good case for Barrie's theme.

The cast had Gerald's old colleague 'Forbie', Sir Johnston Forbes-Robertson, as the father, and Faith Celli in another of her lyrical performances as the sweetheart. Gerald was the son, a rôle he played as a voice-off and thereby set himself a unique problem. Being denied the visual aid of gesture and facial expression, he had to delineate emotion and character through his voice alone. His tone was light enough to suggest that of a young man, and within the limits imposed he covered a wide range of poignant effect. All unawares he anticipated the methods of the radio play which had not yet been invented.

Wyndham's kept him very busy although he did find time to take the family on holiday at Whitby, the scene of many boyhood vacations and of his honeymoon. The weather proved unforgiving, wind howled, waves grumbled, and he was melancholy. At every step there were memories of happy days that seemed now only to increase his discontent. He remembered his father there, and his brother and his sisters on carefree expeditions in golden summers that had long since vanished. Both his father and mother were gone, and so were his beloved Guy and two of his sisters. He poured yet another tiny measure of soda into his double whisky and lit up his twentieth cigarette that day to peer through a window at the drizzling rain. Men were being killed by the thousand and suffering agonies out there. What had he done throughout the war? He had put on slap and made a lot of money by pretending to be a murderer, a policeman, a prince, a failed artist, a patriotic Cockney, a disembodied voice. There was surely something better for him to do. He would, he decided, join the army.

At the absurd age of forty-five he volunteered and was accepted in the Irish Guards. He reported to Bushey in Hertfordshire and was kitted out with all the unglamorous implements of his new trade: thick overcoat, scratchy uniform, mess-tin, button stick. Cadet du Maurier, Gerald Hubert Edward Busson, became known to apoplectic drill sergeants as 'Demerara' or 'Demure'. He could distinguish, after careful thought, between his right and left foot, and, at a pinch, could set off in step with the others, but it was not long before he slithered and stumbled. Drill remained a mystery to him and he earned the dislike of one NCO in particular. Once he did something heinous and was rebuked in volcanic terms. Stoic, expressionless, he looked blankly in front of him. 'What are you staring at me for?' shouted his tormentor, red-faced, bull-necked. 'I'm not Gladys Cooper!' It was too much. Gerald's mouth quivered and he gave way to uncontrollable laughter.

When, under instruction, he took a gun to pieces and tried to reassemble it he invariably found he had several bits left over and did not know where to put them. Maps told him nothing and, so far as he was concerned, represented a mass of incomprehensible jiggles and squirls. During an exercise he thought that at last he might have found a use for his special talents. A mock battle was launched and Gerald received instructions to spy on the enemy and return with details of their positions. Mo was briefed to hire a car and to meet him at a certain rendezvous with items of disguise bought in nearby Watford. They made contact and Gerald donned an unbelievable fake beard, heavy spectacles and a voluminous coat, the whole topped with a hat drawn down over his eyes. Off they went to be almost immediately stopped at an outpost where the disguise was penetrated and the spy taken prisoner. Even his gift for acting, it seemed, was of little use to the Brigade of Guards Training Corps.

His one excellence lay in dress. Khaki was a brutal change from white tie and tails but he made the best of it. His belt sparkled with a loving sheen, his brass buttons twinkled, his uniform was sharply creased in all the right places. Long before reveille sounded early in the morning he would creep out and slip through windows to reach the officers' bathrooms which were out of bounds to lowly cadets. There he wallowed in constant hot water and blessed the impudence that enabled him to escape the communal wash-house the likes of him were allowed. Being in the army, he soon realised, was like school again. If you could not follow a lesson, and there were none that he could, being utterly unteachable, you just copied down what the fellow next to you was writing. The simplest article of strategy escaped him and the most basic theory of manoeuvre was outside his grasp. Surrounded by youths of eighteen fresh from school, he was outstripped as an ignorant quadragenarian by their brains and the speed they showed in divining the secrets of the military art. Only one other man was as old as he was, a neat and systematic character with whom he shared a room. This room was ever spick and span, the delight of orderly officers on their inspection rounds. They were not to know that a loose board under Cadet du Maurier's bed concealed a stock of whisky and port, nor that, after lights out had been sounded, many parties were held, the cadets like boys celebrating in the dorm.

As at Harrow, he could not learn and decided the best thing to do was accept the situation and, whenever possible, outwit authority. Although he claimed to dislike the training, he enjoyed being a ringleader and encouraging escapades. At weekends he brought gangs of his young companions to the house he had rented for Mo and the family and threw uproarious tea parties. The twenty years' or so difference in their ages meant nothing to him. He was as natural, as easy with them as with his own nephews. Angela du Maurier, at the age of fourteen, fell desperately in love with one of them. It was the suspicion of side-whiskers on his face that captivated her.

Things were, after all, a great lark. The horror of early rising, the marching through rain and mud, the grappling with obstacle courses, even the baffling arcana of the drill square, were things he knew he would look back on with amusement, as he did on the far-off experiences of school which had been awful enough at the time. Had his mother still lived she would have been horrified at the ordeals of her 'ewee lamb'. A stream of food parcels, warm clothing and patent medicines to stave off his colds would be arriving for him. Mo, however, was there to keep up the tradition, and the goodies she sent were ample enough for the midnight dormitory feasts he organised with his youthful companions. In time he was thankful that he had not obtained a commission straight away as he at first hoped, and he saw wisdom in the regulation that demanded service in the ranks beforehand. He did not sleep well, in fact he never slept all that well as a civilian, but he felt better. Even golf had not been so effective in keeping his figure slim and lithe as army training had. Most of all he appreciated the blessed monotony of routine. Each day fell into well-ordered sections and the hours slipped smoothly away in the fulfilment of petty tasks which gave a pleasant regularity to existence. No edgy first nights disturbed his peace of mind, no temperamental actors annoyed him, no agonising dress rehearsals plagued him. His nerves, for once, were at rest.

Towards the end of his training the cadets put on an amateur performance of Anstey's famous old comedy *Vice-Versa*. It was an appropriate choice for Gerald, the older man surrounded by young people, since the theme is that of a middle-aged character who becomes a boy again and sees life through the eyes of the lad he once was. The piece does not go so far as the French proverb which observes 'If youth only knew, if age only could,' or even the one that declares 'Old men give good advice only to console themselves for no longer being in a position to set bad examples,' but so far as Victorian convention allows it has some ripe moments.

Gerald directed with a special glee because one of the actors was an Adjutant whom he disliked. Gerald gave orders and the Adjutant did as he was told.

Another reminder of his professional life came when he mounted a concert at which his co-star Lily Elsie and others were to perform. As the Commanding Officer ushered her into lunch she glimpsed Gerald, a meek figure in a corner. 'There's darling Gerald!' she cried and made towards him.

The Commanding Officer restrained her. 'That's all right,' he said, 'you'll be seeing him later. We're going in to eat first.'

'But surely Gerald is joining us for lunch?' she asked.

He told her the cadets ate apart, and, puzzled, she was taken unwillingly to the officers' mess. Gerald shrank into embarrassment. He wished, how he wished, that at a moment like this he could have reached for the blessed, the all-comforting cigarette.

The Armistice of November 1918, found him still in training. He was never to see the battlefield where his brother Guy and his nephew George were cut down. The inability to dig trenches and his fumbling attempts to handle a shovel were not to be tested in the mud of Flanders. Mo, for one, was relieved, though he could not hide a certain disappointment. Still, it had been fun, his experience in the ranks had corrected any pomposity which the famous actor-manager might have been tempted into displaying, and, physically, he felt better. The greatest relief of all was the knowledge that he had at least tried to do something useful. Even though he would have turned out to be a hopeless soldier, he had proved that a mummer could be as well-intentioned and patriotic as the thousands of ordinary fellows who marched off to their death in the slime of the trenches.

[iii]

Bull-Dog Drummond

He gave up the house he rented at Bushey for Mo and the three girls and took them back to London. Home now was a large and rambling establishment in Hampstead which he bought in 1916. *Diplomacy, The Ware Case* and *Dear Brutus* one after the other earned large sums at the box-office and his management at Wyndham's prospered. He could afford to move from Cumberland Terrace and settle in

Hampstead, a district he loved for its association with his childhood and early years. There stood New Grove House, today marked with an ivied plaque recording that 'George du Maurier lived here.' The connection with Hampstead went even further back. Gerald's notorious great-grandmother Mary Anne Clarke also lived in the area, in a house at New End Square which was to be demolished during the air-raids of the 1939-45 war. He felt he was coming home.

New Grove House, which he would have liked to buy and so complete the circle, was not available. He found the next best thing in Cannon Hall, a period house once the property of the physician to King George III. The long façade, extended by a later addition, displayed three rows of over a dozen elegant windows glinting in the sunshine and framed by a wealth of ivy. At the front there was a courtyard and, before the main entrance, a small ornamental pool where a Peter Pan-like figure dispensed a trickle of water from a shell. A spacious garden lay at the back, its lawn enclosed with bushes. Beyond a parapet was a kitchen garden some feet lower. The woodshed had once been a gloomy dungeon, the Hampstead 'lock-up', and the room which the local Justice of the Peace used as his court became Gerald's study. In the garden reposed a strange machine, ornate and complicated of manufacture, which could be identified as the earliest Hampstead fire-engine.

Gerald took Lady Tree to view Cannon Hall while he was negotiating the purchase. They stood in silent admiration of the magnificent green staircase which led down to the ground floor. Their actors' instinct told them that here was an excuse for making the grandest entrance imaginable. The eye was led up irresistibly by the imposing sweep of the curve. It was held by whoever appeared at the top and dominated those below. On the right-hand wall Gerald was to hang a picture of King Charles I. Next to the monarch, covering the wall entirely, he decided on a prospect of a great battle. At the summit Queen Elizabeth I looked down with imperious features.

Around the house he put up theatrical prints from Shakespeare plays, and somewhere hung the portrait of him by Augustus John. He did not like modern art of any description. The painting, the music, the architecture of his own time were repellent, and his aesthetic appreciation stopped short in the middle of the nineteenth century. He hoped his daughters would imbibe his own taste and he gave them presents of beautifully illustrated art books which brought their education up to the Pre-Raphaelites and no further. Literature meant *Treasure Island* and *The Count of Monte Cristo* which he discussed enthusiastically with them.

In art, then, he preferred safety, and he filled Cannon Hall with Georgian furniture, mellow, gracious, and old pictures and old silver. On Sundays when there was no matinée or evening performance he would take his girls on the walk over Hampstead which his father used to enjoy. It was the Hampstead of Jack Straw's Castle and the White Stone Pond, the Spaniards Road and Keats Grove, Squire's Mount and Lower Terrace. Nearby was Church Row where he was born and, at the end of it, the parish church and the graveyard where George and Emma and Sylvia and Guy du Maurier lay. He honoured their birthdays and the anniversaries of their deaths by putting flowers on the graves. The little ceremony done, he stood, head bowed, in silence. On the mantelpiece of his bedroom at Cannon Hall were photographs of them all. In front of them he had placed a silver cross.

A tennis court was soon built in the grounds. His passion for the game was almost as intense as his love for golf, and he played it in a manner that verged on the demoniacal. Sometimes, when preparing for a match, he would hoist the net with such violence that a pole collapsed. An ordinary man would have given up after a few minutes' tinkering. Not Gerald. He dug holes frantically. He hurried off to the woodshed and returned bearing hirsute pieces of rope which he attached to anything that offered. He laboured hotly, twisting rope around the post, trees, seats, even garden rollers until a monstrous and ungainly tapestry had been created. Meanwhile the net went on collapsing again and again. Long after the other players had withdrawn to the consolation of whisky and soda he slaved in a frenzy of tireless, and quite pointless, exertion.

Cannon Hall gave him roots. It provided a solid background to the shadow show of the theatre and set in their right perspective the crises which flared up at rehearsals, each one seeming as fateful as the last yet only to be succeeded by dramas even more exciting than what was supposed to be mimicked on stage. When he drove back to Cannon Hall in his Rolls-Royce after the evening performance he left behind him the overheated egos and the nervous squabbles that are inevitable in the theatre. With Mo he could unwind, pass on the latest funny story and relay new developments in some affair that intrigued them both. Relaxed, he went to bed. But not always to sleep. Often a sense of unease kept him awake. Had he really made the best of his life?

The war changed everything. The theatre Gerald knew up to 1914 no longer existed and the day of the actor-manager was nearly over. Vanished was the age when Sir George Alexander referred cosily to 'our little parish of St James' and Tree welcomed patrons of 'my lovely theatre' as guests rather than customers. Gone, too, were the intimacy and the respect that existed between those knights of the theatre and their audiences. An actor-manager was once a figure to be recognised with awe if glimpsed outside his theatre, his port grave, his eye hooded, his manner distant as he made his stately way along Piccadilly or Bond Street. No one would look twice at their successors, sharp-faced men who had done very well out of the war and regarded the theatre only as a medium for investing their profits so as to make yet bigger ones.

During the Edwardian period and up to the war taxes were small and the cost of living was low. An ambitious actor could put aside enough from his earnings to set himself up, perhaps with the help of a few comfortably off friends, as a manager. He was able to rent a theatre, pay his company, mount the plays that interested him and draw a fair income into the bargain. His personality was stamped on the productions he undertook and he built up a following which, with luck, remained loyal to him. Certain theatres were closely identified over a period of time with the men who ran them. When you bought a ticket at His Majesty's you knew the sort of thing Tree was likely to have on offer and you were rarely disappointed. Likewise at the St James's, where Alexander reigned, or at the Haymarket, fief of Cyril Maude, or at the Garrick, home for a while of Violet Vanbrugh and her husband Arthur Bourchier, you could be sure to find a characteristic brand of play. Audiences liked this and so did playwrights who came to know what was expected of them and the sort of leading rôles that were needed. Above all they had the assurance that their work would actually be produced. By the end of the war the great actor-managers no longer held sway and the system was disintegrating. Its place was taken by syndicates, groups of entrepreneurs who, not confined to one theatre alone, found backers with money and presented single plays in the hope of making a profit wherever they could.

War had also transformed the economic background of the theatre. Rents increased enormously and the cost of everything, from cleansing cream to scenery, went up by as much as four or five times. Wages spiralled and so did production expenses. Gerald was one of the few actor-managers to carry on. At Wyndham's he felt reasonably secure and, more than ever, thankful that Frank Curzon was by his side to handle financial problems. Even in the easy-going pre-war days Gerald would have been incapable of handling that side of the operation. Now, in a strange new world, he left Frank to cope with the dreary figures and concentrated on the artistic matters which were his forte. That, after all, was the way they had agreed to work from the very beginning of their partnership.

In the year after the war ended he made a silent film with Gladys Cooper. He was as diffident about the cinema as his partner was. *Unmarried*, as the melodrama was laconically entitled, dealt with the problem of the single mother. Gerald's contribution added nothing to his glory. He went back to the stage and produced a new play by Alfred Sutro at Wyndham's. Sutro had been a neighbour of his at Chester Terrace, a large benevolent man who paraded an equally large dog on walks in Regent's Park. Over some twenty years Sutro had proved himself to be an efficient dramatist who knew what audiences wanted and could supply it. Would his formula work as well, though, in the changed atmosphere that now prevailed? It did, and *The Choice* ran for more than three hundred performances.

It was a drama in which Gerald played the part of a strong man, the Right Honourable John Ingleby Cordways, a magnate whose only weakness is, paradoxically, his strength. He dismisses one of his employees, a war hero, for some trifling offence and, despite pleas from those he respects and loves, stubbornly refuses to think again. Cordways's very strength makes him a martyr. As a result of maintaining his decision he loses the love of his life to a former admirer. Inflexible to the end, he unselfishly tells his successful rival: 'You're young, my dear Dalman – I'm not. That's all. Perhaps you'll take that job now – that I offered you? . . . And you can tell Lord Sandhills that, within a year or two, you'll be in the running for a directorship in Lordways Limited.' To his brother, by way of valediction, he says: 'There goes my romance, Tim – the one woman I've loved – and, my God, how I love her! There she goes – and a lot of me with her. But I suppose – for the work I've to do – it's better to be alone.' Is strength just another word for obstinacy? And when, asks Sutro, does justice become tyranny?

Gerald in a mood of noble renunciation was irresistible. Having skilfully created throughout the play an impression of strength which, however misguided, earned grudging respect – 'There's something about you that holds me and fascinates me,' says his fiancée, 'because you're a man, a real man' – in the last act he gained overwhelming sympathy for his stoic self-denial. The part of Clarissa, the woman he loses, was taken by Viola Tree. She was Sir Herbert's favourite daughter and inherited much of his waywardness. This took the form of never quite knowing what went on around her and ignoring all awareness of time. One Friday she was supposed to play her namesake in *Twelfth Night* but could not be found. Sybil Thorndike, at the last moment, was pushed on in her place, and Viola remained unseen. On Saturday, which was an opera evening, the prima donna arrived to find her dressing-room commandeered by Viola making up for *Twelfth Night*. The actress refused to believe Saturday had come, argued vehemently that it was still Friday and insisted that she would play *Twelfth Night*. The whole company exhausted themselves in proving that Friday was over and done with. At last they convinced her. She smiled gracefully and as she departed waved them a cheery farewell innocent of malice.

Tree was devoted to his big gangling daughter, perhaps because he saw much of himself in her. They had the same whimsical temperament and an identical sense of humour. At rehearsals of *The Tempest* when she, as Ariel, hovered around the stage suspended from a wire, he suddenly called a half-hour break and left her dangling in the air. She laughed as much as he did. A father's pride led him to cast her in important rôles for which she had neither the technique nor the experience. This little weakness in the great man caused amusement. A revue at the time featured a comedian dressed as Shakespeare who sang:

> How's your pretty Miss Viola?
> Fair and so beautiful she
> And a very short time
> It will take her to climb
> To the top of the Beerbohm Tree.

He would give her a major rôle and leave her to sink or swim without the benefit of advice or criticism. To oblige an American friend he cast the latter's mistress in his production of *Orpheus In The Underworld*. She was no good, so he replaced her with Viola, who at least had trained as a singer. The American came to rehearsals and protested: 'I don't think so much of your goddam daughter, Tree.' Sir Herbert equally replied: 'Neither you as a lover nor I as a father are unbiased judges.'

She married a handsome man called Alan Parsons who for a time pursued an absent-minded career at the Home Office, though he was much more interested in the theatre. Administration bored him, official Minutes in particular, and there was one that haunted him day and night. He did not have the slightest idea of what it meant or of what he should do with it. At last he decided to quit the Home Office and become a drama critic. On the day he left he found a solution:

the Minute was put on the fire and smouldered into extinction. There were problems in his new career, too. As critic on the *Daily Mail* he had trouble in catching the early editions which started printing before the play was over. Again he showed the ingenuity that distinguished his Home Office career: theatre managers were persuaded to give him in advance a full synopsis of the plot which enabled him to meet his deadline. He was the perfect husband for Viola, though he never quite knew what his father-in-law really thought about him. 'Be sweet, dearest Viola, during all the years,' Tree wrote to her, 'as you have been to me during all the years that have passed . . . and do remember to spell holiday with one "l"!' She married Alan Parsons at a fashionable ceremony in St Martin-in-the-Fields amid crowds and traffic diversions. Even on a great day like this Tree was thinking of his beloved theatre. On their way to the church he asked Viola whether she would mind if they made a small detour for him to look in at His Majesty's. While the bride in her wedding car sat patiently outside the stage door, he hastened in to make sure the theatre was still there. It was. Having satisfied his anxiety he came out and they continued the journey. As they were nearing the church he suddenly enquired, with apparent earnestness: 'Do you like Alan, dear?'

She called the memoirs she eventually wrote *Castles In The Air*, an apt description of life with her fantastical husband. He died at the age of forty-five and she not long after, having got from their brief existence more fun than most of those who attain the Biblical span. Angela du Maurier remembered her as 'the most brilliant, most witty, most amusing – and at times most maddening – woman it has been my pleasure to have known . . . she swept across the lawn of Cannon Hall in mauve and black, her gestures large and expansive like her father's and her voice a woman's echo of his voice.' Gerald would have agreed, for she soon became one of his closest friends, a butt for his teasing and practical jokes. To it all she responded with gaiety, devotion and entire lack of self-consciousness. He knew she adored him and he took advantage of the fact to play outrageous tricks on her. She called him 'Sir, sir, sir dear,' and ejaculated in staccato phrases and a deep, deep voice, 'I know, I know, I know,' and 'Yes, yes, yes.' In *The Choice*, though unfortunately no visual record can be found, she dressed up for one scene in the uniform of the Bluecoat School and astonished the audience with her flapping coat and bright yellow stockings. Careful perusal can reveal no justification in the play for this. It must have been another of Gerald's pranks.

'Poor Viola! God knows why she stands for it!' he would remark after some especially elaborate joke had been played on her. She was without vanity and could mock herself as well as other people. Yet while she evoked tears of laughter with her mimicry and her wit, she sang also, accompanied by her husband, lieder and ballads in a voice that went to the heart. She had many talents but not quite enough to put her in the front rank. Like her father she relied on the inspiration of the moment. Personality rather than technique was her chief resource as an actress, and it was this that won her the friendship not only of Gerald but also of Ivor Novello, both of whom put her into their plays on the slightest excuse. She could be vulgar in the extreme and, the next minute, deeply moving. She did not care how foolish she might seem as long as she amused the people she loved. Impulsive, spontaneous, she was utterly enslaved by Gerald. She visited him one year at Fowey where he was on holiday. While attempting to get out of her motor boat she stumbled and fell, wearing a tight satin skirt and large picture-hat, into the harbour. Once in the icy water she decided she might as well treat herself to a swim, and round and round she circled, the picture-hat bobbing majestically as she struck out through the waves to applause from Gerald and the rest. Typical of Viola was the reward for her exploit, a heavy chill and, later, acute peritonitis which nearly finished her off.

Another *monstre sacré* who appeared in Gerald's next production was Lilian Braithwaite. She had already played under his direction in *Nobody's Daughter* and, as the mother, in *A Well-Remembered Voice*. Her career, which began with the impeccable credentials of Benson and Alexander, was to extend for over fifty years. The only flaw in an otherwise glorious half-century was her abhorred rival Marie Tempest who beat her by a number of years to achieve the Damehood Lilian coveted.

One of her most successful parts was that of an acidulous spinster in the murder comedy *Arsenic and Old Lace* which ran for over three years. She, of course, represented the first half of the title. In private life she had a reputation for witticisms, compact and stinging, which became known as 'Lilians'. At an Ivor Novello first night she praised his leading lady and observed: 'She was wonderful, dear, but could you hear what she said?' With a cherubic expression and in the gentlest of voices she would remark of a veteran actress: 'She's learned all the tricks. The trouble is she doesn't know how to perform them.' When James Agate approached her in the Café Royal and said to her: 'My dear Lilian, I have long wanted to tell you that in my opinion you are the second most beautiful woman in

London,' she answered: 'Thank you so much, my dear Mr Agate. I shall cherish that, coming from our second-best drama critic.'

The title of the play in which she now acted opposite Gerald was *The Prude's Fall*. It was a joint work by Rudolf Besier and May Edginton, his collaborator on a number of other social dramas popular at the time. When young, Besier had been a poet, tall, vague, ambling, and had written a lyrical play called *The Virgin Goddess*. Having cleansed his bosom of this poetic stuff he settled down to turning out well-constructed pieces for George Alexander at the St James's. Always craftsmanlike, always efficient, he was said to write a play only when he needed 'whisky money'. His biggest triumph was *The Barretts of Wimpole Street*, much played, much filmed. A Freudian critic startled him with the observation that a hint of incest could be detected in the relationship between Elizabeth and her father. James Agate did little to soothe his dismay when he wrote: 'What's wrong with incest? It's cheap and it's handy.'

The Prude's Fall was a confused imbroglio in which a man cynically obliges his fiancée to become his mistress because he will not marry her on account of her social snobbery in the past. Up pops another of her lovers who points a gun at him and threatens to shoot unless he goes away. The alternatives, one would think, are quite clear. A third solution is offered by the dramatist, and this involves the first lover producing a special marriage licence with the claim that he was 'only pretending'. There is no need to go further into the plot which has a great deal to say about the woman who has 'sinned' and her place in society. Although produced in 1920 the play looks back to pre-war times and was simply a vehicle for Gerald's talents and those of Lilian Braithwaite. 'Mr du Maurier goes through his part exactly as a conjuror goes through a bag of tricks,' commented Agate. 'But the part has not caused the actor one moment's emotion or thought. It came out of his bag like that because Mr du Maurier is that sort of conjuror.'

The Prude's Fall was an Edwardian postscript to all those comfortable, slyly provoking dramas – a tang, but not too much, of illicit passion, a hint of illegitimacy, a dash of social reprobation – that enabled Gerald to create a loyal following at his theatre and an audience that insisted on the mixture as before. With *Bull-Dog Drummond*, however, he plunged right into the spirit of the 1920s and caught the essence of an age that already had recognisable characteristics. Here were crude thrills, spectacular villainy, titillating horror and sadism unashamed. *Bull-Dog Drummond* was *Raffles* and *Arsène Lupin* brought up to date. The gentleman crook was replaced by a reckless war hero who courted the heroine not in flowery language but in clipped monosyllables because there was no time for anything else. His adversaries, no longer thick-headed policemen or bumbling aristocrats, were cold-blooded criminals who employed modern science in the pursuit of their aims. The prize at stake was not a mere diamond necklace but hundreds of thousands of pounds. Syringes, instruments of torture, drugs and mortal poisons were the weapons used.

Like Gerald's earlier 'thick-ear' melodramas, *Bull-Dog Drummond* took its origin from a best-selling novel. It was a 1920s equivalent of the James Bond adventures. With Ian Fleming the author had in common a gift for mixing a raw cocktail of sex and sadism which went as near to outraging the social convention of the time as it dared. The formula was the same: breathless action, excitement, beautiful girls in appalling danger, repellent crooks and non-stop violence. The author of *Bull-Dog Drummond*, who wrote under the name of 'Sapper', had himself fought in the trenches. War simplified everything and presented choices that were obvious and stark. In pursuit of an objective about which there could be no doubt you killed or were killed. There was no room for elaborate philosophising or speculation on the destiny of man. You acted and reacted without the possibility of deep thought. Good was good and bad was bad. It was all delightfully simple as compared with times of peace when decisions were hard to make and the issue was confused by any number of subtle alternatives.

He showed a touch of genius in the name he gave to his hero. The defiant sobriquet and the hard consonants b, d, g, d and d suggested toughness and determination. Drummond and his creator believed, with Nancy Mitford's Uncle Matthew, that all foreigners were 'bloody'. It followed naturally that the crooks whom Drummond fought came from outlandish parts: heathen Chinese, mysterious Russians, ugly men of vague Scandinavian extraction or, worst of all, Germans and, into the bargain, Jewish. There were few problems that could not be settled with a gun or a sock on the jaw. Popular prejudices were skilfully catered for, and, once launched, Bull-Dog Drummond went through many adventures which gained him a vast readership. Such was his long-lasting appeal that after the author, H. C. McNeile, had died, another writer assumed his mantle and continued writing Bull-Dog Drummond novels to satisfy the demand for them.

Ever alert to the drift of public taste, Gerald saw in Bull-Dog Drummond excellent material for a new type of melodrama. The play was attributed to 'Sapper and Gerald du Maurier', although we may be sure that while the original author supplied the plot the dramatisation was essentially Gerald's work. Each of the four acts builds up to a tingling climax. The plot is kept remorselessly on the boil and the audience is never allowed time to think. *Bull-Dog Drummond* was the thickest of all Gerald's 'thick ear' plays.

The fun begins in Drummond's flat – Mayfair, of course, and Half Moon Street in particular. He is awaiting replies from an advertisement he has put in *The Times* personal column, which, in the days before that paper started carrying news on the front page, was among the most intriguing features of British journalism. 'Demobilised officer, finding peace incredibly tedious, would welcome diversion,' the advertisement reads. 'Legitimate, if possible, but crime, if of a humorous description, no objection. Excitement essential. Reply at once to Box X10.' His chums Peter and Algy cluster round to see what replies have come in. They include an appeal from a schoolboy to kill off one of his masters before an exam and an invitation from an American girl in rut to hit the roof with her. More interesting, and perhaps a little daring for family entertainment in the 1920s, is a German reply which, when translated, emerges as: 'In reference to the advertisement in *The Times* and *John Bull*, I, Mrs Von Stramm, a Prussian lady, will give all the excitement required. If Mr Box is serious he must come to Berlin. We German girls will make sure he does not sit down any more.'

The reply that captures Drummond's attention is from a girl who writes that she saw him at *The Times* office when he was booking his advertisement. He saw her too, and recalls that he has known her all his life but cannot think who she is. When she calls at his flat he at last remembers: she is the sister of Jack Benton whose life Drummond saved in a typical act of bravery during the war. So Phyllis is okay! But, poor girl, she is in trouble. She lives with her uncle, James Handley, gambler, alcoholic and, when necessary, expert forger. He is in the power of three criminals, Carl Peterson, a domineering type of foreign origins, Irma his daughter and Henry Lakington, a crooked doctor. At Lakington's nursing home in Godalming they keep a prisoner, a millionaire whom they are torturing to extract his money. When he refuses to sign the documents put before him they call on Handley to forge his signature. Drummond sees his mission. He must clean up this nasty business and save Jack's beautiful sister from the spot of bother in which she finds herself. His man is ordered to bring out the Rolls and he dashes off to Godalming.

At The Larches, home of Phyllis and her uncle, Peterson is bullying

Handley into forging a draft. He warns Phyllis to stop meddling with Drummond if she wants to avoid unpleasantness. The intrepid Hugh arrives in person and taunts him. Soon afterwards a dreadful scream is heard. 'Somebody trod on a cat,' explains his daughter Irma, a vampish creature who must be very decadent because she uses a cigarette-holder. Drummond persuades Phyllis to seek shelter at his own country house in Goring. He assures her it will all be very respectable. 'Go upstairs and ask your maid to pack you some warm things. My man Denny is going down tonight and his wife's following in the morning. Now will you go for Jack's sake? Yes, of course, I can see you will.' They hear the crack of a gun. Poor disgraced Handley has shot himself rather than fulfil any more of Peterson's criminal demands. At The Elms, Peterson's house which also includes Lakington's consulting rooms, the gang are preparing their final coup to steal a cache of diamonds from the hapless millionaire Travers whom they hold prisoner. This done, they will flee the country, which is just as well, muses Peterson when Irma tells him that the hideous Lakington has been attempting to seduce her. They give Travers another injection. 'You blackguards,' he gasps, 'you infernal blackguards! How dare you keep me here?' After threats of more rough treatment – the dialogue at this point is extremely clever in hinting at unspeakable torture without causing revulsion by naming it – Travers relents and signs the document authorising his tormentors to withdraw the diamonds from his bank. Suddenly Drummond appears at the window and shoots out the electric lamp bulb. When light is restored both he and Travers have vanished.

Drummond returns to Goring with Travers on his arm, having spent the day motoring around London in the hope of shaking off Peterson and his gang who are close on the trail. Even now they lurk in the garden. He asks his chum Peter to ring the police: 'Tell 'em to send up half a dozen men as soon as they can – large men with beards!' Peter cannot because the wire has been cut. Irma makes her glamorous entry and Drummond, to the amazement of innocent Phyllis, flirts with her. This is only a blind which enables him to slip away discreetly. Irma gives Peter a drugged cigarette. When he passes out Peterson's henchman Marcovitch chloroforms Phyllis and bundles the pair of them into the car.

Back at The Elms an American detective engaged by Mrs Travers to find out what has become of her husband is questioning Peterson. He insists, despite their bluff, on seeing their victim. Irma trundles him in, and although he looks the image of Travers he is really Bull-Dog Drummond disguised in ulster, scarf and motoring goggles.

Drummond manages to pass the detective an explanatory note. The latter gets the message and goes, leaving Peterson convinced that he has thrown him off the scent. Soon afterwards Drummond's disguise is penetrated and the furious Peterson resolves to torture him. 'The straps,' he orders Marcovitch, 'the ones we use for violent cases.' At the same time Phyllis is dragged to another room. 'Lakington,' Drummond warns him, 'if you hurt one hair of that girl's head, as there's a God above, I'll get at you somehow and kill you with my own hands.' Screams are heard from the room. Drummond is forced to confess that Travers will be found at his Goring home. Peterson makes off while Lakington jeers at Drummond and throws wine in the face of his helpless, pinioned victim. He goes into his laboratory and makes up a phial of sinister appearance. Phyllis manages to release Drummond's straps. He crouches behind the sofa and puts out the light. The room is illumined only by the crackling fire. Lakington comes back, revolver in hand, and fires at him. The bullet hits a picture which falls with a crash. He fires again, runs out of ammunition and seizes a knife from the mantelshelf. The weapon flies through the air – 'Take that, damn you!' – and plunges quivering into the wall. Drummond hurls a champagne bottle as he exits. Lakington returns, head covered in blood, and wrestles with him as a cupboard full of medicine bottles topples over with a crash of breaking glass. Chairs and desks tumble and clatter around the stage. Drummond forces his opponent to the floor and cracks his spine in half. With a terrible groan the body shudders and is still. Drummond gazes down on him.

In Act IV, the reader may be relieved to hear, the action becomes less furious. Drummond contrives, by means of an electrically operated door, to trap Peterson and his gang inside the room. Although Peterson attempts to buy him off as the price of liberty, Drummond calls the police who duly arrive and take the criminals away. Only afterwards does he learn that the 'police' were actually Peterson's henchmen in disguise and that the master villain lives to fight another day – or to inspire a sequel. Drummond has a lawyer's appreciation of rascality and bursts into laughter at the neatness of the trick. As he tries to get through on the telephone to Scotland Yard, Phyllis murmurs: 'I love you!'

'What did you say, Phyllis?' he replies, juggling with the receiver. 'I love you.'

'My dear girl,' he answers, 'why on earth didn't you say that before?' and he kisses her with all the off-hand elegance of Gerald du Maurier.

The Actor-Manager

It has been necessary to speak of *Bull-Dog Drummond* at some length because the play was very much Gerald's creation and gave him one of his most spectacular successes. For over a year it flourished at Wyndham's Theatre and enjoyed a run of four hundred and thirty performances. Though the first night had been shaky – one of the leading actors continually forgot his lines and had to be prompted over and again – the audience was so excited that small mishaps were forgotten. Most of all they revelled in the magnificent fight scene at the end of Act III. Today this sort of thing is commonplace in films, but then, and particularly on the stage, it was rare. The episode was a triumph of meticulous stage management. When Lakington fired his pistol at Drummond the bullet was supposed to hit a picture on the wall which fell with a crash, the effect being created by a piece of lead on string hanging through a hole in the centre of the glass: at the sound of the shot the string was pulled from behind and the picture obediently smashed to the floor. A second shot was seen to have hit Drummond in the hand which he bound up with a handkerchief thoughtfully bloodstained in advance. Lakington then threw a knife at him and it stuck, vibrating nastily, in the back wall. This was arranged by placing an imitation knife in a steel tube fastened on the back of the flat; on the cue 'Take that, damn you!' a stage-hand pushed it through. The champagne bottle which Drummond hurled at his opponent was caught in a net off-stage and a suitable crashing noise provided. The sound of more breaking glass was supplied while the two men wrestled and the cupboard of medicine bottles, controlled by invisible ropes, swayed and toppled. At the end of it all the audience was almost as exhausted as the actors.

The wicked Dr Lakington was Gilbert Hare, son of Gerald's old mentor Sir John Hare. He had, indeed, studied medicine at Göttingen University and, after a busy career on the stage, retired for a number of years to take up his old profession. His fellow crook Peterson was played by Alfred Drayton, a familiar name in English theatre and films for close on fifty years. Bald, tall, broad-shouldered, hoarse of voice and fleshy of lip, Drayton was equally good at conveying menace or bumbledom as the part required. He later became a permanent fixture, alongside Ralph Lynn and Mary Brough, in the Aldwych farces where he specialised in bullying the timorous Robertson Hare and watching him, with sadistic pleasure, lose his trousers yet again.

With Ronald Squire as the silly-ass type Algy to play his lieutenant, Gerald sailed through this high-spirited farrago in a mood of impenitent gaiety. He knew the sort of goods he was delivering and he made no pretence about it. This is shown by his remark to A. E. Matthews who took over as Drummond when he treated himself to a month off in Cornwall. 'The lines aren't important,' Gerald told him. 'Just get the situation and the fights in the right place.' Matthews's reward was to take the play to America, having recruited new players and rehearsed himself with the stage-manager. A few days later Gerald asked him how he was getting on.

'All right,' said Matthews, 'except for the last act.'

'Don't worry about it,' Gerald assured him. 'I seldom say the same thing two nights running. Have a go at the matinée.'

That afternoon Gerald watched from the stalls, much to the discomfort of his deputy who, as usual, did not know all the lines. At the interval Gerald hastened to his dressing-room. 'I've never seen the play from the front before – it's all wrong!' he exclaimed. Then, naming two famous boxers of the time, he went on: 'Alfred Drayton's part should be played by Jack Dempsey and Bull-Dog by Georges Carpentier. I'm entirely wrong for it, and as for you, Matty, you don't even look like one of Bull-Dog's puppies.' Nevertheless he set off on his holiday in Cornwall. When he returned he discovered, with some annoyance, that despite the absence of himself as the star, the box-office returns had remained buoyant.

A few days after the first night of *Bull-Dog Drummond* he received an anguished telephone call from Barrie. His voice incoherent with sorrow, Barrie told him that Michael Llewelyn Davies had died in what seemed to be a drowning accident. Gerald's nephew, then an undergraduate at Oxford, handsome, clever, a week or so short of his twenty-first birthday, was the second of the 'lost boys' to go before his time. Gerald hurried round to Barrie's flat high up in Adelphi Terrace and did what he could to comfort him. Peter, Michael's brother was there, and so was the playwright's close friend Lady Cynthia Asquith. Barrie would listen to none of them and refused all attempts at consolation. Despite being unable to swim, Michael had ventured out into the Thames with a friend, encountered difficulties which neither seemed to resist, and gone under. There were those who thought that the accident was not an accident but a suicide pact. The two friends had an intense relationship which could not survive the problems it created. Barrie watched over Michael's corpse until the funeral, inconsolable, nightmarish, finding life unbearable without him. 'For ever and ever I am thinking about him,' he was to lament.

He never recovered from Michael's death. Only in his dreams did he see him again, and in his dreams, too, he had visions of that dreadful place beside the river where Michael drowned. Every night of his life, he told a friend, he went there looking for him. True, he still had Jack and Peter and Nico, and soon was to become adoptive grandfather to Nico's daughter. But without Michael there was no savour to life, no excitement, no interest in the future. The hermit of Adelphi Terrace received few visitors in his bleak rambling flat among the roof-tops of London. There, in silence, he often stared at the picture of a twelve-year-old Michael which dominated all the others hanging on his wall. For Barrie this was the greatest tragedy in his existence. For Gerald, who had his own normal family life, the death of a well-graced nephew was sad, though one that he would probably get over in time: what made the incident even more poignant was that he had lost yet another link with his adored sister Sylvia, Michael's mother.

Not long before his death Michael suggested to Barrie that he write a murder mystery. Barrie, always anxious to please, began work on it, for Michael was then passing through a difficult mood, had just begun his relationship with the undergraduate that probably led to his death, and, unsettled, was anxious to leave Oxford and study in Paris. Hoping that the new play would divert him, Barrie wrote the first act of what he entitled *Shall We Join The Ladies?* Michael by then was no longer interested and Barrie anxiously tried to find other ways of holding his attention and ensuring the filial love he craved from the boy.

Shall We Join The Ladies? was chosen as part of the programme arranged to open the new theatre built for the Royal Academy of Dramatic Art in Malet Street. Accompanying it were a Barrie one-acter given by current students and the first act of *Trelawny of The 'Wells'* cast from among graduates of the school. *Shall We Join The Ladies?* was performed by an all-star bill which no commercial impresario, however influential, could have assembled: it included Charles Hawtrey, Fay Compton, Sybil Thorndike, Lady Tree, Forbes-Robertson and Irene Vanbrugh. Gerald took the part of Dolphin, a butler. The play which Michael inspired was first given, eight days after his death, on the afternoon of 27th May, 1921.

Just before the curtain rose on *Shall We Join The Ladies?* an electrical fault cloaked the new theatre in sudden darkness. The distinguished company gathered on stage became apprehensive as they gazed unseeing into the gloom. Already nervous at the thought of performing before an audience which included not only the Prince of Wales but, as well, the leaders of their profession, they remembered that they were thirteen around the dinner table where the action of the play begins and they wondered if the darkness might not be an omen. Light, however, was quickly restored and the piece went forward swingingly.

As in *Dear Brutus*, the central character is a weird personality who has invited a number, in this case an unlucky number, of guests to make up a house party. An atmosphere of foreboding is established when they realise they are thirteen at table, and one of them asks Sam Smith, their host, 'a pocket edition of Mr Pickwick', if Dolphin the butler might not join them for a moment. 'There is a superstition,' explains the rosy-cheeked Smith, 'that if thirteen people sit down at a table something staggering will happen to one of them before the night is out.' A guest adds: 'Namely, death.' Suggesting, by the wrinkle of an eyebrow and the tightening of his cheekbones, disapproval of such fraternisation between the classes, Gerald as Dolphin unwillingly sat among them long enough for his health to be drunk. He then withdrew and went back with obvious relief to his butlering.

It soon becomes clear that whether or not there will be a death that evening, the house party has been assembled to enquire into a murder that occurred some time ago. Sam Smith, whose Pickwickian charm now carries with it a hint of menace, remarks, after his guests have congratulated him on his hospitality: 'And yet, do you really know me? Does any person ever know another absolutely? Has not the simplest of us a secret or other which cannot be revealed without shame or remorse?' He explains that he intends to discover the identity of the person who killed his brother in Monte Carlo two years previously. It could have been a man, it could have been a woman. Since that time he has assiduously tracked down all the people who were playing the tables that night in Monte Carlo. Each one of the suspects is now sitting in this room. Dolphin, imperturbable, goes round the table refilling their glasses.

Sam Smith, licking his lips, tells them that he will know the name of the murderer soon. How soon? Soon after the gentlemen have joined the ladies. Over the past week he has, under one pretext or another, been able to search through all their personal belongings, has studied confidential letters, has found evidence that bears out his remark about everyone having a secret guarded closely within themselves. In the meantime, one by one, he plays cat-and-mouse with them and tricks them into revealing matters they had thought safely concealed for ever. A typical ploy concerning one of the ladies who claims she did not know his brother is to show her a photograph of him. 'That is not — ' she begins, and then falters into silence when she realises how she has given herself away. Another of his revelations causes a hitherto engaged couple to become vicious enemies. Each of the ladies is discomfited in turn, and when Sam Smith has finished with them they are all sent off to Dolphin's room.

The men are left, ill at ease, twiddling their wine glasses. Ungallantly, in the discussion led by Smith, they hope the killer was a woman. The instrument of murder was poison, and isn't that a woman's weapon? Or could it even have been Dolphin who was the brother's butler at the time? They look worriedly into their glasses. Having established that any one of the ladies might have been the culprit, Smith now shows that, with equal probability, so could any one of the gentlemen. They all prepare to join the ladies in Dolphin's room where the solution will be found. At that moment a terrible scream, a woman's scream, is heard from the room. Dolphin appears, livid, unable to speak. He looks with horror at Smith, appeals silently to him and goes. Smith sits down to a glass of brandy, his rigid little back merciless. The curtain falls.

That is the end of Act I and also of the play, for Barrie never finished it, either through a mischievous desire to tease or through a reluctance to give the final word on a piece so closely associated with Michael. He did tell Violet Vanbrugh how he planned to complete it and which of the twelve suspects was guilty, but since he was in the playful habit of giving different accounts to different people the testimony is without value. *Shall We Join The Ladies?* transferred to the St Martin's Theatre with another cast and ran as a curtain-raiser for over four hundred performances. It was Barrie's last *jeu d'esprit* and he was to write little else apart from *The Boy David* which turned out to be his only real failure, though a catastrophic one. He lived on, with small relish for existence, until 1937. Rich in money, honours and success, he would, without a doubt, have sacrificed them all to have Michael back. Welcome death found him at last, a sad and profoundly disappointed man.

He filled an odd and unique position in Gerald's life. First introduced into the du Maurier family as a kind of honorary uncle, he gradually became its benevolent patron, Gerald's adoptive brother-in-law, and, at the end, in legal fact, guardian of the beautiful Sylvia's five boys. His influence was not restricted to the family. During his association with Gerald, an association flavoured by the mutual respect each felt for the other's stagecraft, he gave to him the finest rôles the actor ever had in which to exhibit his talent. These, among the nine Barrie plays in which he appeared, were the Honourable Ernest Woolley in *The Admirable Crichton*, Hook in *Peter*

Pan, the central figure of *Pantaloon*, John Shand in *What Every Woman Knows*, Dearth in *Dear Brutus*, and 'Another' in *A Well-Remembered Voice*. *Shall We Join The Ladies?* may be a trifle, but it is a significant one, for, in appearance no more than a cunning detective tale, it also displays Barrie's shrewd and disabused knowledge of men and women. As the mute butler Gerald supplied a neat postscript to the distinguished succession of rôles Barrie created for him. No other playwright gave him such opportunities as that melancholy Scot who had managed to install himself so lastingly at the very heart of the du Maurier clan.

CHAPTER IV

SIR GERALD

[i]

Tallulah, Audrey and A Costly Nap

In January 1922, the New Year Honours list carried the name of
Gerald du Maurier. He was now Sir Gerald though his wife Muriel
never wholly conquered her embarrassment at being addressed as
'Your Ladyship'. When friends asked the reason for his knighthood
she was apt to murmur vaguely, 'Well, we never quite knew, dear.'
It was, of course, because he stood, at the age of forty-nine, as the
leader of his profession. Just as the public of twenty years ago had
identified the theatre in the person of Sir Henry Irving, so they now
regarded Gerald as its embodiment. He had already accumulated
honorary presidencies and chairmanships at a disturbing rate, and,
a well-known figure, he lent his name to many good causes. Being
Gerald he went further than that, took his duties to heart and
threw himself with gusto into all the activity they demanded. As
President of the Actors' Orphanage he had turned the Theatrical
Garden Party into a yearly event of riotous enjoyment. He was also
a vice-president of the Actors' Benevolent Fund and a conscientious
member of the council which administered the Royal Academy of
Dramatic Art. Soon he was to become chairman of the trustees
at Denville Hall, the home for retired actors and actresses. It had
been founded by Alfred Denville JP, a veteran who in the best
tradition made his first stage appearance at the age of six weeks.
After playing melodramas throughout the country he established
his own organisation which toured as many as twenty companies up
and down the provinces. He later was metamorphosed as Member
of Parliament for Newcastle-on-Tyne Central, a benefactor who,
recording his hobbies as 'work and sleep', invested some of his riches
in the large mansion and pretty garden where elderly persons now
lead an existence of comfort and regularity which their profession

has not always granted them. Sometimes, at the French window, you may discern the ghost of a 1930s matinée idol wearing blazer and flannels and demanding to know who's for tennis. In easy chairs venerable ladies dream of glamorous nights while phantom applause drums in their ears.

Gerald, at the height of his career, prosperous, buoyant, easily moved, felt much compassion for the old folk at Denville Hall. He knew he had talent, but he knew also that he was blessed with luck. As the star, director and part-author of *Bull-Dog Drummond*, besides being manager of the theatre which presented it, he was making large sums of money. He went gaily to Buckingham Palace for the accolade, wore his ceremonial costume with a fine elegance, and knelt gracefully to play the part of commoner raised to distinction. His bills he now paid in sovereigns with an airy instruction to keep the change, and his tips, always generous, attained the level of endowments. It amused him to do everything in the grand manner, and although he pretended to deprecate the obsequiousness of head waiters who automatically escorted him to their best table, he would have been annoyed had they not done so. If only he had been made a baron: what fun he'd have had choosing his title with the same enjoyable dither as he chose the title of a play!

A London home and a country house were not enough. There must also be grand family holidays. They would go to Algiers with the three girls and a retinue which included Gerald's secretary and the complaisant Ronald Squire. Vast loads of cases and trunks were borne by squads of staggering porters burdened also with the floating paraphernalia of golf-clubs, newspapers, Fortnum hampers, walking-sticks and tennis rackets. While the family groaned with sea-sickness on a rolling Channel steamer Gerald walked spritely along the deck and, under their embarrassed stare, pretended to engage an elderly passenger in conversation while pulling the vilest faces behind her back. Or he would suddenly stop in mid-walk, clutch his heart with an agonised grimace, and feign the symptoms of mortal illness to the concern of passers-by.

In their first-class train compartment they sank into a welter of hats and magazines and playing-cards and bottles that littered the velvet seats. Gerald would abruptly remember that he had left all sorts of essential items at Cannon Hall. Perhaps, as the weather showed signs of turning nasty, they'd be better off going back home after all? Their way to the sleeping-car was smoothed by the distribution of notes whose large denomination brought incredulous smiles to the faces of attendants. Gerald's berth quickly took on the appearance of his bedroom at Cannon Hall: row upon row of sachets and unguents and powders and pastes lined up on the basin, clothes hung in mandatory positions, belongings arranged according to well-defined rules. The carriage resembled the sitting-room they had left behind them with the difference that cases had to be disposed so that Gerald could engage one of his daughters in card games.

Mustapha loomed, and the St George's Hotel where they took possession of their suite. It was not quite right, Gerald decided, because the view from the window failed to please him. Would the manager be very kind and provide them with another that looked out on a prospect more genial? If it was necessary to displace a guest already installed, Gerald would declare: 'Send the chap a case of cigars, will you?' The caravan moved on, the hillocks of luggage were transferred, belongings were unpacked and spread around. Once the du Mauriers had taken root and felt at last that they were in a place of their own with all their personal treasures nicely laid out to give the anonymous rooms a feeling of identity, Gerald would grow restless. Had it really been such a good idea to come away so far from home? Would not a few weeks at Birchington have been just as much fun? He knew he wasn't going to like this place. It was too hot. There was too much dust. The people were unsympathetic. The girls looked at each other and at Muriel. The dreaded, the terrible thought gripped them, as it had so often in the past: Gerald was about to be bored!

Then something would happen, a satisfying bout of golf with Ronnie Squire or a chance witticism that pleased him, and he would suddenly be transformed into the jolliest of companions who led them on absurd expeditions and filled the days with laughter. Ever surrounded by what he described as 'a parcel of women' at home, on holiday he always took with him a few of his men 'pals'. If any of them could not afford the trip he would advise: 'See Tom about it, will you?' and Tom Vaughan, his business manager, would discreetly make yet another advance on the royalties from *Bull-Dog Drummond*. This was a small price to pay for the assurance that he could rely on having a partner at golf and a friend at bezique in the evenings to exchange stories with over brandy as the hours lengthened. It made up for the lack of bridge on cosy nights at the Garrick and the latest gossip, which he missed so badly, about all the people he knew back in London. For he was a London person, a metropolitan man, and 'abroad', for all its charms, was not the Garrick, or Wyndham's, or the Ritz, or the foggy streets, or Simpson's in the Strand.

Breakfast was a testing time. No one knew what his mood was

likely to be. He might arrive smiling and bubbling with all sorts of ideas for amusing day trips. He would just as likely turn up dull, uneasy, captious and yearning for home. The holidays, long planned and long anticipated, were a period when nerves became strained to the limit. On the scented heights of Cannes or in the hurly-burly of Monte Carlo he remained the same: unpredictable and wilful. At least in Monte Carlo there was roulette to distract him. He enjoyed the tables although he would never have become the complete gambler – such a type is impervious to the thrill of the game and cold-blooded in his pursuit of it – and found his excitement in the pleasure of anticipation. From time to time he would bet on one of the horses owned by his partner Frank Curzon. He would also fancy a horse purely because of its name. A mount called Felstead won him what was then the enormous sum of five hundred pounds. He had chosen it on account of a name which combined the first syllable of his sister's house at Felden with the last syllable of his own at Hampstead. Another earned him a rich reward because it had the same name as one of the characters he was playing at that moment. But once the momentary thrill of gambling was over he started to fidget again. And the danger, the ever-present danger of boredom hovered once more.

Sir Gerald arrived back in London with relief. In the absence of any new play he revived *Dear Brutus*. This time he cast Alfred Drayton as the coarse-fibred butler Matey and Ronald Squire as the philandering Purdie. They were excellent choices, as James Agate conceded with his description of Drayton as 'masterful and masterly'. Squire's performance, he continued, 'was labelled "England 1912 or thereabouts", as legibly as though it had been emblazoned on his shirt front. Here again was a character with limitless potentialities of annoyance. Mr Squire overcame them all and abounded in the airs of the well-bred scapegrace.' Of the players in the original production Faith Celli remained as the waif Margaret and Gerald himself as her father Dearth.

> Miss Faith Celli, who had a hundred opportunities to be irritating or purposefully charming, which is the same thing, avoided them all [wrote Agate]. She managed that very delicate business of wistfulness admirably, and at the same time made you feel that she was capable of playing a useful game of hockey for her school. She was brilliantly helped by Sir Gerald du Maurier, who played the sentimental father with extraordinary tact. Let those who say that this delicate player does not act, note how nice is the quantity

of emotion conveyed when the father wakes to the loss of his dream-child. Note, too, the subtlety of his earlier degradation, and the moral well-being of the painter in the wood. You would swear the good fellow subscribes to *Punch*, and that the picture on the easel is not altogether bad. Throughout the long duet father and daughter maintained the atmosphere of a dream. Unreality floated about them like wisps of summer.

For Gerald, back in his element, the theatre was a tonic. Reality was not to be found in exotic hotels and wanderings abroad. It began in his dressing-room where he peered into the mirror and smoothed the faintest dabs of Leichner over the face that looked quizzically back at him. It was still a young face, not lined except for the hint of laughter wrinkles at the corner of the eyes, and the cheeks were flat and the hair little touched by grey. His dresser moved discreetly around, holding up a jacket, proffering a tie. 'Sir Gerald, please,' the call-boy's voice intoned. Although his fingers may have shaken a little as he stubbed out a last cigarette, although his heart-beat may have jumped slightly as he prepared to confront the audience, he knew that this was reality, the only reality that meant anything to him.

Dear Brutus kept Wyndham's going until the December of 1922. When the box-office started its inevitable dip Gerald put on a revival of *Bull-Dog Drummond*, which, he judged, would see him through into the New Year when his preparations for the next play would have been completed. This was attributed to a dramatist called Hubert Parsons. Hubert was Gerald's second Christian name and Parsons the married name of Viola Tree. *The Dancers*, as they called their play, was a joint work whose concoction must have given them a deal of hilarious pleasure. The first act had a Canadian setting and opened in a British Columbia dance-hall. The owner was Tony Chievely, heir to an English lord, who like many a scion of the time had been sent for a period of learning and earning in the colonies before taking up his inheritance. Amid a whirl of colour and riotous action Tony falls in love with Maxine, an impetuous but golden-hearted chorus girl. News comes from London that his father has died in an accident. He must leave his adorable *danseuse* and return to assume his duties as the Earl of Chievely. In London he renews acquaintance with Una, the playmate of his infancy, a girl who embodies the post-war generation of neurotic, unstable womanhood. She is a denizen of night-clubs, an addict of fox-trots and Charlestons who, unknown to Tony, is already pregnant by one of her gigolo dancing partners. The susceptible Earl of Chievely loses his heart to her and they plan marriage. Una realises that she cannot go on with the deceit and is unable to forgive herself for having played false with the man who loves her. A few minutes after the wedding reception she takes poison and the Earl finds her dead. Some years later he goes to a theatre in the Champs-Elysees and watches the début of a sensational new ballerina. Who should it be but the voluptuous Maxine? Since her roughneck days in British Columbia she has flowered into a queen of the dance and the toast of Paris. She is reunited with Tony. They have both been deepened and chastened by the experiences of life after their youthful love affair, and, it is suggested as the curtain falls, will be happy together in a wiser and maturer way.

The plot of this madly novelettish drama, which barely stands up to recounting, doubtless came from Viola, whose inconsequential trademark it clearly bears. Gerald trimmed and shaped the dialogue, worked up the climaxes and devised effective curtains. Yet Viola was the originator who spurred him on and gave him the impetus. They needed a youthful, flamboyant and preferably American actress for the part of Maxine. She was difficult to find. The impresario Charles B. Cochran thought he could help. On one of his frequent trips to New York he had gone to a party and been struck by the personality of an audacious girl whom he saw there. Among the guests was Ethel Barrymore, queen of the American theatre, a national monument. The girl, noted in a small circle of friends for her mimicry, was urged to do her impersonation of Miss Barrymore. This she did and, afterwards, asked that stately woman to forgive her impertinence. 'But my dear,' said Ethel with a Gorgon stare, 'you make me look so fat.' The girl blurted out: 'But Miss Barrymore, I was imitating *you*.' Ethel slapped her face.

The name of the girl was Tallulah Bankhead, and what Cochran saw of her convinced him that she had star quality. With Gerald's agreement he invited her to London. The rôle offered, he told her, was

somewhat of a siren and in one scene she has to dance. She must be a lady, and altogether sounds like you. She is, in the play, supposed to be of surpassing beauty. I have told the part-authoress and Sir Gerald that I believe you are 'the goods'. They are quite excited about you and I think there is little doubt that if you care to take the risk of coming over you will be engaged . . . In favour of your coming I would say that the management is the best in London for comedy actresses. It is the ambition of every young actress to be with Sir Gerald. Moreover, Sir Gerald is the best stage director in this country and Miss Gladys Cooper and several other actresses owe their present positions to his help.

Not many days later a cable arrived: 'Terribly sorry. Du Maurier's changed plans.' Tallulah wilted. Why be upset? a friend assured her. Go to England anyway. She was certain to be offered a part in some other play because her hair was so beautiful.

Ignoring Cochran's urgent advice not to come she borrowed a thousand dollars from an elderly admirer and took the first boat available. Cochran met her at Waterloo station and she booked an apartment at the Ritz, the only hotel she knew of in London. The impresario lunched her and escorted her to a matinée of *Bull-Dog Drummond*. Afterwards, in his dressing-room, she met Gerald for the first time. 'My dear girl,' said he, 'I cabled you I had engaged another girl for the rôle, that she was already in rehearsal. I'm terribly sorry. We're opening in a fortnight, you know.' Well, replied Tallulah undaunted, it had been a pleasure to meet him: perhaps the girl would break a leg?

One evening at dinner Cochran remarked that du Maurier had never seen her with her hat off. 'I don't think he's aware of your unusual beauty. Your hat masks your unusual hair,' he mused. By now he was very much on her side, admired her nerve and appreciated, himself a gambler, her willingness to risk all. They visited Wyndham's again and Tallulah, radiant in evening gown, her hair a golden cascade, displayed herself to the actor-manager. Daphne, Gerald's daughter, was also there. After they had gone she said to her father: 'Daddy, that's the most beautiful girl I ever saw in my life.' Next day Tallulah was engaged at a salary of thirty pounds a week. The girl originally contracted for the part had to be paid a fifty-pound weekly wage for the whole run of the play and, since she had just given birth, was able to nurse her child in luxury.

Tallulah was sent off to Leonid Massine who told Gerald she was a natural-born dancer. In a buckskin costume glittering with beads, her head waggling immense feathers, she jigged a wild Indian dance that sent the first-night audience into a frenzy. On that evening a new cult began, the cult of Tallulah Bankhead. Large numbers of fans would queue up as much as thirty hours before the performance began, frozen, hungry, but determined to applaud their goddess.

They are a mysterious lot, these stalwarts of the cult [wrote Arnold Bennett]. Without being penurious, they do not come from Grosvenor Square, nor even Dorset Square. They seem to belong to the ranks of the clerk class. But they cannot be clerks, typists, shop-assistants: for such people don't and can't take a day and a half off whenever their 'Tallulah' opens. What manner of girls are they? . . . All one can say is that they are bright, youthful, challenging, proud of themselves and apparently happy. It is certain that they boast afterwards to their friends about the number of hours they waited for the thrill of beholding their idol, and that those who have waited the longest become heroines to their envious acquaintances.

'Talu', as intimates called her, soon developed the persona which made her not so much a leading actress as a heroine of the gossip columnists and one who scattered her natural gift in the careless manner of a junior Mrs Patrick Campbell. Since she did not appear in the second act of *The Dancers* she had forty idle minutes to kill and used them for entertaining her friends and admirers. Their revelry made so much noise that Gerald had a door put in the stairway to close off her dressing-room. After, when the first act had ended, she would rush off in full make-up for dinner at the Savoy and come back, breathless, just in time for the third. One day, in a fit of caprice, she decided that her hair was too long, unbearable in hot weather and difficult to control. She decided to have it shingled in the new fashion and summoned a French hairdresser. (His name, she swore, was Monsieur La Barbe.) The locks were shorn during the second act and she made her entry. At one point she had to let her hair down to the knees and brush it up in a flamboyant gesture. She waited for Gerald's reaction when he saw what she had done, but he, his mind too preoccupied with acting and with the holiday he was about to take, did not notice. Afterwards in his dressing-room she wiggled her shaven head at him. Still he failed to realise. Then, as he did, he burst into tears. 'You have ruined the play!' he groaned.

He put on his understudy and left to take a holiday which the combined strain of the new production and Tallulah's antics had made so needful. At his return she demanded an increase in salary. Every penny of her thirty pounds a week was usually spent by Tuesday, and, setting a pattern to be followed for the rest of her existence, she could never live within her salary. He, startled by her presumption but aware that much of *The Dancers'* success was her achievement, raised the sum to fifty. Not content with this she insisted on a holiday too. If he could have one why couldn't she? It was pointed out that such things were an actor-manager's prerogative and not a supporting player's. She insisted. He offered to increase her salary to seventy-five pounds. No, she wanted her holiday and he could act with her understudy as he had left her to do with his. Gerald's cool, knightly style could not survive her passionate arguments and he let her go. She went to Venice and promptly collapsed with sun-stroke and a temperature of a hundred and six.

Gerald had for once met a creature whose temperament was even more capricious than his own. He always, moreover, went into battle with her handicapped by the undeniable fact that, although his own drawing power brought thousands to see *The Dancers*, Tallulah's incandescent appeal enticed many, many more, and that her conquest of London had made her a star in her own right. Viola Tree, watching the turmoil from a thoughtful distance, commented on the girl who now wore slacks under her mink coat:

She had green dowdy clothes and wore a rat's tail fur when she landed here. But she must stay at the Ritz. She has Ritzed it ever since. This is typical of her. She earns a larger and larger salary and spends it all. She lives well, gives much to friends and servants. In appearance Tallulah is like a Greek fragment – or, rather, an Egyptian head put on a Greek torso. Her head is a little large for her body, and for this reason she cuts off her immense chevelure of fair waving hair. She now scrapes it back, Garbo-like, from her high forehead. Her eyes are hieroglyphics, and her eyelashes are as long in reality as Greta Garbo's are artificially. When nervous, she blinks them, which is foolish, but she has no other mannerisms – except, perhaps, her voice. Like a cricket, she chirps all day and half the night, and gets hoarse in the process . . . The inanities and sex-appealing affectations which have been set down as hers have nothing in common with her at all. She is direct to a degree, and, according to herself, 'as full of faults as any woman'. If I may throw a stone, albeit through a glass window, I would say she gets through life too quickly (she has lived about four lives already in her short one) . . .

Gerald sighed and let her have what she wanted. You had to admit that she was outrageous and that, in later years, her playing of acidulous, drawling bitches was type-casting of the most obvious sort, but at the same time she was amusing and rarely failed to illumine a scene with her extravagant personality, even though she went against all the rules of gentle behaviour. The girl who acted Gerald's suicidal bride in *The Dancers*, a twenty-three-year-old player called Audrey

Carten, provided an exquisite contrast with Tallulah's thunder and lightning. Gerald had earlier picked her out and cast her in his revivals of *Dear Brutus* and of *Bull-Dog Drummond* where she was the gentle heroine. She fulfilled his hopes of her with a sensitive and moving portrayal. Although *The Dancers* was blatant melodrama, Daphne du Maurier recalls, 'acted by Gerald and Audrey Carten with a wonderful sense of delicacy, restraint, and sincerity, these two characters lived and were human, were painfully agonisingly human, playing upon the emotions of the audience in a fashion that could be vouched for by wet handkerchiefs and swollen eyes.' Also in the large cast of twenty-three – for *The Dancers* was produced in great style and had four scene changes – was Nigel Bruce. He often appeared under Gerald's management and you did not need to know he was the son of a baronet to appreciate his aristocratic manner and deep, port-wine voice. After a busy career on the West End stage he emigrated to Hollywood and made an international name for himself as an amiable bumbler, a dear, chubby old fellow who always lost his wife to a more unscrupulous lover. His best rôle was that of Dr Watson to Basil Rathbone's gaunt Sherlock Holmes, a part he acted many times with a nicely proportioned blend of incredulity and dull-wittedness. He had been badly wounded in the trenches of 1914-18. This was something which, in Hollywood during the wartime 1940s, he would often mention in a throwaway line to young British actors of military age.

The Dancers ended its run with the three hundred and forty-sixth performance on 15th December, 1923. Although busy during the day preparing a successor, Gerald could at least treat himself to a leisurely Christmas and free evenings over the period. Sunday was the only day when he could rely on such a luxury – except, of course, when a country-house weekend party inspired him, rather slyly, to put on his understudy for the Monday evening performance so that he could return without needing to rush, as a gentleman should. He was firmly opposed to Sunday performances, not through religious conviction but because, in general, none other but the seventh day was available to him for relaxation. In the morning he would devour the newspapers and take the children for a walk or a trip to the zoo. Then came what made Sundays at Cannon Hall famous in theatrical circles: a big luncheon party at which the guests around the table were likely to include Marie Tempest and Gladys Cooper and Herbert Marshall and Ronald Squire and, on occasion, Sacha Guitry with his wife of the moment.

Afterwards, if it were summer, there was a hazard which, should you be reasonably fit and not too shaky, you found difficult to avoid: unending games of tennis organised by a tireless host. Even at the age of fifty, which he was in 1923, Gerald played like a demon, whirling a brand-new racket at each set and darting around the court with unforgiving energy. He wore out his opponents not so much through his skill as through the relentless vigour that powered his lean frame and the determination with which he led the assault. In winter things were more quiet. People gathered to look at the newspapers, to talk, to stay on until tea, until supper, and to play bridge or perhaps a hand of bezique. It was decidedly less exhausting to be a Sunday guest at Cannon Hall when the trees were leafless or snow lay on the ground.

The Christmas of 1923 followed the pattern set by earlier Christmases, and took the form of Sunday in a more expansive mood. The day itself was tranquil, and the household staff were left to enjoy themselves in their own fashion while Gerald conducted the family to lunch at the Savoy. Evening, back in Hampstead, was the time when fun began, with a table laid for anything up to eighteen guests, presents at every cover, and a turkey weighing twenty-six pounds that Mo sliced up at dexterous speed. Perhaps a conjuror would entertain after dinner, and there would be roulette to end an evening lit by many candles and a gleaming Christmas tree. Gerald, as usual, dominated the occasion with a brittle vivacity and drank, it may be, too much, and smoked excessively.

On more intimate occasions, when visitors were absent and only Mo and the girls sat at table and Gerald ate his favourite cold beef, the talk was of family jokes that outsiders would not have understood. One of these concerned Gerald's 'stable', the name the children gave to the select band of young women admirers by whom he was always surrounded. X, he would tell them, was becoming a little too forward, and Y, oh dear, Y had been quite boring with her demands for his favours, and as for Z, well, the sooner he was able to give her the slip the better. It was all, Mo would tell him with an indulgent sigh, because he encouraged them in the first place, and if things turned out awkwardly, if hearts were broken, then he had only himself to blame. He enjoyed flirtations and, in his actor's way, delighted to create make-believe romantic situations that brought amusement and diversion into life. Or were they always restricted to make-believe?

One reason for his compulsive flirtations was increasing age. He hated the thought of growing old and, now that he was a quinquagenarian, he had to prove to himself that he could still attract and conquer women. Each pretty face was a challenge to be met, a new experience to be embarked upon. Audrey Carten was not beautiful but she had very pretty eyes and an elegant long face. The moment he saw her at RADA, where he was a member of the council, he had been fascinated by her Pre-Raphaelite looks. Her voice, her movements, her personality, had something which caught his attention and held it. He could not say exactly what it was, but he knew that here was a girl with the promise of star quality. As we have seen, he groomed her with a series of engagements which culminated in *The Dancers*. He took her out to intimate little dinners and learned that she was of Dutch extraction, that her family had no theatrical background, that her gift for acting had shown itself with a natural spontaneity and come, apparently, from nowhere. She absorbed him. Soon she was a prominent member of the 'stable' and, being not much older than his own girls, their companion and a frequent visitor to Cannon Hall.

Angela du Maurier thought her a witty friend and a daring practical joker. She remembered how one evening they went to a concert and, on the stairs, passed other members of the audience talking among themselves. One made a remark to which Audrey, walking by, mischievously replied in an undertone.

'Did you say something?' enquired the speaker.

Whereas most people would have fled in embarrassment, Audrey stood her ground. 'You don't remember me?' she said brazenly. 'How shattering.'

The woman, puzzled, racked her brains.

Audrey continued, drawing on her riotous imagination: 'Don't you remember Shanklin?'

Danger loomed, for the woman, unexpectedly, said: 'Yes.'

Audrey fought on: 'I can't bear it. It *is* Peggy, isn't it?'

'Yes,' came the reply.

This was too much, even for the inventive Audrey who could now foresee terrible complications. She gave the stranger an affectionate kiss, muttered 'I must fly,' and rushed away.

Upon the handle of her umbrella she wrote incongruous sentences and words that might come in useful as conversation-stoppers. Among them was: 'Do you get much tennis at the convent?' Once she had a slight grievance against Angela and her family and repaid it by stocking with innumerable empty champagne bottles the fountain that stood outside the front door of Cannon Hall. When the innocent household awoke next morning it was to a scene that implied a night of licentious revelry.

If Gerald's daughters asked him what the latest 'form' of the 'stable' was, Audrey Carten's name often cropped up as a leader. The situation was, however, not so frivolous as he cared to suggest. She was profoundly in love with him. If he did not have the dazzling good looks of Henry Ainley he had the charm and the prestige of Gerald du Maurier, and those were more than enough to enchant her. She found his manner irresistible. He had only to stare at her in his mocking, quizzical way for her defences to crumble absolutely. And, like all the other actresses who capitulated to him, she was flattered that her lover should be England's most famous actor-manager. Mo, who had seen this happen so often before and knew that it would happen again, many times, kept her counsel. Such diversions were essential to her husband's ego and there was never any danger that he would break up their marriage. They had been together too long, were bound by their children too closely.

Yet his love for Audrey went deeper than usual. He admired her talent as well as her body and spent hours tutoring her in the craft of the theatre. Her gift was encouraged by long letters which he wrote to her about the art of acting and how to adapt her approach in the light of his own vast, intuitive knowledge. These letters have since disappeared, which is a pity, for they would have given us the only permanent record he ever compiled of his methods and techniques. He may, to a certain extent, have overawed her professionally. After *The Dancers* she only appeared in two other plays, and these at wide intervals. Her success with *The Dancers* inhibited her and she had an uneasy thought that everything afterwards would be an anti-climax, that she would not be able to live up to the first sensational triumph. In her mid-twenties she virtually retired from the stage, although she kept her theatrical interest alive by writing plays and adaptations from the French in collaboration with her sister Waveney. The emotional cost of her involvement with Gerald was high. It was compounded by a sentimental association with Tallulah Bankhead during the run of *The Dancers*, for Audrey was also bisexual and loved women as intensely as the other sex. In later life she found a durable relationship with Lady Caroline Paget, herself divorced from a husband whose taste inclined to men. By now Audrey was an alcoholic, perhaps as a legacy from those hard-drinking theatrical parties of the twenties. She declined into senility and would lie in bed all day reciting speeches from the plays she had done when young. In 1977 she died, as old as the century, her five-year stage career and her passion for Gerald a vague, distant memory.

Gerald did not forget her and even, a few years later, directed and appeared in a play she had written with her sister Waveney. A more urgent matter was to find an attraction to succeed *The Dancers*, and he solved it by putting on *Not In Our Stars*, an adaptation of a novel which drew its title from the same Shakespearean couplet as Barrie's *Dear Brutus*. The plot was ingenious and opened in the prison cell of a man about to be hanged for having murdered his rival in a love affair. The events which led up to the situation were then told in reverse order to the moment when the lover contemplates murder. At this point he is allowed a glimpse into the future and realises what will be his fate if he commits the crime. Shall he stay his hand? He resolves to break off the affair. The girl, however, persuades him against his will to remain her lover. So he knows that he will go ahead with the murder and be hanged in consequence. As a variation on Barrie's theme – that even if we had a second chance in life we would make the same mistakes all over again – *Not In Our Stars* generated a certain macabre power. This was emphasised by Gerald's performance as the condemned lover, grey-faced, haunted, his eyes speaking guilt. His admirers, though, did not want that sort of thing from him and *Not In Our Stars* faded after two months.

If, then, the clientèle he had built up at Wyndham's preferred the mixture as before, that was what he would give them, light comedy in which he purred and posed with the nonchalance they expected of him. He approached A.A. Milne, a reliable trafficker in gently amusing entertainments that had a vogue in the twenties and thirties, and was offered *To Have The Honour*. It was, like all of Milne's work, a neat and craftsmanlike piece imbued with quiet humour, not too demanding and well designed to show off the talents of Gerald and a cast which included Faith Celli, his partner in *Dear Brutus*, and Madge Titheradge. This, too, failed to please and vanished from the posters before six months were up.

While he cast about anxiously to find something that would keep his theatre open he was side-tracked into directing the annual revival of *Peter Pan* at Christmas, 1924. Gladys Cooper was, for the second time, to play the title rôle. He had his own idea about Wendy.

'Do you know who is to play Wendy this year?' he asked his daughter Angela.

'No, who?' she asked.

'You.'

She already knew the whole play by heart, or so she thought, having seen it every year since she was two. Rehearsals taught her differently, although she enjoyed them. 'I was never happier than sitting in dust-sheeted stalls,' she remembered, 'watching Daddy conducting rehearsals on a bare and empty stage, the actors with their parts in their hands (sometimes), and going over and over the same scene until perfection was reached. To watch a play shaping . . . it's like watching a child growing up. If a good play, or an attractive child, quite absorbing.' Gerald, as always, directed with open-minded sympathy. An actor would sometimes remark: 'I don't feel *natural*, Gerald, when I say so and so.' He would answer: 'Right. Do it your way and let's see what it's like.' Should the actor's way be an improvement he would say: 'Far better. Do it like that.'

The one thing that perturbed Angela was the flying. For this she was trussed up in a fearsome harness with a steel plate at the back to take the wires. What she had always feared came to pass one afternoon as she and the others swung out through the window to land mid-stage. She flew into the yawning void, crashed over the footlights and landed in the orchestra amid an avalanche of toppling instruments. An understudy was hastily brought on. After she had got her breath back she stood up and promptly cracked her head against someone else's. Gerald, who had looked in to see how things were going, was saluted with frenzied shouts of, 'Wendy's gorn!'

He needed light relief at this time. Towards the end of the year his sister May died. She and Gerald had always been thought of as the weak ones in the family and this brought them even closer together. Witty, athletic, brainy, she often put Gerald in his place when he became too exuberant, though he never minded, for he loved her and respected her judgment. Now, with May dead, he was the only du Maurier left. He tried to forget his depression in the search for a new play, could not find one, and stopped the gap temporarily with a revival of *The Ware Case*, an old dependable which he had done that year for a charity performance in aid of King George's Pension Fund. The sets were all in place, rehearsals had freshened his memory and it seemed the obvious thing to do in an emergency.

Early the following year, by which time his theatre had been 'dark' for too long a period, he settled on *A Man With A Heart*, a play by the veteran Alfred Sutro who up to then had never disappointed. It failed. In 1925, at the age of fifty-two, he wondered if the time had come at last to give up after fifteen years of management. His alone had been the responsibility of choosing plays and casting them while his partner Frank Curzon stayed discreetly in the background and provided finance. If any practical matter caused annoyance he could rely on his business manager Tom Vaughan to help him out. 'Oh, ring up Tom; he'll settle it,' Gerald would say, and Tom always did, relieving him of the need to parley with agents over fees and royalties and to handle all the commercial problems that were, and ever had been, enigmas to Gerald. But Tom was ill, very ill, and failing. So was Frank Curzon. Gerald no longer had the zest to carry on. The fun had gone out of life.

Was he losing touch with the public? Had his taste faltered? He looked at the type of play which had come into vogue and he did not like what he saw. In particular he was scandalised by *The Vortex*, a new melodrama by the young Noël Coward which dealt flamboyantly with drug addiction and an ambiguous mother-son relationship. Genuinely revolted by the subject, and, at the same time, fearing that his leadership of the theatrical profession was under attack, he denounced the new trend. 'The public are asking for filth . . .' he declared, 'the younger generation are knocking at the door of the dustbin . . . if life is worse than the stage, should the stage hold the mirror up to such distorted nature? If so, where shall we be – without reticence or reverence?'

Coward replied with a spirited newspaper article.

Sir Gerald du Maurier, having – if he will forgive me saying so – enthusiastically showered the English stage with second-rate drama for many years, now rises up with incredible violence and has a nice slap all round at the earnest and perspiring young dramatists. This is awful; it is also a little unwise. Art demands reverence much more than life does – and Sir Gerald's reverence so far seems to have been entirely devoted to the box-office.

It was ridiculous, Coward went on, to say that this age was degenerate and decadent. Every age was, the only difference now being that people were not so hypocritical about it. For his part he intended to write 'as honestly and sincerely as possible on any subject that I choose'. If the public did not like it they need not come to see it.

When the self-advertising denouncers of the stage describe the English theatre as being 'in a disgraceful state', they speak a little truth without being aware of it – for a theatre-going public which cheerfully tolerates such fake and nauseating sentimentality as has been handed out to them recently can hardly be acclaimed as judges of what is right or wrong, moral or immoral, in the theatre or out of it.

Sir Gerald

The whirligig of time brought in his revenge. Twenty-five years later Coward was to find himself occupying the embattled position of a Gerald du Maurier. By then he was become, like Gerald, a symbol of fashionable dinner-jacket theatre. He had even succeeded him as President of the Actors' Orphanage, and his feelings about the plays written by his younger rivals were the same. In a much-publicised attack he spoke about 'dustbin drama' and the need to respect the public. He continued:

The prevalent assumption that any successful play presented by a commercial management in the West End is automatically inferior in quality to anything produced on a shoestring in the East End or Sloane Square is both inaccurate and silly. It also betrays an attitude of old-fashioned class-consciousness and inverted snobbism which has now become obvious to the ordinary playgoer.

Such a declaration might have been Gerald speaking from beyond the grave.

After his skirmish with Noël Coward and his unsuccessful attempts to find a play for Wyndham's Gerald decided it was time for a holiday. Daphne was at school in Paris so he took Mo, Angela and Jeanne with him and set off in the family Packard driven by his chauffeur on a tour of Italy. They journeyed by way of the châteaux on the Loire. The Simplon tunnel was blocked by snow so the car went by train into Italy. At Como the rain hurtled in solid sheets while Gerald stumped up and down the hotel lounge volubly regretting the mad idea of going there. He would give it another twenty-four hours, he swore, and if the rain continued they would all return to England. Next day, it appeared, Heaven listened to his threat, for the morning dawned sunny and bright. He was suddenly accosted, to his apprehensive surprise, by a pair of formidable sisters who descended upon him and revealed that their brother had once been on the stage with him in his youth. Their father was the vicar of a London parish, and they, tall, forthright, uncompromising, carried the banner of the Church militant. Sister Agnes had a Christian love for all humanity save lesbians. 'I can smell them a mile off,' she insisted to Angela. 'Dear child, why do you *know* such people? And do wipe that stuff off your pretty lips.'

The du Mauriers left their hotel and moved into a villa up on the hill which they rented from the British Consul. Nightingales sang, there were leisurely rounds of golf all day long, and Viola Tree joined them to enliven the holiday with her zany humour.

After two months Gerald grew restless and the party moved on by way of Milan and Grenoble to Paris where they stayed at Versailles and were reunited with Daphne. Gerald was impatient for London. During his absence from the town he worried about all he must be missing and the projects that were being launched without him. He was glad when he got back.

His first engagement on his return was to direct Gladys Cooper in a revival of *Iris*, the Pinero drama that had been one of Mrs Patrick Campbell's successes at the turn of the 1900s. It was too long for a modern audience and Gerald struggled to reduce it, not much helped by the author, who, present at every rehearsal, cavilled at any suggestion of cutting his beautiful dialogue. Another problem was the romantic lead, a young Irish actor called Anew McMaster who did not respond well to Gerald's method of direction. At the first night he changed his style so completely that there was unexpected laughter during the key love scene. He was replaced with another young actor, Ivor Novello, and although Ivor's acting technique was immature his film reputation helped the box-office considerably. *Iris* was not an entirely happy welcome back to London for Gerald.

Worse followed. Freddy Lonsdale heard that he was looking for a play and rang up to say he had just the thing for him. Gerald invited him to Cannon Hall for dinner and Freddy arrived with the manuscript under his arm. Despite their close friendship Gerald had never appeared in one of his plays, but this one, Freddy was convinced, gave him just what he wanted. They ate well, they drank even better, and after dinner retired to the library where Freddy prepared to read the play which he called *The Last of Mrs Cheyney*. Gerald settled down comfortably in an armchair beside the roaring fire, Mo sat opposite, and Freddy took out his manuscript. 'Act I,' he read aloud in his clipped Old Etonian voice. 'A room at Mrs Cheyney's house at Goring . . . The orchestra plays one verse of "A May Morning" – at the rise of the curtain the song is being concluded and is heard off to the accompaniment of a piano . . . William, a footman, enters from door L . . .'

The reading aloud of a play, unless it is done by a versatile actor, can be a tedious affair. Just as composers are rarely good conductors of their own music, so dramatists are not always the best readers of their plays. Freddy droned on, his epigrams falling by the wayside, his voice beginning to crack a little. Gerald snuggled deeper into the chair and his eyes started to glaze over. He did not seem to laugh much when Freddy declaimed, with an author's pride, one of his smoothest exchanges:

WILLIE: Oh! Lord, how I hate my face!
JOAN: Supposing you had to live with it, like your wife has.
WILLIE: I never thought of that. I'll give her a present.

The dramatist came to his second act. 'Room at Mrs Ebley's house,' he read. 'After dinner on a warm summer evening . . . The orchestra plays one chorus of "Poor Little Rich Girl", which, at the rise of the curtain is taken up by the piano on stage, at the repeat, as the orchestra finishes . . .'

He was not very far into the second act when he heard a strange noise. He looked up from his manuscript and across at Gerald. He heard the noise again as Gerald's chest rose and fell at a relaxed and steady pace. He realised it was a snore and jumped to his feet, threw the manuscript at Angela, told her to read it, and flew out of the door. Mo followed him in distress. As he stamped down the grand staircase she pleaded: 'Please, Freddy, please come back. He's so terribly tired. He couldn't help it. Please, Freddy, come back.' He ignored her and jumped into the car he had parked outside. On the way home he vowed that he would never speak to Gerald again and that he would never work with him in the theatre.

Next day he started making other arrangements. Did Gerald really doze off? Or was the incident another of his practical jokes? 'It is most likely that Gerald did genuinely fall asleep,' says Freddy's daughter, 'but that, when he was awoken – as he inevitably would have been – by Freddy leaving the room, and he realised what had happened, he decided that, rather than have a humiliating scene of apology, he would continue to play it as though he was still asleep.'

Gerald took action. What little he had heard of *The Last of Mrs Cheyney* convinced him that he needed the play for Wyndham's. Gangling Viola Tree was sent to plead his cause with Freddy. She met Freddy, his daughter and the novelist Michael Arlen for a prickly dinner at the Embassy Club. Why not, Viola proposed, offer the play to Gerald again?

'Give me one good reason why I should do as you suggest,' snorted Freddy.

Viola, good-hearted, bungling Viola with her talent for the incongruous, decided on an appeal to Christian charity. Her scriptural knowledge was, however, a trifle scanty, and in the heat of the moment there was only one phrase that floated into her mind. 'Wasn't it Christ,' she asked, 'who said "Suffer little children to come unto me"?'

At least she silenced Freddy. Michael Arlen replied on his behalf. 'I take it,' he replied venomously, 'that *we* are the little children.'

Viola ambled off to report the failure of her mission.

Soon afterwards Gerald was driving his car up the steep incline which led to Cannon Hall. He saw Tom Vaughan walking down towards him and stopped.

'Tom,' he said, leaning out of the window, 'I think I shall have to have that play of Freddy's.'

'You're too late, old boy,' answered Vaughan. 'Gladys is going to do it with Gilbert Miller.'

According to Freddy's daughter, Gerald probably had his foot on the brake when Vaughan spoke, for at that moment the car began to slide back down the hill carrying a stricken Gerald with it.

[ii]

The Last of Mrs Cheyney and the First of Edgar Wallace

A young Parisian on his first visit to England was startled to see newspaper headlines announcing 'Collapse of Kent'. At least, he reflected, as he looked around him after coming off the ship, Dover had been spared. Some earthquake, some natural cataclysm must have sent the rest of Kent slithering into the English Channel. It was quite a time before he became sufficiently acquainted with British customs to realise that the headline meant nothing more dire than the insuccess of the Kent county cricket team. A similar misunderstanding afflicted the young American impresario Gilbert Miller. When first he arrived in London he saw 'Close of play' and figures of runs displayed on newspaper placards. 'This is a dreadful season, with a play closing every day,' he wrote to his father back in America, 'but there is great interest in the theatre when the end of a run is given huge headlines by the newspapers.'

His father, Henry Miller, was an English-born actor-manager who early in his career emigrated to America and made himself a prominent figure on Broadway where he is commemorated by the theatre named after him. Among the hundreds of rôles he played the strangest was doubtless that of Oscar Wilde in *The Poet and The Puppets*. Since it belonged to the year after *Lady Windermere's Fan* the piece must have been a satire on a public figure who was not yet notorious. Henry's son Gilbert also went into the theatre and for many years operated successfully both in London and New York. He divided his time between the West End and the Henry Miller Theatre, and in the course of his long life presented many famous plays from Barrie to Rattigan, from Emlyn Williams and J. B. Priestley to Dylan Thomas and T. S. Eliot.

By the 1920s he had the St James's Theatre under his management and it was here that *The Last of Mrs Cheyney* was to be produced. Gerald now saw that he had no hope of presenting it at Wyndham's. He was determined, though, to appear in it and said as much. All the main parts were cast except for that of Lord Arthur Dilling. Gladys Cooper was to play Mrs Cheyney and Ronald Squire had been selected as Charles the crooked butler. Freddy decided that Gerald must be forgiven. As a further gesture everyone agreed, Ronald Squire included, that he should be offered the choice between playing Charles or Lord Dilling, the two leading male rôles. He chose Dilling. It is a longer part than that of Charles, but the latter is probably the more rewarding of the two. So thought Ronald Squire, as did Freddy, and when Gerald made his choice they looked at each other significantly.

The reunion with Gladys Cooper was, for Gerald, among the pleasantest things about *The Last of Mrs Cheyney*. Since helping her career early on he had become a close friend. She was, indeed, one of the very few women he knew with whom he did not flirt, did not engage in light-hearted romance or whom he did not try to seduce. Firm-minded, clear-eyed, she stood no nonsense from him and he respected her for it.

Every matinée during the run of *Cheyney* [Daphne remembers], they met for lunch like two men at a club, silent, shoulder to shoulder, Gerald with his cold beef and Gladys with a chop: now and then discussing the affairs of the day, brief and matter-of-fact, or comparing notes about each other's children. No lingering over coffee for her, no long stories, no confessions, no declarations of private misery, no mysterious revelations. No hammering down her great reserve: no indirect questioning, no sudden suggestions, penetrated the wall she had so wisely built around herself. What lay at the back of her mind, what remembrances, what past endeavours and what future goals only God and Gladys ever knew.

They often took holiday homes at Birchington with their respective families. Every night, when the curtain fell on *The Last of Mrs Cheyney*, they would drive down to Birchington. Next day, around the middle of the afternoon, following cricket and games on the beach with the children, Gerald's three and Miss Cooper's three, they would drive back to the theatre. Gladys and her family were, of course, frequent guests at Cannon Hall, where much tennis was played and the tea-table was set with a plenitude of home-made cakes, scones, jam and honey. The room looked, said one observer, like a stage-set for a comedy by Freddy Lonsdale. Gerald would treat Mo as if he had only just seen her and fallen in love with her. It was, he would assure people, the only proper way to approach your wife. There were, naturally, many return visits to Charlwood, Gladys Cooper's ancient and beautiful country home. In its rambling grounds dwelt cows, sheep, ponies and, her tastes embracing the exotic, a snake, a monkey and wallabies. Gerald, once, was bitten by the monkey. This did not annoy him quite so much as did Miss Cooper's habit of naming her uglier pets after his stage rôles.

When Lonsdale offered her *The Last of Mrs Cheyney* she formed a partnership with Gilbert Miller to present it at the St James's. Gerald, besides playing a leading rôle, was invited to direct. He had, therefore, emerged as best he could from the terrible mistake he made on that drowsy night at Cannon Hall. Even so, he had done himself grave harm, for, had he put on the play himself at Wyndham's he would have drawn not only his salary as actor and director but also a share of the profits. This would have been considerable, for *The Last of Mrs Cheyney* was to run some eighteen months.

Rehearsals went agreeably. Freddy lounged in the auditorium munching boiled sweets from a paper bag while Gerald supervised the action on stage. Sometimes he did not bother to come at all and was happy to let Gerald carry on. After a week of rehearsals, though, Gerald and Ronald Squire felt uneasy. They came off the stage and down into the stalls.

'Freddy, this third act is no good,' said Gerald. 'We shall have a flop unless you can do something about it.'

Freddy remained cheerful and no whit offended. Like a grocer who knows the customer is always right, he was ready to adapt the goods if necessary. 'I know,' he said calmly. 'I know. You are perfectly right.'

Perhaps, Gerald suggested tactfully, they might all three break for lunch and talk things over.

'I'd rather go by myself,' he replied. 'I must think about it.'

He did. When the others came back from lunch he greeted them with a triumphant 'I've got it!' While the cast rehearsed the first and second acts he rewrote entirely the ineffective third and, by the time the players were ready to start work on it, he presented them with a final act which is one of the most ingenious he ever constructed.

The play opens in the Goring home of Mrs Cheyney, reputedly an Australian widow who now frequents a high society which has eagerly accepted her. Among the guests in the large house party she currently entertains is Lord Arthur Dilling. 'He has a reputation with women that is extremely bad,' observes her butler Charles, 'consequently, as hope is a quality possessed of all women, women ask him everywhere! I would describe him as a man who has kept more husbands at home than any other man of modern times.' Another guest is the not so bright but very rich Lord Pilco. The rest of the company discuss him:

MARY: Being Lady Pilco would have certain advantages?
JOHN: Heavens! Think of waking up in the morning and finding Pilco alongside of one!
MARY: One wouldn't!
JOHN: That's true!

They comment wistfully on the pearl necklace that one of the husbands has given his wife: 'If a man is prepared to give the woman he married such divine pearls, what wouldn't he be prepared to give the woman he loves?' Happiness is money, diamonds, a rich husband, a generous lover. Lord Arthur Dilling, who has a reputation for cynicism, listens complacently to the sort of talk he hears everywhere he goes. Meanwhile he thinks he recognises Charles, the oddly well-spoken butler. He is positive he has seen him somewhere else, perhaps at Oxford. No sir, comes the answer, they have never met before. In a reply which shows how neatly Lonsdale could blend satirical wit and dramatic point, Dilling says: 'I assure you we have! I was educated – I mean, I was at Oxford.'

The guests drift away and leave Dilling alone with the beautiful Mrs Cheyney. It is clear that Dilling has, for the first time, fallen genuinely in love. He will not readily declare it, and in a long virtuoso scene he feints skilfully with Mrs Cheyney who proves equally adept at parrying his advances. At last Dilling retires, not worsted, it is true, but certainly, thanks to her adroitness, even more captivated than before. When he has gone her butler Charles and all her other servants gather round her. Now comes the *coup de théâtre*: they reveal themselves to be a gang of international crooks who plan the theft of a pearl necklace belonging to one of her guests, Mrs Ebley. They will strike on the evening when Mrs Ebley has invited her to dinner. Mrs Cheyney begins to have scruples: all these people are so nice, they have such charming manners, it would be a pity to harm them. The rest of the gang do not take long to talk her out of this benevolent mood.

Act II begins to the strain of Noël Coward's 'Poor Little Rich Girl', a characteristic twenties touch, and is set in Mrs Ebley's country house where her guests come out from dinner. While bridge is played everyone speculates about Lord Pilco and his obvious designs on Mrs Cheyney. The pair of them are at that moment enjoying a romantic tête-à-tête in the garden. Is she, wonders a guest, flirting with Pilco merely to encourage Dilling? Once again Dilling finds himself alone with Mrs Cheyney. In the course of this return match he confesses that he is desperately in love with her. 'To me,' he says, 'the idea of marriage has always been the death and burial of all romance in one's life! And God knows I have done all I can to persuade you that is so, but you don't agree. Very well, as I like you so much — ' He is ready, now, to offer the supreme sacrifice: marriage. And he makes the lover's classic declaration: 'For the first time, I don't understand myself; I'm unhappy when I'm not with you; I'm unhappy when I am!' Still she keeps him at arm's length and still she meets his pleading with ironic banter.

After this frustrating encounter Dilling remembers where he has seen Charles before: it was at Monte Carlo, and Charles was a crook, an amusing rogue with an Oxford accent. He suspects what is afoot and, fabricating an ingenious excuse, persuades Mrs Ebley to exchange rooms with him, for she keeps her pearl necklace at her bedside. At three o'clock that morning the door opens and Mrs Cheyney appears. He knows what she has come for and confronts her with the knowledge that he can identify Charles her butler. Over a bottle of champagne they duel once more. Even though he has penetrated her secret he still adores her. Despite her angry pleas he refuses to unlock the door. She calls his bluff by ringing the servants' bell and throwing champagne over him. He retaliates by slapping her face. Mrs Ebley and Lord Pilco enter, astonished. In a last attempt to protect her Dilling claims that he invited Mrs Cheyney to the room so that he could seduce her. But she, defiant, avows bluntly that she came to steal the necklace.

The rewritten third act, a product of Freddy Lonsdale's lunchtime inspiration, depends for its resolution of an apparently insoluble crux on the device of a letter. It appears that the dim Lord Pilco has not only been foolish enough to ask Mrs Cheyney to marry him: he has also put his proposal in writing together with very unflattering, if not libellous, comments on each one of the other house guests. He dislikes them all and has only tolerated their company for the sake of being with her. Dilling suggests that Pilco buy back the letter in order to prevent their being exposed to ridicule when Mrs Cheyney comes up in court. Will she accept a return ticket to Australia and a hundred pounds? No, says Mrs Cheyney, she and Charles are ready for gaol. Anyway, she doesn't come from Australia . . . she comes from Clapham, and she wants ten thousand pounds for the letter. Pilco writes the cheque. She promptly tears it up, just, she tells them, as she tore up his imprudent letter this morning. Then Mrs Cheyney reveals that she it was who rang the bell and delivered herself into their hands. As a girl she had been a shop assistant, she goes on, who wanted lovely things and the glamour of society. Her dear friend Charles took her in hand and trained her up for a life of crime. The other guests relent, impressed by her honesty and relieved that they will not now be made to look fools in public. Lord Pilco even offers to set her up in a shop. Charles tells Dilling that after Eton and Oxford he found life very dull. Starting, in a small way, as a blackmailer, he gradually worked up to bigger prizes. He returns Dilling's gold watch that he stole from him five years ago in Monte Carlo. 'My dear Charles,' replies his victim, 'I've always wanted to meet the man who took it, and I hope you will do me a favour – keep it!' Charles does and makes a gracious exit to regretful adieux from Mrs Cheyney. She turns to Dilling and remarks that he has made an honest woman of her. 'I've always believed that most of the good things done in this life were unintentional,' he assures her. He flourishes a marriage licence and kisses her eyes:

MRS CHEYNEY: What's that?
ARTHUR: That is the last of Mrs Cheyney.
MRS CHEYNEY: I'm so glad. (*He embraces her and kisses her on the lips.*) What's that?
ARTHUR: That's the beginning of Lady Dilling.

The Last of Mrs Cheyney had a shock value in the 1920s which it does not possess today. It was then thought very novel for a product of Eton and Oxford to be a crook, and a butler who spoke with the accent of the upper classes was something quite audacious. Yet Lonsdale's construction and dialogue remain effective. Interest is sustained and expectation aroused. The audience wants to know what happens next. Indeed, after the curtain to the second act there seems to be no play left, and the third act is a sparkling example of

Lonsdale's gift for the unexpected twist. As for the acting, Gerald and Gladys Cooper made an exquisite partnership. Their three scenes alone together were played with unerring delicacy, cleverly paced and imbued with a teasing quality that hinted at true emotion. They made it all look so simple. But it was not. 'Lonsdale is not easy to play,' says Rex Harrison, who is in the line of direct descent from Gerald. 'I'd rather have Bernard Shaw any day. Shaw worked for his actors: Lonsdale made them work for him. He gives you practically nothing: he wrote in a weird style all his own.'

There were ovations at the end of the first performance on that September night in 1925. Ronald Squire showed himself to be the ideal Lonsdale exponent in his portrayal of the butler's rascal charm. Did Gerald ever regret not having chosen to play the part? The audience refused to go until Lonsdale made a speech. Dragged, with much reluctance, on to the stage, he said, mischievously: 'Ladies and gentlemen, this morning I composed a most brilliant little speech to make to you this evening, but this afternoon I read it to Sir Gerald du Maurier in his dressing-room. He liked it so much that he insists on making it himself.' At which he turned and left. Gerald, utterly taken aback as Freddy intended, gaped in silence. Then he pulled himself together and, in a rusty tenor, croaked the song which had been heard in the first act:

> I want to be happy
> But I can't be happy
> Till I've made you happy too.

A short while before the memorable first night of *Cheyney* he went into a nursing home. He had been feeling, as he would have put it, a little 'seedy', and the Italian holiday did not seem to have done him much good. Doctors advised, consultants diagnosed, surgeons probed. It was, they told him, nothing to worry about, a minor condition which would soon right itself after a small surgical intervention to help it along. He hoped that their expensive opinions were justified.

These days, it may be, he did not have quite the same vitality as before. He was, after all, fifty-two, which was not middle age: it was being old. The threshold of middle age is thirty and he had long since passed that ominous mark. Yet he still played a ferocious game of tennis and spent strenuous days on the golf course and sat up late at night and early into the morning drinking brandy and playing cards. He smoked, his family thought, much more than was good for him.

Yet he refused to grow old. The tennis racket was flourished with grim force and the golf-club handled with stern resolution. He got more breathless than he used to but would not admit it. Secretly he acknowledged the onset of the years by giving up his reign at Wyndham's. The operation and the loss of *Cheyney* through his expensive nap had convinced him that he could not go on. He went into partnership with Gilbert Miller whom he had come to know and like during the production of *Cheyney*, and became his associate at the St James's Theatre.

Before, however, he moved over to the St James's there was one last production at Wyndham's, now under the sole charge of the invalid Frank Curzon, that proved to be a rewarding swan-song. It came about through an unusual chance and linked him with a partner who, at first sight, would appear to be the most improbable of collaborators for him. He happened to read a newspaper article entitled 'The Canker in Our Midst'. It was a blustering attack on the immorality of modern times and hinted, in particular, at the depraved habits of certain well-known theatrical figures. Gerald, who had conventional sexual tastes, secretly approved of such views, and, especially since the arrival of Noël Coward, believed also that the theatre was plunging into degeneracy. He detested homosexuality and always avoided, wherever possible, engaging actors whom he suspected of harbouring the tendency.* On the other hand, as the head of his profession, he was anxious to protect it and to make it 'respectable' in the eyes of society. He telephoned the author of the article whose name was Edgar Wallace.

Wallace held an unrivalled position as England's most famous and prolific novelist. The critic who once made the often quoted remark that 'It is impossible not to be thrilled by Edgar Wallace' spoke for millions of people throughout the country. His industry was astounding and the number of books and plays he wrote can only be rivalled by the equally fertile Alexandre Dumas – with this exception, that while Dumas employed a factory of 'ghosts' to keep up his productivity, every word that appeared under Edgar's name had been written, or dictated, by himself. Such was his prolificacy that people began to joke about 'the monthly Wallace' and then 'the weekly Wallace'. Soon they were talking of 'the midday Wallace'.

---

* This accounts for the gratified astonishment of Eric Portman when he learned that Gerald had engaged him for the revival of *Diplomacy* in 1933. Portman was notoriously gay and had a taste for coprophagy. Gerald knew this but paid him what must have been the supreme professional compliment by taking him on nonetheless.

'Hello, Sir Gerald,' said Wallace in answering the telephone, 'I hoped you'd ring up. Of course, you've had my letter.'

Gerald was taken aback. Prepared to remonstrate with the author of the sensational article and to defend the slur on his profession, he had not been expecting this friendly response. In any case, he had received no such letter. Edgar explained that he had written to him care of Wyndham's. They agreed to meet for lunch the next day. As they dawdled over soup, Edgar talking fast and excitedly all the time, Gerald saw the vulgarian he at first suspected. By the time the main course sat on the table his reserve had melted under the warmth of Edgar's haughty charm. At coffee and brandy they were speaking like old friends. Edgar's letter to him concerned a play he had just written, a crime melodrama featuring a villain whose identity was not disclosed until the final minutes of the last act. Gerald would be prevented from taking the part since, obviously, his appearance as star would give the game away too soon. Still, he was intrigued by Edgar and by his play. The only small criticism he had to make concerned the title. *The Gaunt Stranger*, title of the novel on which Edgar based his plot, was rather dull, he thought. Why not, he suggested with infinite box-office wisdom, call it *The Ringer*?

Edgar Wallace came into this life as the bastard son of a small-part Cockney actress in Greenwich. Since her career made it difficult for her to bring up a small child she boarded him out with the wife of a Billingsgate fish porter at five shillings a week. There came a time when she could no longer afford even this small sum and thought of sending the infant to an orphanage. The warm-hearted foster mother, who knew what such institutions were like, protested that she would keep him free of charge as one of her own family. It already numbered ten children and lived, together with her fish porter husband, in a four-roomed cottage. By the age of eleven the boy was obsessed with the stage. He sold newspapers in Ludgate Circus, where a plaque now records that 'he knew wealth and poverty', and on the proceeds haunted the cheap seats at local theatres. A gallery ticket cost fourpence, a bottle of ginger-beer a penny, and, given another penny for the tram ride home, sixpence would cover a good evening's entertainment.

He worked as a printer's apprentice, a cabin boy, a milk rounds-man, a builder's labourer. Then he joined the army and, for the first time, enjoyed regular meals and regular pay. The evenings were given over to the theatre. A first little triumph came his way when the popular comedian Arthur Roberts sang a song he had written for him. It was called 'A Sort of a Kind of a – !' Edgar went absent without leave to hear him sing it one night. On his return to Aldershot he found himself sentenced to ninety-six hours' hard labour. The penalty was cheerfully paid and thought well worth it for the sublime happiness of hearing his words sung in public.

On a posting to South Africa he began contributing in his spare time to magazines and wrote jingoistic poems which Kipling himself read with approval. Gradually he slipped into journalism, reported the Boer War as a freelance, departed from the army to become editor of the *Rand Daily Mail* and formed a connection with the *Daily Mail* in London. Back in England he was appointed editor of the *Evening News* and, in between, wrote a novel called *The Four Just Men*. With the irrepressible self-confidence that marked all his ventures he was convinced it would be a best-seller. To make absolutely sure he published and advertised it himself. He took a whole page in the *News Of The World* and other papers, arranged for posters to be displayed all over London, and offered prizes totalling five hundred pounds to readers who solved the mystery set by what he immodestly described as 'a story of enthralling interest'. Unfortunately too many of them did, and the prize money and advertising expenses engulfed all his profits. In the end he persuaded his employer, Alfred Harmsworth, to advance him the amount he owed and repaid it with monthly deductions from his salary.

Not long afterwards Harmsworth found cause to regret his benevolent gesture. Edgar's exuberant style of journalism involved the newspaper magnate in two very expensive libel suits, one of them with the giant Lever soap company which extracted heavy damages from the *Daily Mail*. Edgar, decided Harmsworth with little reluctance, must go. No other newspaper would employ him, since, despite his brilliance, he was considered unreliable. What next? He turned for advice to the Bible, opened it at random and dropped a key on the page. It came to rest on that chapter of Ezekiel which read: 'Thus saith the Lord God, set on a pot, set it on, and also pour water into it . . . make it boil well . . .' Here was unmistakable advice from on high to write a pot-boiler. He thought of his recent newspaper assignment reporting atrocities in the Belgian Congo and put together *Sanders of the River*. Another source of ideas was racing. This had long fascinated him as much as did the theatre. The raffish atmosphere and the possibility of winning huge sums of money mesmerised him. He placed his bets with the same harebrained nonchalance that inspired his handling of fact in the journalism he wrote. Yet he remained the classic punter, devoted to the study of form and believing, with pathetic credulity, in the hot tips supposed to be passed on direct from the stable. However much money he lost, and he threw away vast amounts even when he owned horses himself, hope always sprang eternal when the starting gate lifted.

Usually he rose at six o'clock in the morning after a deep sleep of five hours or so, which was all he needed, and put on a dressing-gown ready for work. He and his writing table became shrouded in a heavy mist from the cigarettes he chain-smoked through a long holder. These holders were made in dozens to his favourite specification and kept the smoke out of his eyes while he worked. By eight o'clock a pile of handwritten sheets and dictaphone cylinders awaited his secretary. He took time off for a bath and returned to his desk. Constant smoking made him so thirsty that he drank large quantities of tea, heavily sweetened and much diluted with milk. A fresh pot was made every half-hour to satisfy his appetite. All he needed to keep him going was a desk and chair, a dictating machine and unlimited supplies of cigarettes and tea. In later years he added a glass screen which protected him on three sides from the draughts to which he thought himself especially vulnerable. Before he dictated a story he would have worked out a broad sketch in his mind. Apart from this he had no idea how the tale would unfold. Unplanned developments occurred to him as he went along, and he seized on them to give his plot new interest. When writing a serial he did not know, any more than his readers did, what the next instalment would bring forth. Everything depended on the agility of his imagination. The flow of invention went unchecked. A friend once bet that he could not dictate a novel in the course of a weekend. Edgar accepted the bet and won.

In the early days he was not above strewing veiled advertisements throughout his stories. One of them concerned a vital murder clue which happened to be a carton of insect powder manufactured by a well-known firm. For this he received twenty-five pounds. Another, more ingenious device netted him two hundred pounds. Soon, though, he did not need to do this because he was the greatest best-seller of his time, if not of all time. His flow was unstoppable. As in the novels of Agatha Christie, the characters are cut from the flimsiest of pasteboard, the psychology is crude and the style hackneyed. Interest lies wholly in the tantalising mystery propounded and in the swift action of the plot. Journalism had trained him in writing to a deadline, capturing the reader's attention immediately and holding it until the very end. His formula worked. In 1928 he was making fifty thousand pounds a year.

He spent it all. Extravagant, as generous to others as he was to himself, he bought a vast country home and staffed it with twenty servants. In a strange fit of economy he moved his London headquarters from a luxurious flat in Portland Place to a suite at the Carlton Hotel. Every day he spent a minimum of a hundred pounds on racing bets as well as keeping up a large stable of horses which ran under his own colours. He loved making lavish gifts to others. His sense of drama was gratified when he astonished a friend with the present of a handsome cheque or an exotic holiday for no other reason than that he enjoyed making sensational gestures. In three days at Ascot he once lost twenty thousand pounds. It did not worry him.

A few days' work easily recouped all he had lost since he was producing books at the rate of two a month. The photograph by which his readers knew him showed pallid features, a hawkish nose, a long cigarette-holder clenched between thin lips. The eyes were cold and hooded, the eyes of a gambler. He still had not lost his passion for the theatre and contributed sketches to revues where his sense of topicality brought him many a reward. The theatre, for him, was as thrilling a gamble as the racecourse, and as instant. By the time of the first interval you knew if you had a success or a failure on your hands. Books took a little longer. He wanted very much to be a dramatist. Already he had written several plays, none of them a hit despite his strongest endeavours which included, on one occasion, a machine which recorded the number and length of laughs scored with the audience. He was more than ready to learn from Gerald.

The two unlikely collaborators, the bastard Cockney and the Old Harrovian, set to work on *The Ringer*. Who was this mysterious figure?

His exploits had terrified London. He had killed ruthlessly, pur-poselessly, if his motive were one of personal vengeance. Men who had good reason to hate and fear him, had gone to bed, hale and hearty, snapping their fingers at the menace, safe in the consciousness that their houses were surrounded by watchful policemen. In the morning they had been found stark and dead. The Ringer, like the dark angel of death, had passed and withered them in their prime.

Edgar enjoyed crooks. Villains are more interesting than honest people and easier to write about. He saw them at racecourses and, as a journalist, relished their company. The society of thieves, con-men and shady tipsters amused him and supplied valuable material for plots. Sometimes he would give them a fiver in exchange for the anecdotes they passed on to him. Once, asked to do a burglar a favour, he innocently found himself a receiver of stolen goods. Yet although he dreamed of one day unearthing a master crook, a Napoleon of crime such as he often depicted in his novels, he never did. The supporting cast of *The Ringer*, therefore, was made up of the small-time practitioners whom he knew through experience and through the medium of the *Police Journal*. The most substantial figure is the crooked lawyer Maurice Meister. He flourishes by defending criminals on apparently hopeless charges and, through his intimate knowledge of defects in the law, bringing off acquittals. How is he paid for his advocacy? From, it is said, the proceeds of robberies carried out by his clients, though no one can prove this. 'A sallow, thin-faced man with dark fathomless eyes, there was something of the aristocrat in his manner and speech. "He looks like a duke, talks like a don and thinks like the devil," was not the most unflattering thing that had been said about Maurice Meister.' We know he is a crook because he has an un-English name, lounges about the house wearing a pale green dressing-gown, plays the piano exquisitely and smokes cigarettes through an amber holder. His villainy is confirmed when he takes a pinch of white powder from a gold box in his pocket and sniffs it. The bounder is a cocaine addict.

More representative of the humble burglars Edgar actually knew is the old lag Sam Hackitt. This cheerful Cockney imbued with a nonchalant cynicism has unexpected interests. In a discussion about history with the golden-coiffed heroine he remarks: 'I don't take any notice of history – that's lies, too. Lor', Miss, you don't know all the hist'ry books I've read – 'ume, Macaulay, Gibbons, the feller that wrote all about Rome.'

'You've read them, Sam?'

'Studied 'em.'

'You're quite a student: I didn't realise you were such a well-read man.'

'You have to do something in stir.'

The one flaw in the existence of the otherwise contented history student and snapper-up of unconsidered trifles is Mrs Hackitt. She is a shrew that cannot be tamed, a virago who pursues him along Deptford High Street broadcasting his imperfections in a shrill voice to passers-by. He contemplates emigration to Canada and, for that purpose, burgles Meister's home in search of his cash-box. Unfortunately he chooses the very night when the Ringer calls to murder the lawyer.

Sir Gerald

The Ringer was thrown off, as usual with Edgar, in a matter of days. Gerald put it into rehearsal, rewriting and adjusting as he went along. In Gerald's hands the play became a neat and economical affair, each scene tautly organised and leading on breathlessly to the next revelation. There were no loose ends, no improbabilities to distract the attention, and the plot developed with rigorous logic up to the supreme moment when the charming old Scottish police doctor snatched off his grey wig and showed himself to be none other than the vengeful Ringer. In performance this scene came as a totally unexpected incident and scored the maximum dramatic impact. The only man not to be hoodwinked by Gerald's cunning happened to be that wily old bird Sir James Barrie. Gerald invited him to the dress rehearsal thinking it would be useful to have his technical opinion. Barrie sat through the play in utter silence. At the final curtain Edgar asked him what he thought. The artful dramatist had much to praise. He added: 'What impresses me most is the original and skilful way you take the audience into your confidence so that *they* know from the start who the criminal is: and yet the excitement is sustained throughout the play!' Edgar was shattered. The whole point of the drama lay in the unexpected disclosure of the villain. As soon as the curtain went up Barrie had predicted to himself that the next person to sit in a certain chair would be the disguised culprit. He was right. Fortunately subsequent audiences possessed neither his uncanny stagecraft nor his malice.

The part of the Ringer was taken by Leslie Faber, an Old Bensonian of elusive charm and a versatility that enabled him to play the whiskery Scottish doctor as convincingly as he did graceful heroes. He died young soon afterwards and is not much remembered now. Leslie Banks, who had a slight facial imperfection that gave his handsome features a rugged pathos and an air of silent command, played a tenacious detective alongside Nigel Bruce as a well-meaning police inspector. Mrs Hackitt, raucous and unforgiving, was Naomi Jacob, a name better known in the field of popular literature than the stage. She began as an actress specialising in character parts. Ill health dictated early retirement from the theatre and exile in Italy where she wrote a stream of novels and autobiographies that had many admirers at the time. She once played a cook opposite C. Aubrey Smith and had, in a comic scene, to catch a lemon he threw at her. He launched it with a slight off-spin and she always, to his delight, caught it immaculately. As an author she was a 'character' herself with her short black hair, heavy horn-rimmed glasses, mannish suits and, occasionally, a cigar. Her husband in *The Ringer*, Sam Hackitt, was the real discovery of the play, an actor called Gordon Harker, member of the well-known scene designing family. This was the earliest of the character rôles for which he became famous, that of the wry Cockney who is never startled by the depths to which human nature can descend. The bored eyes had seen it all before, the ears had heard every possible excuse that could be trumped up. The lower lip jutted out from a frog-like face in a permanent sneer of disbelief. Whether inside the law or out, the world-weary visage regarded everyone with sly mistrust. The reluctant Cockney whine gave a characteristic edge to his utterance. Edgar tailored many such parts for him. An extensive career impersonating low criminals, dubious bookies and copper's narks brought Harker prosperity and an expensive Knightsbridge address.

The Ringer opened in May 1926, just after the start of a coal strike. Within a few days the general strike swung into full blast. There were no newspapers and no public transport, so that prospective audiences could neither read about the play nor travel to Wyndham's. Edgar raged bitterly. At the very moment when every auspice was good and theatrical success looked like being his at last, circumstances appeared to be ruining everything. He remembered what he once had written of the playwright's lot:

> For months his hopes and ambitions have been centred upon this child of his; he has watched it develop in the hands of the producer, and has gone to the theatre for the first night full of faith. And halfway through the evening, or probably before, his heart begins to sink. Instinctively he knows that this *tour de force* of his has, in some way, failed to realise his rosy hopes.

But *The Ringer* did not let him down. Early in the evening Edgar saw that the triumph he had worked for so long had been granted him. Curtain calls were lengthy and ecstatic. A long run, in the event more than four hundred performances, could safely be predicted. After the first night he gave one of his splendid parties at the Carlton with over a hundred guests. His total royalties amounted to seven thousand pounds, half of which, in a typically warm-hearted action, he gave to Gerald as acknowledgment of what he had done to help bring about the success. He noted, however, that Frank Curzon put up the money for the production and, as a result, drew thirty thousand pounds from his investment. This made him thoughtful. In future Edgar did the same and financed and managed all his own plays. Over the next half-dozen years he wrote and produced seventeen of them. They earned him a hundred thousand pounds. He no longer had trouble in paying the rent of his Portland Place flat which, at a time when the average weekly wage amounted to something less than a pound, he had taken at an annual rent of sixteen hundred.

Soon afterwards he hit on an idea for another play which he hoped to do with Gerald. It hinged upon a particularly abstruse point in racing procedure and had been the subject of a friendly test case he brought in the Chancery Division. The problem involved the rule that if an owner died before a classic race was run the horse he had entered should automatically be withdrawn and a forfeit paid. In the play the hero deliberately arranges for his mount to lose at Ascot because among its rivals is a horse which will obviously beat it, the trick being to enter it for another race which does not include the rival so that it will start at a long price and win a substantial sum. The plot was garnished with blackmail, a beautiful but treacherous heroine, a great deal of racing lore and Gordon Harker as a one-time burglar transformed into a butler. Edgar offered it to Gerald inviting him to direct and to take the part of the hero.

Gerald had reluctantly to turn it down.

Dear old Edgar [he wrote], I have got myself into such awful trouble lately with authors promising to do their plays and then not doing them that I shall soon be cut by the county . . . In the meantime, what we consider a very good play has come to hand, which can go straight into rehearsal, and I think that to be the wisest thing to do. I think you are an extraordinary brick, seeing that I was in a hole, to gallop the play through for me the way you did, and I am tremendously grateful, but then you are a very great friend in need.

That, though, was not the last Gerald heard of *The Calendar*, as Edgar had entitled his new play. After it had been produced by another hand a Mr Lewis Goldflam, a manufacturer of cardboard boxes who wrote under the name of L. C. Gould-Flème, accused Edgar of plagiarism. The plot of *The Calendar*, he declared, was stolen from his own novel called *Lucky Fool*, and Edgar showed himself to be no more than 'a mean cribber'. The novel was published some time before *The Calendar*, although it had taken Mr Goldflam, alias Gould-Flème, six months after the opening night to make his claim and circulate his letter to many well-known people. Edgar brought an action for libel and Gerald featured among his witnesses in court.

His letter was quoted and he testified that *The Calendar* had been ready for the stage some months before the appearance of the novel. Edgar won his case easily and Mr Goldflam, not so lucky as the hero in his work of fiction, retired into obscurity. At the same time, pursued by annoying accusations that he used a factory of 'ghosts' to sustain his phenomenal production rate, Edgar seized the opportunity to issue a public challenge offering a reward of five thousand pounds if this charge could be proved. No one dared take him up on it.

For a while, thanks to *The Ringer*, Gerald had much money in the bank. Now, said his family, was the time to buy that home in the country they had been dreaming about. Mo and the girls took the train to Cornwall and, at Bodinnick, saw the very house they wanted. It was called Swiss Cottage, a name which, to lofty denizens of Hampstead, recalled suburbia. They quickly renamed it Ferryside. After six months of enthusiastic labours they turned into a charming retreat what had once been a derelict sail-making workshop on the edge of the river. Walls came down. The stream which flowed through the ground floor was diverted. The boat store changed into a sitting-room and the sail loft was metamorphosed as bedrooms and bathroom. Chintzes were bought, and new carpets and curtains while Gerald benignly disgorged his proceeds from *The Ringer*.

The play he spoke about in his letter to Edgar was called *Interference*. It had been written by Roland Pertwee and Harold Dearden, a team who often worked together. On his own, Pertwee was responsible for a number of West End pieces, the most successful being *Pink String and Sealing Wax*. There may even be people who can remember the early television soap opera he devised about the adventures of the Grove family which, featuring a quite awful grandmother, complied efficiently with the requirements of a new populist medium. *Interference* had an excellent part for Gerald as a Harley Street specialist. Into his life comes Philip Voaze, his wife's former lover and ex-husband whom everyone thought, wrongly, to have been killed in the war. Voaze is now carrying on an affair with another woman who starts to blackmail the specialist's wife and threatens disclosure of the love letters she sent Voaze during their affair. Sir John Marley, the husband, has a dramatic interview with her and declares: 'You are interfering with the happiness of myself and the woman I love, and I mean to put a stop to that interference – permanently.' His wife, however, determines to resolve the situation by murdering Voaze with prussic acid. Somehow, by coincidences which only the most ingenious dramatist could have imagined, Voaze gets possession of the phial. After a violent disagreement with his blackmailing mistress he contrives in a moment of fury to kill her with it. Sir John Marley arrives, discovers the corpse, assumes that his wife is the murderer and rearranges the evidence so as to give the impression of suicide. But while he suspects his wife, she, at the same time, suspects him. In an effort to protect him she claims responsibility for the crime. Husband and wife are cleared when Voaze, doing the decent thing, owns up and is taken into custody. As the *Play Pictorial* demurely remarked, 'there is ample material in *Interference* for an evening of sustained excitement.'

Interference, which Gerald presented in joint management with Gilbert Miller at the St James's, ran for over a year. This was largely due to the scene, played in complete silence, where Gerald as Sir John sought to fake an alibi for his wife. After a long look at the dead woman he inferred the cause of her death. Having put on gloves to conceal any fingerprints, he wiped the rim of the tumbler which had contained prussic acid. Then he slowly decanted the remains of the liquid into a flower-bowl, after which he placed, with meticulous gestures, the emptied phial between the corpse's fingers. John Gielgud well remembers *Interference* and how Gerald 'played a long dumb-show scene in which he found a murdered woman before the police arrived. It was a ten-minute episode during which he kept the house enthralled. If only he had brought such skill and expertise to Ibsen and Chekhov!' James Agate wrote:

One might say that Sir Gerald du Maurier's performance gives infinite pleasure. But that would be to speak loosely. His acting last night gave one pleasure of a finite, definite, almost concrete sort. You could pin down, and nail to the counter, each and every one of its many admirable qualities – vigour, ease, precision, attack, balance. He did what only an actor of extreme accomplishment could have done; he remained ten minutes alone on the stage without speaking. There are other rôles besides the philosopher's in which one can be bounded in a nutshell, and count oneself a king of infinite space.

The evil Voaze was acted by Herbert Marshall, or 'Bart' as he was known to his five wives of whom Edna Best was the second. In youth a reluctant trainee accountant, he made his first stage appearance at Buxton Opera House and played a hundred or so parts in the London theatre before becoming a permanent fixture in Hollywood. He had lost a leg in the war but arranged his movements nonetheless with elegance and precision. Suave, round-faced, speaking with ripe enunciation, he usually embodied sympathetic rôles in which his rather startled expression bespoke sincerity and warmth. Voaze must have been one of the few villainous parts he ever took, and for it he dyed his then black hair with becoming streaks of grey. Although genuine grey hairs came quickly enough, they served only to enhance the aura of amiability which he radiated with seeming naturalness.

Soon after *Interference* began its run in January 1927, Gerald directed Gladys Cooper in *The Letter* which Somerset Maugham had adapted from his short story. Beverley Nichols happened to watch him at rehearsals and was impressed by Gerald's way of doing things. He witnessed, he later wrote,

> a curious sight – a sort of human chameleon, marching up and down the stage, changing the entire colour of his personality according to the rôle which he is for the moment illustrating. For when he is producing he plays any part at a second's notice. He can change his sex more easily than I can change my trousers, and listen to the amorous declarations of a juvenile lead as though he really liked it. He can precipitate himself into a state of hysteria with the speed of a sporting Bugatti, and the moment afterwards is playing a love scene with admirable timing and sentiment . . . For one thing, he does not impress his own version of the rôle upon any actor until it is absolutely necessary to do so. One hears this sort of tuition: 'Just a minute, old chap. I shouldn't make this man quite such a brute if I were you. After all, he is supposed to be an attractive sort of stiff. Couldn't you – well – like this?' And then the human chameleon steps forward, the face alters, the voice alters, and you have a beautiful little cameo of acting . . . If I myself had to do that sort of thing for a living, on a cold, dusty stage, before a quantity of strangers, I should throw myself into the Thames; but that is beside the point. The point is that du Maurier does it extremely well.

Gerald's direction of *The Letter* was eased by Maugham's willingness, unusual in a dramatist, to alter his work if necessary. A curtain line gave trouble, and both Gerald and Gladys decided that something had to be done about it. Maugham was told of the problem. 'If you don't feel it's right,' he answered agreeably, 'change it.' He would even attend rehearsals prepared to censor anything that might not work. 'I've had so many of my lines cut that I think I shall collect them together and make a whole play of them some day,' he commented.

For once he lived up to the image of the resigned man of the world he always strove to project.

Within a few months Gerald again visited the Chancery Division where he had lately given evidence for Edgar Wallace's libel case. Sir Squire Bancroft, who had died at last aged eighty-four, left him in his will all the rights to *Diplomacy*.* Ten days before his death Bancroft sold the film rights through an agent to an American company for fifteen hundred pounds. Whose was this sum: Gerald's or the other beneficiaries under the will? The court decided for Gerald. Six years later, at the Prince's Theatre, he revived the old thing with himself in his original part. Although the speeches were discreetly modernised for a 1930s audience, the construction of the ancient melodrama remained so sturdy that it once more succeeded in thrilling those who saw it.

So many of Gerald's friends both old and young were now dead or dying. A few weeks after the Bancroft will had been settled Gerald's comrade and mentor Frank Curzon died at the age of fifty-nine. Like Sir Squire, he left what was then a fortune of over a hundred and eighty thousand pounds, in his case the harvest not only of long-sighted theatrical management but also, uniquely, of lucrative racing stables. But leave-takings were not always sorrowful. There was the supper Gerald presided over at the Garrick in honour of Sir Johnston Forbes-Robertson. Affection, wit and humour flowed warmly. At the end of it all 'Forbie' rose to his feet and gave a speech. Though well over eighty his noble voice had lost none of its plangency, the syllables were as crisp as when he played a youthful Romeo. He spoke without notes and recalled events amusing and touching in his career. In conclusion he referred to the beautiful ladies with whom he had been privileged to act. 'How those dear names crowd in upon me!' he said, quoting the names of Mary Anderson, Madame Modjeska, Kate Rourke, Mrs Patrick Campbell, Genevieve Ward. 'And last but, oh, not least,' he added, 'the lovely lady who has been my inspiration and my comrade in so many theatre ventures, my dear wife – eh – h'm . . .' Alas, he could not remember the name of his dear wife. He stood in silent perplexity, a look of baffled surprise on his face. Would he miss his cue? Perfectly timed, from the president's chair, came Gerald's

---

* The only slightly disapproving remark Sir Squire ever made to his favourite protégé Gerald occurred when the latter played in *The Admirable Crichton*. It dealt, he said gloomily, 'with the juxtaposition of the drawing-room and the servants' hall, always to me a painful subject'.

discreet prompt: 'Easy does it, Forbie – Gertrude Elliott!' The old gentleman smiled in relief as everyone stood up and cheered.

Gerald could not visualise himself at the age of eighty. It was a prospect he wanted to ignore, and the advancing years filled him with anguish. At fifty-five he still felt like the baby of the family. He was the youngest son who never grew up, a Peter Pan whose figure was as lithe as it had been in his twenties, the hair but lightly flecked with grey, the eyes clear, the step light. Yet the skin of his face had roughened, there were wrinkles on his forehead, a suspicion of jowl marred the once clear line of his chin. The bitter truth that he had grown into an ageing man was driven home to him by Gracie Fields.

In 1928 the girl from Lancashire was England's most bankable star. She sang and danced and clowned to the pleasure of millions who worshipped her, and she earned six hundred pounds a week. During the run of *Mr Tower of London*, a revue with which she captivated the town, a calling card embossed with the name of Sir Gerald du Maurier was handed in to her dressing-room. It bore the message: 'I would like to see you.' Impressed, flattered, she had him shown in. He said he wanted her as his leading lady in his next play.

'Me?' she gasped.

'Yes,' he replied. 'I want you to play the part of Lady Weir in *SOS*.'

With her Lancashire accent, she argued, she could never be a posh lady. She must, he agreed, speak in her normal voice. How big, she asked, was the part?

'I'll send it to you tomorrow.'

'Right. I'll measure it.'

'*Measure* it?'

'Yes, I'll measure the speeches; if they're not too long, I know I'll be able to keep up the right sort of voice without dropping back into Lancashire.'

Years ago his spur-of-the-moment decision to engage Gladys Cooper for *Diplomacy* had startled everyone but, in the event, confounded those who foresaw disaster. Now he planned to do the same thing with Gracie Fields.

On their second meeting she wore her favourite tartan kilt, a purple Hungarian blouse, a fur coat and a Scots Tam o' Shanter. After a stunned silence Gerald walked round and round her murmuring: 'Good God! . . . Good God! . . . Good God! . . . Why a kilt?'

'I like 'em.'

'And the . . . the blouse?'

'I like that too. I like anything with a bit of colour.'

She told him she had measured the part and could do it. At the first rehearsal in the St James's Gladys Cooper and Tallulah Bankhead looked on. 'Do you mind, darling,' said Tallulah sweetly, 'I love to watch people closely at rehearsals.'

Gracie, nervous and sick at heart, was led to a chair and Gerald gave her the cue: 'Are you all right, darling?' He bent over and kissed her at length. The kiss was not in the script, and, not knowing what to do, she took out her handkerchief, blew her nose and wiped her mouth. The watching actresses tittered.

Determinedly she worked her way through the lines. Then he sent her off with Viola Tree to observe a real Duchess who happened at the time to be running a Mayfair dress-shop. She returned and mimicked the accent so faithfully that he shook with laughter. She dined at Cannon Hall and visited the Cornwall home they called Ferryside. On the lawn she flipped cartwheels and rowed out across the harbour singing in her strong Northern voice. When she got back she offered to buy the place and suggested a very large sum. Gerald, politely, refused, and asked her to perform some of his favourite ballads instead.

SOS had a fair run which it chiefly owed to the presence of Gracie Fields. Gerald's unorthodox casting had worked yet again. One evening at Cannon Hall after dinner with Mo and the three girls he was left alone in her company to rehearse. He immediately put his arms round her and kissed her. She let him do so, not liking to push him away. When he withdrew she looked at him and said: 'Ee lad, don't be soft, you're older than me dad!'

He could no longer avoid reality. His eyes, there and then, filled with tears.

THE FALL OF THE CURTAIN

Gracie Fields's bluntness told him something that others, through respect or kindness, had never dared mention. When other actresses said to him, 'Gerald, darling, you don't look a day over thirty,' she would remark, with complete innocence, 'They're real daft, aren't they? You *do*, you know!' He learned to smile ruefully. A photograph of himself he gave her was signed: 'To Gracie, from Old du Maurier.' They lunched every Wednesday at the Green Park Hotel, where, beside her plate, there was always some small present, a lace handkerchief or perfume or flowers or a trinket of jade. She began to wish he had been thirty after all.

King George V came to see *SOS* and spoke with Gerald afterwards in the royal box. Why, asked the King, had he engaged Gracie Fields who didn't seem at first an obvious choice for a straight play? Because, Gerald explained, there was something refreshing and sincere about her: the play was a tragedy, but it took a great comédienne to play great tragedy. 'Yes, du Maurier,' said the King, stroking the royal beard, 'I think I know what you mean.'

Since Gracie, as Lady Weir, 'died' in the first act of *SOS*, she was able to leave in time for the second house at the Alhambra music hall. Afterwards she did late night cabaret at the Café Royal. During the day she made gramophone records. Her vitality astonished Gerald. She belonged, she told him, to music hall, she felt at home there giving people a song and a laugh. Would she ever change her way of speaking? No, she said, that would be daft. 'Grace,' he reflected, 'you're a lucky girl. I wonder if you know just how lucky? You have enough in you not to *have* to change, you *can* stay as you are.'

If he had taught her how to perform in a straight play she, with her blundering sincerity, had taught him an unwelcome but inevitable fact of life. He realised that the actresses he pursued automatically and with such lazy confidence were often the same age as his own daughters, those grown women whom until now he looked on as little girls. His children were no longer children.

They had a world of their own into which he could not enter. When they came back late from parties he would question them, angrily, worriedly, and feel jealous of the young men who dared admire them, who might, horrible thought, venture even to kiss them and take unmentionable liberties. It disturbed him to think that the women whom he stalked also had fathers in the background, perhaps still younger than himself.

He could never resign himself to age and faced life with desperation. One way of relaxing the strain was practical jokes, an immature taste he preserved from youth. His friends would receive fake telegrams bringing news that left them angry and alarmed until they realised that Gerald had been at work. There would be press cuttings, specially printed in secret, which contained ghastly revelations and inspired whole families with dismay. Once he turned up an old photograph of himself as a boy and posted it, with a begging letter from a so-called illegitimate child, to Mo. She was not deceived. 'How absurd you are, darling,' she said quietly, having seen and recognised the photograph from years past.

Even on stage he could not resist these puerilities. He would set clockwork mice hopping over a table and defy the cast not to laugh. Further tests of their endurance came when they sat down at a meal and found that the plates tended to slither mysteriously around or the apple from which they took a large bite was made of soap or the knife bent in their hand. They never knew, if they sank on a couch to play a sentimental episode, whether the cushion would not emit a vulgar squeak. When the plot obliged an actor to sit in a chair and carry on an important piece of dialogue for several minutes without moving, Gerald took infinite pains to arrange for a steady drop of water to fall regularly on the man's forehead. Such tricks, thought Gerald, were very, very funny, and afterwards in his dressing-room fits of laughter reduced him to helpless tears.

There was nothing much to laugh about in his career at that moment. *SOS* was followed by an Arnold Bennett play called *The Return Journey* and based on the Faust theme with Gerald as a modern 'Dr Henry Fausting'. It ran for a month or so. He put on *The Play's The Thing* by Ferenc Molnar, the Hungarian dramatist who never had much success with London audiences until one of his comedies was adapted as the musical *Carousel*. It failed. Then Gerald turned to his old love Audrey Carten. She, with her sister Waveney, had written a play which he thought had possibilities. In *Fame* he was Paolo Gheradi, a violinist who, at the height of his celebrity, is stricken with paralysis and deprived of the virtuoso skill which has earned him renown. Since Waveney had a penchant for high society Acts I and IV of *Fame* were placed among the country house set, as Gheradi is supposed to have married into the hunting and shooting community. They made an odd contrast with the other acts which explored the psychological effect of the disaster on the gifted musician. Daphne du Maurier thinks that in Act III, where Gerald displayed the bitterness of a frustrated artistic temperament, he gave one of his best performances. However penetrating the study it was not what his public expected of him, and the notices went up after little more than a hundred performances.

So they did after a brief revival of *Dear Brutus* which lasted no longer. At Christmas 1929, he played again his old rôles Hook and Darling in *Peter Pan*. Barrie had already made over his royalties from it to the Hospital for Sick Children, and on this occasion a single performance of the nursery scenes was given in the building itself at Great Ormond Street. 'Sir Gerald's impromptu linking-up was delightful,' wrote a journalist, 'and I am sure Sir James, when he slipped in unobtrusively before the start, approved of the way the story was told.' Back in the theatre Gerald managed to rediscover some of his original zest, despite the by now tattered scenery and threadbare costumes.

What a moment it was for those with long memories [exclaimed *The Times*] when there appeared again in the middle of the piratical sledge team that skull-like head with the glittering eyes, when the hornpipe was stepped again with the old dainty diablerie, when again the old Irvingesque mask of horror greeted the defiance of the Doodle-doo in the cabin. There have been so many excellent Hooks, yet only one Hook, and this is the one . . .

This was the last time he played the part he had made so much his own and he was glad to be shot of it. In January 1930, he left with Mo and Angela for a holiday in Italy. The cold winter air made him cough a lot. Or was it no more than the chill that irritated his lungs? He needed the warmth of Sorrento and Capri and Amalfi. At Naples he and his family were received *en prince* by a flagship of the Royal Navy. On Capri the rain poured down with non-stop vehemence and he shivered in icy winds. His return to London was darkened by the pile of income tax demands that awaited him. He had never put money aside, had spent it all as soon as it came in, and now that the good years were over there was nothing to meet the clamant requests of the Inland Revenue, which, like a delayed-action time-bomb, had been ticking away remorselessly until the moment of explosion fell due. His sister-in-law 'Billy', who was also his secretary, came in to show him a final threatening letter. 'I can't be bothered with income tax, Billy dear,' he said. 'They're probably quite decent fellows. Write and tell them I haven't any money.' And he poured himself yet another very large brandy.

Windfalls such as materialised from giving his name to a cigarette were unfortunately rare. 'Du-Maurier cork-tipped', as the brand was called, were sold in square packets of a bright red colour and striped with a large silver band. Advertisements showed a man of vague distinction, neatly moustached, who might have been an ambassador or a high-ranking military officer. Occasionally he wore over his white tie and tails an evening cloak whence glinted the star of some rare knightly order. Always, he carried in his hand a cigarette which had just been lighted. Whether Gerald himself smoked them we do not know. Perhaps not, as the cork tip, he would have found, spoilt the raw tang he needed to feel curling down his throat and into his lungs, a vital stimulus and, at the same time, a very present comfort in moments of stress.

Where could he earn, and quickly, the money to satisfy those fellows at the Inland Revenue and to keep up his two establishments, his family, his social life at the Garrick and the Savoy, his golf, his gentlemanly weekends in the country? He had ended his association with Gilbert Miller and there was no new play in prospect. The cinema might give an answer to the question that harried him during his wakeful nights and stubbornly survived the anaesthetic of brandy. The arrival of the sound film had doubled the number of stage people who appeared before the camera, and in the mid-thirties over sixty per cent of the profession were regularly working in studios. The new medium called for actors and actresses able to speak lines and deliver them in a pleasing tone. The studios were easily reached by car from London, and performers could work there during the day and return in time for the theatre that evening. Gerald was one of the earliest distinguished names to follow this routine, although he did so with reluctance and detested everything it involved.

He was persuaded into films by Basil Dean. This formidable man knew from practical experience every branch of the theatre and, later, of the cinema. As an actor he played in a variety of styles from Shakespeare to Galsworthy. He helped found the Liverpool Repertory Theatre, was technical adviser to Barry Jackson in Birmingham and even survived a strenuous twelve months as assistant to Beerbohm Tree. After the 1914–18 war, a period when he organised entertainments for the services and ran ten touring companies, he went into partnership with a quiet tycoon called Alec Rea. As ReandeaN they formed a prominent theatre management which sponsored some of the finest productions the West End saw in the post-war years, Rea supplying the money and Dean providing vigorous leadership. Dean could not resist a challenge and once, bravely, took on control of Drury Lane, a white elephant that few others would have cared to tackle. During the 1939–45 war he founded and directed ENSA, the Entertainments National Service Association designed to brighten the off-duty hours of the armed forces. It was not his fault that a wag dubbed it 'Every Night Something Awful'.

Dean began making films in 1928. All of Gracie Fields's very successful pictures were directed by him, and he showed a flair for handling others which starred George Formby and Will Hay. Despite working on a small budget he managed to turn out popular films that earned their keep and sometimes made big profits. For a while he was London representative of an American concern but quickly tired of working for an employer and set up his own firm. He plunged into the maze of City finance with the bravado he showed in all his ventures only to discover that one of his fellow promoters was an undischarged bankrupt. So he started all over again and eventually founded not one company but three: Associated Talking Pictures, British Film Distributors and Ealing Studios. He was a big, blustering fellow, impatient to achieve his ends and easily irritated by duller associates who did not at once grasp his drift. The paradox was that his rough exterior and bull-like manner cloaked a personality that was very shy and very sensitive.

He wanted someone of distinction and authority to be chairman of Associated Talking Pictures Limited and he thought of Gerald. There were many visits to Cannon Hall, many exhausting Sunday games of tennis and many roast-beef lunches before Gerald agreed. He disliked films and he disliked commerce which, for him, remained an impenetrable mystery. Dean, as he usually did, got his way and even talked him into playing the major role in *Escape*, a film he based on Galsworthy's play. 'Apart from his money problems, to which the engagement might have provided a partial answer,' Dean later wrote, 'it was a generous gesture on his part, for I knew he hated films . . .'

Gerald was to hate them even more after his experiences with *Escape*. His part was that of a convict who escapes from Dartmoor. One of the scenes showed him fighting with a policeman in Hyde

Park. This was made at night on location with a crowd recruited from among fashionable Londoners to save the expense of hiring extras. A small-part actor dressed as a constable allowed Gerald to knock him down with feeble blows, each take being less convincing than its predecessor while Dean, perched on a rostrum, pitilessly demanded through his megaphone re-take after re-take. By early morning, when nannies were beginning to wheel their prams into the park, Dean wanted to record some hunting songs played by the band of the Welsh Guards whom he had engaged for the purpose. At that moment a determined thrush flew down and sat squarely on the microphone. It sang loudly and ruined all efforts at recording. The exasperated musical director threw a piece of wood at it, missed, and smashed the microphone into pieces, thus ending the day's, or night's, shooting.

Other location shots were just as trying. There was an episode on the banks of the River Dart when Gerald as the convict was supposed to come across a retired judge fishing for trout. The actor who played the part was himself an expert fisherman and insisted on reeling in his prey each time Gerald looked through the bushes. The trout caused endless problems. 'It must have been drowned half a dozen times before we got a satisfactory take,' Dean commented grimly. There was trouble, too, with the elementary sound recording equipment. A gentle breeze came over like a tempest and the soft rustle of leaves created the effect of a thunderstorm. At last the ardours of *Escape* were over and the film was released to critical praise. It had the most notable cast of any English film made up to then, for Dean had raided the West End and called not only on Gerald but also on Madeleine Carroll, Gordon Harker, Felix Aylmer, Edna Best, Nigel Bruce and Ian Hunter. The film turned out an honourable failure and did not recover the forty-two thousand pounds it cost to make. Yet it had other distinctions. Hitchcock's *Blackmail* is usually accepted as the first British talking film, although it was wholly planned and largely made as a silent, the sound being added on re-shooting afterwards. *Escape*, entirely conceived and produced as a talkie, has a greater claim to the honour. And, as Dean stoutly argued ever afterwards, remembering his problems with the intrusive thrush and the booming breeze, it was the earliest sound film to be shot in the English countryside.

That countryside, when Gerald and Mo arrived on Dartmoor, seemed an agreeable enough place. They stayed at a local inn and admired noble prospects. Gerald took his binoculars and went on bird-watching forays. His delight in what had at first seemed like a holiday quickly vanished. As the escaped convict he had to crawl through mud for the benefit of the camera, run along ditches and leap over walls. A cloud passed over the sun and ruined the shot. Again he crawled, ran, leaped. This time the film jammed. Once more he heaved himself over rocks and gulleys. Something was not quite right and Dean ordered a re-take. By this time the sun had gone in and the light was poor, so Gerald, shivering from his exertions, endured several hours' wait until it reappeared. When it came back, too dim and watery for shooting, Dean called a halt. Gerald returned to the inn knowing that yet another day of scrambling through the heather awaited him. He longed for the elegant discipline of the theatre, the warmth of the footlights and an audience. In the theatre you did your piece and walked off. In films you sweated alone save for the presence of a pitiless director and a cynical camera crew. The money, of course, was splendid, but he saw little of it since it went to the Inland Revenue in payment of those cursed back taxes.

Accustomed to a leisurely rise at eleven in the morning, he now had to be up at unheard-of hours. Once arrived on the set he would be condemned to interminable periods of waiting: a previous shot was taking longer than expected, a camera had broken down, a cable had frayed. He lounged about, his face daubed with heavy make-up (in the theatre he only used the lightest of touches), and smoked cigarettes continuously as his nerves grew tauter and tauter. The call would come at last and he had to walk down a passage once, twice, ten times, twenty times until the director was satisfied. He came to loathe the film barracks out at Ealing Green which, factories in truth, were dignified by the name of studios. On the flat roof was painted in big white letters a message warning aeroplanes to keep away. He wished, sometimes, that one would come and drop a friendly bomb on it.

Amid the turmoil and discomfort he kept up a bright façade. He was Sir Gerald du Maurier, famous man of the theatre and a good sport. There were pleasantries with the make-up man, flirtations with the continuity girl, manly badinage with the sound engineer. Practical jokes abounded. The most ingenious tricks he could find at Hamleys were avidly bought and tried out. Clockwork mice alarmed secretaries, flowers spurted water into unsuspecting faces, strange and apparently indelible stains appeared on valuable dresses, chairs collapsed. Tedium was replaced by uproar as baffling telegrams evoked perplexity and outlandish telephone calls sowed apprehension. Gerald discovered a fellow amateur of practical jokes in Alfred Hitchcock when he made *Lord Camber's Ladies* with him.

The director had a morbid talent for devising escapades of thoughtful elaborateness. One Christmas Eve, while Gerald was playing at the St James's Theatre, Hitchcock arranged for a cart-horse to be sent round there as a seasonal present. In Gerald's absence on stage a group of conspirators knocked down a part of the wall to his dressing-room. Gerald came off at the end of the act and saw the large, placid animal staring at him through the hole. Around its neck hung a board which read: 'A Merry Christmas and A Happy New Year.' That horse soon became well-known in various London theatres, for Gerald had it sent on to Herbert Marshall. He, in turn, passed it on to another friend's dressing-room, and the game of pass-the-horse brightened the season more vividly than any Christmas tree.

Lord Camber's Ladies was one of Gerald's better films. It came from a play by the once popular writer Horace Annesley Vachell and told the melodramatic story of a nobleman who marries a music hall actress. Her sudden death is thought to have been caused by poison, and one of her previous lovers is suspected though afterwards cleared. Gertrude Lawrence was the unfortunate wife and Benita Hume played the slighted mistress. In *I Was a Spy*, a true adventure based on the exploits of a heroic Belgian nurse during the 1914–18 war, Gerald had second billing after Conrad Veidt, the German actor of sinister good looks who, after filming, most notably, in his native land *The Cabinet of Dr Caligari*, had a much applauded career in England and America. Cast ineffectually as a doctor, Gerald was overshadowed by the younger rising star of Veidt.

Even more humiliating for him was *Catherine the Great*. The period drama, which Alexander Korda hoped would repeat the success of his earlier historical extravaganza *The Private Life of Henry VIII*, starred Elisabeth Bergner and Douglas Fairbanks Junior. Among the cast were Gerald's old friend Irene Vanbrugh, like him a reluctant trespasser in the world of film, and a young Flora Robson. Gerald played the part of a valet and flitted, uneasily, without conviction, across the screen. He had earned, with great pains and much inconvenience, his dues to the Inland Revenue and also a laconic entry as 'the famous stage actor' in *The Picturegoer's Who's Who and Encyclopedia* which noted:

Du Maurier, Sir Gerald. b. March 26, 1873, Hampstead, London. 6 ft; brown hair; grey eyes. Father George du Maurier, artist and author of *Trilby*. Educated Harrow. Married Muriel Beaumont. Hobbies: golf, motoring. Received Knighthood, 1922.

The Fall of the Curtain

Gerald's excursion into films under the guidance of Basil Dean embroiled him in other farcical events. To celebrate the release of a new production, Lady Warwick, Dean's neighbour in Essex, organised a lavish fête. Its climax was to be a performance of one-act plays given by 'Sir Gerald du Maurier and full West End company' on a wooden stage built out into an ornamental lake. The rustic backdrop recalling Marie Antoinette's model farm included a summer-house in the shape of a Chinese pagoda and a fringe of willows drooping over water lilies. Someone had forgotten to anchor the stage securely, and as soon as Gerald stepped on to it the floor swayed so alarmingly, the scenery trembled so ominously, that he had hastily to step back and give up the idea of performing at all. Another function Dean engineered him into was a charity matinée attended by the King and Queen. Thomas Beecham whisked through *The Marriage of Figaro* overture in a record time of one minute and fifty seconds while the King was taking off his coat and settling down in his seat.

'That was Sir Thomas Beecham conducting Mozart,' the Queen informed him.

'Oh, was it?' said George V looking up to greet the musician who had already disappeared.

Ronald Squire compèred, 'Monsewer' Eddie Gray juggled disastrously, and Anton Dolin pirouetted.

George V scanned his programme and said: 'Ha! Here is du Maurier palming off that old sketch where the revolver doesn't go off – I've seen it about five times. They think they can fob me off with anything.'

'Hush, dear,' whispered his consort, 'let us see.'

They saw. The sketch, *Bachelor Party*, was, contrary to what the King expected, a new one, and on this occasion the revolver was definitely supposed to go off. But it misfired six times and the affair limped to a disappointing close.

'What did I tell you?' grumbled the King as he stumped away for tea.

It was heaven for Gerald to be back on the stage with Gladys Cooper in June 1930, when they acted together in *Cynara* at the Playhouse. The building, in Northumberland Avenue and remote from the traditional West End, had been put up last century as the Royal Avenue Theatre by a speculator, according to legend, who hoped that the owners of Charing Cross railway station next door would eventually need to buy the site. They never did, the mirage of big profits dissolved, and the theatre remained. It opened with a run of French operetta and was managed in turn by George Alexander,

Charles Hawtrey and Cyril Maude until the roof of Charing Cross station fell in and badly damaged the structure. Beautifully restored, decked out with balustrades and Italianate decorations, the renamed Playhouse continued as a theatre until 1951 when the BBC took over and broadcast from it, among other delicacies, *The Goon Show*. It opened once again, in 1987, with excellent sight-lines and acoustics, and the painted act drop, unique to London, exquisitely recreated. The Playhouse still, though, has to find a success that will equal the triumphs of Gladys Cooper's management sixty years ago.

She had her failures, true, but with *The Letter*, for example, which Gerald directed, she made a profit of forty thousand pounds on the four hundred she put into it. The famous partnership with Gerald in *The Last of Mrs Cheyney* would, she hoped, cast its old spell for *Cynara*. The title came from Ernest Dowson's famous lines, 'I have been faithful to thee, Cynara, in my fashion.' The play showed obvious signs of its origin, a novel which was adapted by the veteran dramatist H. M. Harwood. The first act lasted an hour and twenty-five minutes. Other episodes were so brief as to imply a film scenario. Gerald played a barrister, Jim Warlock, who falls in love with the shop-girl Doris. He is, however, inconveniently married, and Doris, unable to secure her man, commits suicide. Gerald directed the play with great care and skill, though even he could not atone for the authors' oversight in making the hero a barrister since, as James Agate waggishly pointed out, 'barristers do not fall in love except under proper safeguards, covers and other indemnities.'

Cynara failed to duplicate the effect of *Cheyney* because it was not such a good play and because Gladys Cooper limited herself to the relatively minor part of Mrs Warlock. She tended to be outshone by the pathetic fragility of Celia Johnson as the shop-girl, a rôle that helped make the latter's reputation. Despite these handicaps the piece ran for seven months and showed a profit. This encouraged Gerald and Gladys to chance their hand again with a revival of *The Pelican*, a play which was already old-fashioned when it appeared some years before. Gerald was a French lover, complete with a nasty little moustache, and Gladys the married mistress. After only a few months *The Pelican* had to be taken off. Gladys then decided she was in need of a holiday and left Gerald to direct and play in *The Church Mouse*. Here he portrayed a German baron. His change of nationality did no better at the box-office and the Playhouse went dark again.

What could he do next? No one at that moment was writing the sort of play he wanted. It was too early for yet another revival of *Dear Brutus*. He went through all the proved successes in his repertory and lighted on *The Ware Case*. For over thirty years he had been domiciled in the West End. Why not take *The Ware Case* on a tour of the provinces? He had not seen them as an actor since the days of his youth, and it would be amusing to put up at luxury hotels where once he had stayed in dingy lodging houses. What is more, as President of the Actors' Benevolent Fund he decided that on the tour he would raise no less than a thousand pounds for the charity. At Southsea, where he began his four months of travel, he made a little curtain speech as he was to do after every performance. Those in the audience who had not spotted the identity of the murderer until the third act were asked to put money in a collecting box or to send him a cheque. He threw in an extra attraction by dressing up as Henry Irving, founder of the Actors' Benevolent Fund, and giving his famous imitation of him. At luncheons and dinners he spoke for his charity and with impersonations and funny stories charmed contributions out of the guests. He made a bet that he would raise at least a hundred pounds in every town he visited. The bet succeeded.

His tour of *The Ware Case* did not make a great deal of money for him personally but it raised well over his ambitious target of a thousand pounds for the Actors' Benevolent Fund. He returned to Cannon Hall jubilant and with a feeling he had not known for a long time of work well done in a good cause. The Christmas of 1931 was a particularly joyful one. He served the mince pies with a flourish and led the celebrations in such a boisterous way that the Inland Revenue might never have existed.

That troublesome organisation was also pursuing his friend and collaborator Edgar Wallace. He owed them, in income tax alone, twenty thousand pounds, and to clear himself entirely he needed a sum of about four times that figure. He decided, like Gerald, that in films lay his salvation and took up a lucrative invitation to Hollywood. Before he left he started work on *The Green Pack*, another crime play which he hoped the du Maurier magic would doctor into a profitable run. The writing machine, though fed on a permanent diet of cigarettes and weak tea, showed no sign of running down, even if the owner now was bronchitic and weakened by diabetes. On the sea journey, before even reaching Cherbourg, he had written a newspaper article. In the ten days that covered his preparations and the trip itself he wrote a novel, a twenty thousand-word story, his new three-act play *The Green Pack*, a scenario, sixteen articles and a broadcast. There was also, he added to his list of work done, 'something else which I can't remember.'

The Green Pack was to be presented at Wyndham's, the place where Gerald and Edgar had worked so happily together in the past. Edgar, now fully committed to the stage, had taken a flat above the theatre itself. It is today an office where there still may be found an unusually spacious armchair which, so they say, was constructed to accommodate his large bulk. On the high seas en route for Hollywood he revised *The Green Pack*. 'I think I shall change the play so as to make it less real and more theatrical,' he wrote to his wife. 'After all, people want to be pleased and not harrowed; so the lady must be altered, though I am afraid I cannot make her respectable . . . We did some more work yesterday, and I think I have just about paid my passage.'

Gerald was dismayed when he received the script of *The Green Pack*. It bulged with improbabilities, the dialogue was flat and the action diffuse. Edgar, meanwhile, had arrived in Hollywood and signed his profitable contract with the RKO film company. Once installed in the battery system which corralled writers there, he found that his record productivity was absorbed with discomfiting ease: the stories and ideas he produced in a ceaseless flood were gobbled up into the giant maw and never heard of again. Such conditions exacerbated already high-strung nerves, and he responded with anger to suggestions from London that *The Green Pack* needed extensive alterations. He cabled irritably to his wife: 'SUGGESTED CHANGE DOCTOR'S WIFE AND END GROTESQUE FANTASTICAL STOP CANNOT RISK HAVING PLAY RUINED BY ILL CONSIDERED WHIMSICALITIES STOP SUGGEST ABANDON PRODUCTION UNTIL MAY LET THEATRE GO DARK.'

Even in the best of moods he disliked criticism, however discreet and constructive it might be. A few minutes later he shot off another cable: 'FURTHER TO MY PREVIOUS WIRE FEEL THAT BOTH YOU AND GERALD READ AND LIKED PLAY NOW ELEVENTH HOUR WANT WHOLE PLOT AND MOTIVES CHANGED STOP FEEL PERFECTLY HELPLESS ABOUT IT RATHER NOT PRODUCE UNLESS ON LINE WRITTEN STOP DON'T MIND INTERPOLATING SCENES BUT CANNOT POSSIBLY RECONSTRUCT PLAY AT THIS DISTANCE.'

He had reached the second stage where criticism of his work was involved, that of despair. Another cable arrived for Mrs Wallace announcing that he would telephone her at Wyndham's that night. When he did he sounded more relaxed and amenable to the changes proposed. The next stage in the cycle was reached when he cabled, workmanlike and professional, the revised situations and dialogue. By then he was penitent over this show of temper. 'Don't get rattled,' he wrote to his wife, 'even when I go off the deep end. The only thing that matters is happiness, and especially your happiness, and what the hell does it matter what happens at the theatre?'

It did matter a great deal to Gerald, who both directed and played a leading rôle in *The Green Pack*. The plot was original and made a change from the customary Wallace milieu of burglars and the London underworld. The setting was Africa and the villain a businessman who sets up a partnership in a gold-mining project with three friends. They learn that he plans to dupe them of their share once they are no longer useful to him, so they decide he must be killed and draw lots as to who shall murder him. After he dies an inquest is held and a verdict of suicide returned. The three friends are left to enjoy their legal share of the venture. 'Do what you like with the play,' Edgar had cabled, 'and God love you, Gerald.' This was precisely what Gerald had to do, for even with the revisions it still needed pulling together. At rehearsals actors wrestled with the dialogue and altered speeches as they went along. 'What about this?' they would say, pencil and paper in hand. If the suggestion proved remotely acceptable it went into the script.

Edgar, in Hollywood, nurtured ambitions of directing a film and was immersed in what he called a 'horror picture' about prehistoric monsters. It eventually reached the screen as *King Kong*, an epic which, originally scheduled as a thrifty way of using up miles of film shot for *Trader Horn*, became, to everyone's surprise, an enduring classic. Edgar was not to know this. On 6th February, 1932, three days before the première of *The Green Pack* at Wyndham's, he planned to give a party and then, on the opening night, to surprise the audience with a broadcast from Hollywood relayed to the theatre before the curtain rose. Despite what he thought was a slight cold he looked forward with childish excitement to springing his little ruse. A violent headache developed, the worst he had ever suffered, and he retreated to bed. While the dress rehearsal took place at Wyndham's he lay delirious and incoherent. A doctor arrived and found evidence of sugar diabetes. A second medical man confirmed the diagnosis, a result of those thousand upon thousand cups of heavily sweetened tea. Double pneumonia set in. The first night of *The Green Pack* was clouded by the message on newspaper placards in the Charing

Cross Road outside the theatre: 'EDGAR WALLACE GRAVELY ILL.'

Next day he fell into a coma and died at the age of fifty-seven. His estate showed debts of a hundred and forty thousand pounds and no assets. A private company he had set up in a move to reduce income tax emerged as principal creditor. In law, since he was managing director of the company, he therefore owed fifty thousand pounds to himself. Additional tangles came to light when the owners of Wyndham's claimed for the rest of the lease he had taken on the theatre: Edgar's company was lessee, but since he had given his personal guarantee for the rent his estate became liable. There was, however, no estate worth mentioning. Other claimants were, implacably, the Inland Revenue, and, vociferously, tradesmen who had supplied Edgar with the means of his grandiose existence. Unexpected absentees in the queue of debtors were the bookmakers, for Edgar always settled his mammoth gambling debts with pious regularity each week.

Over the next two years an ingenious arrangement by Edgar's solicitors and the formation of a new company settled all his debts. Royalties were still surging in and, after a short time, the company began to pay dividends. Until 1982, when by the unjust and vicious laws of copyright which govern a writer's work Edgar's books fell into the public domain, his descendants were able to enjoy the rewards earned by an author whose extravagance was only equalled by his generosity. No English novelist, except perhaps for Barbara Cartland and Frank Richards, the creator of Billy Bunter, can have entertained in his time so many millions of readers.

The Green Pack certainly contributed towards the happy solution of Edgar's complicated affairs. Although a sadness was cast by his early death and Gerald went through his rôle as Larry Deans with a professional briskness that concealed personal sorrow, the play ran for a good seven months. He found, too, reassurance in the surroundings at Wyndham's that he knew so well, in the familiar old plush curtains and the narrow passages backstage he had trodden so many times before making his first entrance as Henry Beauclerc in *Diplomacy*, as Raffles, as Sir Hubert Ware, as Harry Dearth, as Bull-Dog Drummond. He remembered the kindness of Edgar Wallace, the man his family nicknamed 'Krazy', his pugnacious will, his refusal of defeat. Above all he treasured the dedication of *The Ringer*: 'My dear Gerald, this book is *The Gaunt Stranger* practically in the form that you and I shaped it for the stage. Herein you will find all the improvements you suggested for *The Ringer*

– which means that this is a better story than *The Gaunt Stranger.* Yours, Edgar Wallace.'

As soon as *The Green Pack* ended its run he went over to the St James's Theatre and took the lead in John van Druten's new play *Behold, We Live.* Van Druten, the son of a Dutch father and an English mother, had been a solicitor before gaining notoriety with *Young Woodley*, a play centred on the infatuation of a schoolboy for a married woman, a theme which also in the 1920s inspired Raymond Radignet's *Le Diable Au Corps.* He favoured 'strong' dramas which hushed the tinkle of afternoon matinée tea-cups. Among them was his adaptation for the stage of Rebecca West's novel *The Return of the Soldier*, although he could when required, as in *There's Always Juliet*, write effective comedy. *Behold, We Live* presented an unhappily married woman in love with a famous barrister. His wife is jealously protective and refuses him his freedom. The news of his affair becomes public and he is denied the judgeship that would have automatically come his way. The mistress contemplates suicide but her lover dissuades her, only to die himself as the result of a dangerous operation. The message of this profoundly depressing entertainment is that the most solid of human relationships endure and cannot be dissolved by death itself.

The gloom was lightened by the presence of Dame May Whitty as the barrister's mother. Gerald knew her of old, for she had appeared opposite him in *The Last of Mrs Cheyney*, and he valued the impeccable technique she evolved over what, by 1932, already amounted to fifty years' experience on the London stage. Her special line was upper-class ladies, absent of mind and feathery of mood, who blundered through life armed with vast floppy handbags and cloaked in billowing flowery dresses. Her endearing vagueness was matched by apple cheeks and a plump presence. On occasion an incisive flash of practicality would shine through the dimness and startle an audience. In *Behold, We Live* she played what she really was, a Dame of the British Empire, having gained the honour for wartime service in 1918. Hitchcock's film *The Lady Vanishes* brought her celebrity on the screen as the elusive Miss Fay. At the age of seventy-one she launched on a Hollywood career and, for the next decade or so, was to personify America's baroque ideal of English damehood.

As her son, the barrister, Gerald gave a performance that was acutely detailed and subtly observed. One scene in particular much impressed the young Charles Laughton who then regarded Gerald as an idol. This occurred when the barrister came in from seeing a doctor to reassure his mistress, Gertrude Lawrence, that he had nothing to fear.

> She knelt by him with her head in his lap [recalled Laughton's wife Elsa Lanchester]. Charles always said afterwards that it was one of the most beautiful pieces of acting he'd ever seen – the way du Maurier very quietly looked at all the things in the room, fireplace, pictures, ceiling, tables, chairs, and silently communicated his feelings to us, the audience. We knew he was saying, 'Goodbye, goodbye.' The audience knew he had cancer, but she did not.

Despite the tragic nature of the play Gerald, behind the scenes and even in front of them, went on unleashing practical jokes. In this he was aided by his leading lady, Gertrude Lawrence, for she had as keen an appetite for mischief as he did. At the time they were also making the film *Lord Camber's Ladies* with Alfred Hitchcock, and the three of them spurred each other on to see who could engineer the most inventive put-down. To Gerald must go the palm. Gertrude Lawrence had a splendid entrance to make in *Behold, We Live* when she came down a staircase wearing a beautiful evening dress. At every rehearsal, as the script enjoined, he murmured the set line: 'You look lovely.' On the opening night she made her shimmering descent of the staircase. As she reached the bottom step he looked at her and drawled: 'You know, you look pretty awful.' He brought the house down.

Another view would suggest that here he was not perpetrating a joke but, through his technique of deliberate under-playing, was suggesting in a teasing manner the intense admiration the character he impersonated really felt. Charles Laughton would probably have thought so. Gerald was to direct *Alibi*, a play from the Agatha Christie novel, and Laughton had been suggested as the detective Hercule Poirot. Until then his name was associated with bizarre rôles such as Hugh Walpole's creepy *The Man with Red Hair*. Gerald had the impression that he was one of the new degenerate sort now infesting the theatre and declared he did not want a fellow like that in any production of his. Laughton heard of this and paid an indignant visit to Gerald in his dressing-room at the St James's. 'I hear you've been saying I'm a pervert?' he angrily accused him.

'Well, are you?' asked Gerald calmly.

'No!' he shouted.

'Good,' Gerald replied. 'Have a drink.'

Laughton won the part and his professional admiration for Gerald became personal friendship.

After *Behold, We Live* ended its six-month run there was little for Gerald to do until the November of 1932 when, yet again, he was called in to arrange a Command Performance on behalf of King George's Pension Fund for actors. He had, in his time, organised many of these functions, and only his sense of duty spurred him on. They were rushed, last-minute affairs, anathema to one who always took meticulous care over his productions. His feelings were not helped by knowing that King George V, the bluff sailor monarch, disliked the theatre and only attended with reluctance.

The play chosen was *Bull-Dog Drummond* with Gerald in his famous rôle and a cast which included Cedric Hardwicke, Gladys Cooper, Edith Evans and Gordon Harker. The young Canadian actor Raymond Massey also took part and was involved in an agonising experience. Gilbert Hare returned to the stage as the villain Dr Lakington, having spent five years on biochemical research at Cambridge. He seemed a little out of touch with the theatre, as might be expected after so long an absence. *Bull-Dog Drummond*, it will be remembered, depended for its effects on accurate timing. At the appropriate moment, Massey, as the American millionaire, duly trussed up and drugged, took his place in the wings and saw, in the gloom, a figure he thought was Hare standing beside him. As the time for his cue neared he whispered: 'Here I am, Mr Hare.' The figure turned round and he saw, with alarm, that it was a stagehand. He warned the stage manager who ran up to Hare's dressing-room on the second floor. An eternity of three minutes or so followed.

During that endless wait Edith Evans as Irma Peterson and Alfred Drayton as her father Carl were on stage. Edith Evans, Massey recalled, kept things going 'in one of the most astonishing improvisations I have ever seen'. Since she was supposed to be Russian she poured out a torrent of gibberish in wild Slavonic tones. Overcome with astonishment, Drayton panicked and made his exit. Alone on stage she swept around toying seductively with a long cigarette-holder. Gently she hummed the song of the Volga Boatmen. The audience was spellbound. Finally the breathless Hare rushed on. From the royal box a gruff voice was heard enquiring testily if this was another of those 'damned, dramatic pauses'.

A duty Gerald also assumed out of civic-mindedness, and one of a very different nature, was to join the council of the actors' trade union Equity. That body had been formed three years previously, one of the most active leaders being a pugnacious Dame May Whitty.

Early meetings were often held at her flat in Bedford Street around the enormous dining-room table which could seat up to forty actors. For many years afterward the business of Equity council committees was transacted over its mahogany expanse. The impetus to organise a union came, not as usually from below, but from the top and soon the names of John Gielgud, Cedric Hardwicke, Gertrude Lawrence and Sybil Thorndike confirmed that this was no left-wing conspiracy. Gerald's politics, if he had any at all, leaned to a vague acceptance of everything to do with the established order of things, and he was reassured by Godfrey Tearle's declaration: 'Neither I nor any other council member of British Equity is politically minded. If we vote at all we vote Conservative simply because ours is a luxury business that caters for the leisured classes. The theatre itself is innately Conservative, but frankly we have no time for politics.'

More private matters absorbed Gerald behind the scenes. His second daughter Daphne showed signs of her grandfather's literary talent and published at the age of twenty-four a novel called *The Loving Spirit*. A year later, in 1932, she brought out another, *I'll Never be Young Again*, which was followed in the next twelve months by *The Progress of Julius*. Then she fell silent for three years until she produced *Jamaica Inn*. He did not live long enough to read this, or *Rebecca*, which placed her among the leading popular novelists of the day and opened with a paragraph at once haunting and irresistible:

> Last night I dreamt I went to Manderley again. It seemed to me I stood by the iron gate leading to the drive, and for a while I could not enter for the way was barred to me. There was a padlock and chain upon the gate. I called in my dream to the lodge-keeper, and had no answer, and peering closer through the rusted spokes of the gate I saw that the lodge was uninhabited.

He was flattered that his little girl should have grown up into a clever writer and that she should have inherited George du Maurier's gift. He could not help, though, being somewhat disturbed by the love scenes which were thought to be 'daring' for the time. While he was acting in *The Green Pack* she had met a young Guards officer called Major Frederick Browning, otherwise known as 'Tommy' or 'Boy'. The very handsome military man was first observed cruising the river near the du Maurier home at Ferryside in Cornwall. It later emerged that, having read Daphne's first novel *The Loving Spirit*, he decided to visit the district which inspired her. Daphne and Angela spotted him through Gerald's bird-watching binoculars, intrigued, as his motor boat chugged up and down the river. They christened him 'Harold Alexander' because at the time they mistakenly thought he resembled the distinguished soldier. Months afterwards Daphne met him in more formal circumstances and heard that his late father had known Gerald. Friendship quickly turned into love and Mo dreamed of her beautiful daughter in white satin being married at a glamorous wedding in the Guards' Chapel.

In fact, since they both disliked publicity, they insisted on a very quiet wedding. Early one July morning in 1932, when both her sisters were away, Daphne and her small party of groom, best man and parents embarked in two motor launches up the river. They were married at the church of Lanteglos and Daphne wore blue serge instead of the glittering satin Mo hoped for. After a wedding breakfast of sausages and bacon they went off on their honeymoon. On their return they settled in a small Queen Anne house attached to Cannon Hall which Gerald gave them as a wedding present.

He was both pleased and depressed, pleased for Daphne's sake and depressed for himself. The horrid prospect of grandfatherhood loomed. When it arrived, in the shape of a granddaughter whom he delighted in, he felt the same mixed emotions. He was an ancient now, a thing of the past. He could no longer keep up the show of being young. He was tired of acting, tired of the theatre, tired of life. Apart from a revival of *Diplomacy* in 1933, the year of his sixtieth birthday, he was to do no more on the stage. Even practical jokes had ceased to entertain him or to divert his thoughts from the gloom that shrouded him. Cedric Hardwicke, who thought him 'one of the most attractive personalities I ever met', was baffled one evening to be told how wretched Gerald felt beneath his assumed gaiety. They sat up all night while Gerald in a fit of impassioned melancholia avowed that he hated acting and everything to do with it. And how he despised the hacks who provided him with successes like *Bull-Dog Drummond* and *Raffles*! 'I have never,' he declared, 'had a happy day in the theatre.'

This was, of course, wrong. Like his father, he had aged before his time and was anxious for death to release him from a world that had given him so much but not quite enough. Few people are ever satisfied with their achievements. Often they discover, as Bernard Shaw observed, that there is only one thing worse than not getting what you want, and that is getting what you want. Gerald had fashionable success and much adulation. Having fulfilled his ambition he remained a disappointed man.

When Voltaire came to England he anticipated with delight the prospect of meeting Congreve and talking theatrical shop with the leading English dramatist of the age. He was outraged and perplexed to find that Congreve dismissed his plays as the trifles of an idle hour and talked of other things, insisting that he was a gentleman and not a mere playwright. Such was Gerald's attitude. He liked to give the impression that the theatre was little more than a pastime in his life, that if need be he could do without it. Yet he could never have been anything else but an actor.

He was one of the most naturally gifted performers to appear on the English stage. No drama school, no tutor, ever taught him any-thing. His technique sprang wholly from intuition and observation. What lessons he learned came from practical experience with Tree, Forbes-Robertson and, especially, Mrs Patrick Campbell. She, more than most, was responsible for his initiation both as man and actor. Traditionally handsome looks were not among his attributes. If Mrs Pat had a love scene with him she would say to herself: 'Good God! To have to play a scene like this with a face like that!' What he did possess was the much rarer gift of star quality. He not only acted, he reacted. When silent he continued to embody the character he was playing and to create an aura that made the traffic of the stage a warm, coherent whole. You could not take your eyes off him and you believed in him completely.

Gerald was not an intellectual. Theorising bored him and he avoided books about acting as he avoided books in general except for the classic adventure stories he read as a boy and perhaps the occasional thriller. Nonetheless, relying on intuition alone, he arrived at techniques which have been the subject of learned manuals. Those who read the long letters he wrote to Audrey Carten say that, all unconsciously, they outline the same theories as did Stanislavsky, a figure of whom Gerald had doubtless never heard. He also anticipated 'Method' acting. While preparing his rôle as Bull-Dog Drummond he was Bull-Dog Drummond at home, charging around Cannon Hall with boisterous daring and imagining villains behind every panel. As Raffles he was a smooth Gallic charmer at the dinner table. When he played the broken Harry Dearth his sadness overwhelmed the household. During the period when he was acting the tragic violinist Paolo Gheradi his black mood depressed everyone who came in touch with him.

Everything seemed to come easily to him, an impression which, like Congreve, he encouraged, although in reality he worked very hard to give the illusion of naturalness. As we have seen, he spent hours in front of the mirror perfecting his nonchalant style of lighting a cigarette or pouring a drink. Each word, each phrase in his speeches was analysed and gone over many times in the attempt to make his delivery as fluent and realistic as possible. If he seemed to throw away a line in his casual staccato voice, he only appeared to be doing so and achieved the effect by varying stress and inflection: his enunciation remained clear and audible in every corner of the theatre. His imitators overlooked this, did not realise that he had the art of concealing art, that his effortless manner hid a formidable technique. Gerald, said Laurence Olivier, '. . . brilliant actor that he was, had the most disastrous influence on my generation, because we really thought, looking at him, that it was easy; and for the first ten years of our lives in the theatre, nobody could hear a word we said. We thought he was being really natural; of course, he was a genius of a technician giving that appearance, that's all.'

No actor can properly be assessed until he has attempted the great classical rôles. Gerald played none of them, and his acquaintance with Shakespeare was limited to a few minor parts which he took in his youth. He preferred to choose mediocre plays and to transform them with his creative flair into something apparently worthwhile, much as Thomas Beecham would conduct a minor piece and persuade his audience that they were hearing great music. Gerald's contribution to the theatre lay in the revolutionary style of acting he perfected. This arose partly in response to the new type of play that was being written and partly as a reaction against the flamboyant manner of his predecessors. Irving could not have managed the subtle understatement of *Dear Brutus* nor the delicate suggestiveness which impressed Charles Laughton in *Behold, We Live*. As John Gielgud has pointed out:

> I always thought that acting meant panting and crying and laughing and being very impressive, fighting duels and jumping up with enormous impressiveness . . . and yet when du Maurier came on in the last act of *Dear Brutus* . . . his face when they told him that the child was a dream was so extraordinary and yet he appeared to do absolutely nothing. I remember thinking what a pity it was that he never played in Chekhov or Ibsen. He was such a great actor, but in those days leading men like du Maurier had such vehicles provided for them, and they were themselves such an enormous draw with the public that anything they bothered to put on was always a success, and so they had no urge and no particular temptation to go into the classical field.

The actor leaves only a memory behind him. Whereas the writer, the artist and the composer are remembered by the tangible evidence of their works, the actor lives on, if at all, in the mind of those who saw him and in written accounts of his performance. Films are, at best, a monochrome substitute for the real thing, and those in which Gerald appeared offer no reliable guide to his skill on the stage. His father George du Maurier left solid proof of his achievement which posterity could recognise in drawings and books. Gerald had nothing to bequeath. His awareness of this accounts for the bitter despair he felt at the end of his life and the contempt he had for the third-rate dramatists upon whose plays he lavished his gifts. 'I am a professional actor,' he would say in the days of high success before disillusionment set in, 'not an interpreter of great dramatists or anything like that. What I have to do is to have material to act. I've got to collaborate and put in my part of it.' That, of course, is what Irving did, with the result that some of his greatest performances were in plays of abysmal quality. But Irving also took the precaution of acting in Shakespeare as well.

Gerald was a very emotional man. He could easily be moved to tears, and often, as a member of an audience, he wept at touching moments in a play. His mask of light-heartedness concealed a depth of feeling that was quickly roused. Despite being an adult in years he remained, for the rest of his life, a boy at heart with all the spontaneous and unthinking reactions of youth. The tragedies of human existence found him unprepared. The early success he won so easily blinded him to reality and he did not have the resources to grapple with it. He was left puzzled and frustrated.

On 26th March, 1934, he reached his sixty-first birthday. Peter Pan was old, irrevocably and incontrovertibly old. Two years previously he had made his will. It was a simple affair in which he left everything to his wife Mo, including the income from his share in his mother's residuary estate. Should Mo die before him everything went to his three daughters. In that event his sister-in-law 'Billy', otherwise Sybil Mary Beaumont who had been his loyal secretary for many years, was to be guardian of the under-age Jeanne du Maurier. It was right that Mo should be sole beneficiary. She was the one fixed point in his life, as his mother had been for George du Maurier, quiet, self-effacing Mo who gave up all her own ambitions and devoted herself entirely to him and to raising his family.

For some time now he had been complaining of a pain in the region of his heart. There were days when he looked pale, haggard even. He took to consulting medical dictionaries and avidly studying the more hideous diseases. Advertisements for patent remedies were scanned with care. Dozens of bottles and tubes bearing mysterious names filled his bathroom cabinet and jostled the lotions and sachets and cartons already there. He saw his doctor who passed him on to a specialist. An operation was necessary, they informed him, and a week or so after his birthday he went into the clinic at 20, Devonshire Place. The family came to see him afterwards and were told that the operation had been successful. What, they thought as they beheld the ravaged features and the hands no longer strong enough to hold a cigarette, would he have looked like had the operation been unsuccessful?

His grandfather Louis–Mathurin died at the age of fifty-nine and his father George at sixty-two. Gerald was to observe the tradition of short-lived du Maurier men, for he died on 11th April, of cancer, sixteen days after his sixty-first birthday. Eleventh April was also his thirty-first wedding anniversary. This was another melancholy tradition he involuntarily followed. Had not his own mother died on her wedding anniversary too?

Late one evening his coffin was borne into Hampstead Parish Church. Lit only by candles that were carried before it, the small procession trooped over the cold stone floor in darkness except for pinpoints of light that flickered and threw grotesque shadows. It was a setting the actor-manager would have appreciated. The bier was set up in the Lady Chapel and engulfed in a mass of flowers, their scent heavy on the chill air. Next day, after the funeral, he was buried in the du Maurier family grave beside his mother and father, his brother Guy's wife, and his sister May and her husband. Mo was later to follow him there.

His estate was valued at the modest sum of £17,996 4s 3d, an unusually small figure even in those days. He had never invested and never saved. The one big asset was Cannon Hall, which, sold in due course, helped to keep Mo reasonably comfortable for the rest of her life. In 1967 a plaque recording Gerald's residence there was put on the wall. He lies in the parish churchyard only two hundred yards away from 27, Church Row where he was born. The simple inscription bears no other detail than his name: GERALD.

BIBLIOGRAPHY

Agate, James, *Alarums and Excursions*, Grant Richards, 1922.
   At Half Past Eight: Essays of the Theatre 1921–1922, Jonathan Cape, 1923.
   Ego 6, Harrap, 1944.
   Red Letter Nights: A Survey of the Post-Elizabethan Drama in Actual Performance on the London Stage 1921–1943, Jonathan Cape, 1944.
Allen, David Rayvern, *Sir Aubrey: A Biography of C. Aubrey Smith, England Cricketer, West End Actor, Hollywood Film Star*, Elm Tree Books, 1982.
Alpert, Hollis, *The Barrymores*, W. H. Allen, 1965.
Bancroft, Mr and Mrs, *Mr and Mrs Bancroft: On and Off the Stage, By Themselves*, Richard Bentley, 1888.
Bankhead, Tallulah, *Tallulah: My Autobiograpy*, Victor Gollancz, 1952.
Beerbohm, Max, *Around Theatres*, Rupert Hart-Davis, 1953.
   More Theatres, 1898–1903, Rupert Hart-Davis, 1969.
Birkin, Andrew, *J. M. Barrie and The Lost Boys*, Constable, 1979.
Carson, Lionel (ed), *The Stage Year Book*, issues from 1908 to 1934.
Darlington, W. A., *The Actor and His Audience*, Phoenix House, 1949.
Dean, Basil, *Mind's Eye*, Hutchinson, 1973.
Donaldson, Frances, *Freddy Lonsdale*, Heinemann, 1957.
Du Maurier, Angela, *It's Only The Sister: An Autobiography*, Peter Davies, 1951.
   Old Maids Remember, Peter Davies, 1966.
Du Maurier, Daphne, *Gerald: A Portrait*, Victor Gollancz, 1934.
   The Due Mauriers, Victor Gollancz, 1937.
   (ed), *The Young George du Maurier: A Selection of His Letters, 1860–1867*, Peter Davies, 1951.
   Growing Pains: The Shaping of a Writer, Victor Gollancz, 1977.
Du Maurier, George, *The Novels of George du Maurier*, With Introductions by John Masefield O.M. and Daphne du Maurier, The Pilot Press and Peter Davies, 1947.
(Du Maurier, Gerald, Du Maurier, Guy and Barrie, J. M.) *An Englishman's Home*, By A Patriot, Edward Arnold, 1909.

Du Maurier, Gerald, and 'Sapper', *Bull-Dog Drummond, A Play in Four Acts*, adapted by 'Sapper' and Gerald du Maurier from the novel by 'Sapper', Samuel French, 1925.

and Tree, Viola, *The Dancers: The Beginning and the End of the Story in the Play*, Hodder and Stoughton, 1923.

Fields, Gracie, *Sing As We Go*, Frederick Muller, 1960.

Forbes, Bryan, *That Despicable Race: A History of the British Acting Tradition*, Elm Tree Books, 1980.

Fox, Angela, *Slightly Foxed*, Collins, 1986.

Gielgud, John, *An Actor and His Time*, Sidgwick and Jackson, 1979.

Green, Roger Lancelyn, *Fifty Years of Peter Pan*, Peter Davies, 1954.

Hampstead Museum, *The Du Mauriers: A Hampstead Family*, Exhibition Catalogue, 1984.

Hardwicke, Sir Cedric, *A Victorian in Orbit*, Methuen, 1961.

Hoyer-Millar, C. C., *George du Maurier and Others*, Cassell, 1937.

Irving, Ernest, *Cue For Music*, Dennis Dobson, 1959.

Lanchester, Elsa, *Elsa Lanchester By Herself*, Michael Joseph, 1983.

Lane, Margaret, *Edgar Wallace: The Biography of a Phenomenon*, Heinemann, 1938.

Lesley, Cole, *The Life of Noël Coward*, Jonathan Cape, 1976.

MacQueen-Pope, W., *The Footlights Flickered*, Herbert Jenkins, 1959.

Mander, Raymond, and Mitchenson, Joe, *The Theatres of London*, New English Library, 1975.

Massey, Raymond, *A Hundred Different Lives: An Autobiography*, Robson Books, 1979.

Morley, Sheridan, *Gladys Cooper: A Biography*, Heinemann, 1979.

A Talent To Amuse: A Biography of Noël Coward, Heinemann, 1969, revised edition, Pavilion Books, 1986.

Moseley, Roy, with Philip and Martin Masheter, *Rex Harrison*, New English Library, 1987.

Nichols, Beverley, *Are They The Same At Home?*, Jonathan Cape, 1927.

Ormond, Léonée, *George du Maurier*, Routledge and Kegan Paul, 1969.

Parker, John (ed), *The Green Room Book, 1908*, T. Sealey Clarke and Co.

(ed), *Who's Who In The Theatre*, successive editions from 1912 to 1936, Pitman.

Pearson, Hesketh, *The Last Actor-Managers*, Methuen, 1950.

Beerbohm Tree: His Life and Laughter, Methuen, 1956.

Play Pictorial, The, special issues devoted to productions by or featuring Gerald du Maurier.

Sanderson, Michael, *From Irving to Olivier: A Social History of the Acting Profession in England 1890–1980*, Athlone Press, 1984.

Shaw, Bernard, *Our Theatres in the Nineties*, volumes 1 and 3, Constable, 1948.

Bibliography

Short, Ernest, *Theatrical Cavalcade*, Eyre and Spottiswoode, 1942.
Stokes, Sewell, *Without Veils: The Intimate Biography of Gladys Cooper*, Peter Davies, 1953.
Trewin, Wendy, *All On Stage: Charles Wyndham and the Alberys*, Harrap, 1980.
Vanbrugh, Irene, *To Tell My Story*, Hutchinson, 1948.

INDEX

Index

Index